D1480391

DATE		

HOMER'S ORIGINAL GENIUS

Eighteenth-century notions of the early
Greek epic (1688–1798)

HOMER'S
ORIGINAL GENIUS

*Eighteenth-century notions of the early
Greek epic (1688–1798)*

KIRSTI SIMONSUURI

CAMBRIDGE UNIVERSITY PRESS

Cambridge

London · New York · Melbourne

Published by the Syndics of the Cambridge University Press
The Pitt Building, Trumpington Street, Cambridge CB2 IRP
Bentley House, 200 Euston Road, London NWI 2DB
32 East 57th Street, New York, NY 10022, USA
296 Beaconsfield Parade, Middle Park, Melbourne 3206, Australia

First published 1979

Printed in Great Britain by
Western Printing Services Ltd, Bristol

Library of Congress Cataloguing in Publication Data
Simonsuuri, Kirsti, 1945–
Homer's original genius
Based on the author's thesis,
University of Cambridge, 1972.
Bibliography: p.
Includes index.
1. Homerus – Appreciation – Europe.
2. Literature, Modern – 18th century – History and criticism.
I. Title.
PA4152.E8S5   883'.01   78–56758

ISBN 0 521 22198 6

Contents

Plates

Abbreviations

AJA	*American Journal of Archaeology*
AJP	*American Journal of Philology*
CL	*Comparative Literature*
CLS	*Comparative Literature Studies*
DNB	*Dictionary of National Biography*
ELH	*A Journal of English Literary History*
HSCP	*Harvard Studies in Classical Philology*
JAAC	*Journal of Aesthetics and Art Criticism*
JHI	*Journal of the History of Ideas*
JWCI	*Journal of the Warburg and Courtauld Institutes*
MLN	*Modern Language Notes*
MLQ	*Modern Language Quarterly*
MP	*Modern Philology*
PCPS	*Proceedings of the Cambridge Philological Society*
PMLA	*Publications of the Modern Language Association of America*
PQ	*Philological Quarterly*
RE	*Paulys Realencyclopädie der classischen Altertumswissenschaften*
SP	*Studies in Philology*
TAPA	*Transactions and Proceedings of the American Philological Association*
TAPS	*Transactions of the American Philosophical Society*
TLS	*Times Literary Supplement*
YCS	*Yale Classical Studies*
YFS	*Yale French Studies*

For my mother and to the memory of my father

Preface

This book originated in the research which I started for the PhD degree at the University of Cambridge in 1972, and it may be that the special marks of the doctoral thesis have been indelible. I was, however, fortunate in being allowed to choose a particularly unusual theme for research, and in finding scholars who showed their interest from the earliest stages of my work.

This book offers room for specialists in many fields. I am aware of the gaps that still exist. A further analysis of Italian criticism will perhaps prove useful and important, to mention one of the issues that pertain to eighteenth-century scholarship. Contemporary developments were, however, related to a larger framework offered by the classical tradition, and my main purpose in this book is to study the mechanism of gradual change in the history of the classical tradition. The complex development that characterizes eighteenth-century discussions of the Greek epic, as well as the nature and interrelation of the reasons why Homer was preferred as the model of the original genius during that period, are problems to which no single solution can be given. Hence I argue in this book merely for a new point of view and a reinterpretation of the eighteenth-century material.

I remain grateful to those with whom I have had discussions during the course of my work. Many people have contributed to it in various ways. I am grateful to the staffs of the University Library, Cambridge, of the British Museum and of the Warburg Institute, London, and to Newnham College, Cambridge. My special thanks are due to Professor Noémi Hepp, of the University of Strasbourg, and to Dr Robert Bolgar, of King's College, Cambridge, who has been my supervisor and teacher since the beginning of my work.

London *July 1978*

INTRODUCTION

Ut jam Homeri nomen, non hominis, sed poeseos, sed doctrinae esse
videatur.

> James Duport, *Homeri, poetarum omnium seculorum
> facile principis, gnomologia, duplici parallelismo
> illustrata* (Cambridge 1660)

Introduction

It is not difficult to imagine why Homer has fascinated men's minds to this day: the enigma has its attraction and the blatant commonplace its unknown side. Homer shows us perhaps that the definition of the good poet should be more concerned with the diversity of responses a poet can evoke than with the quality of the verse. Everyone can read his own myths in Homer. For the eighteenth century, Homer had an undoubtedly varied appeal: the aims and aspirations in the aesthetic and social fields were clearly mirrored in the responses to the Greek poet. Homeric criticism of the period is therefore a touchstone of the age which must not be belittled.

The eighteenth-century notions of Homer's originality and genius, which are the theme of this book, belong to the framework of a larger historical development. It is highly characteristic of the eighteenth century that even though Homer had survived in the awareness of educated people from the Athenian Enlightenment to the time of the late-seventeenth-century *querelle des anciens et des modernes* and had been used as a vehicle for the promulgation of educational reforms, literary doctrines and scientific learning – not to mention the imaginative repercussions in literature – it was not until this time that Homer was seen as a type and a representative of current ideas about poetry, history and society.

What made the eighteenth century a remarkable period in the history of Homeric studies was the fact that Homer became the focal point round which some of the major debates of the period revolved, and the way that the eighteenth century built upon the Homeric tradition was wholly characteristic. The issues that emerged in connection with the Homeric epics were varied. Three

3

points must be kept in mind. There was the problem of poetic genius and the kindred problem of originality which were first debated during the *querelle*. There was the question of realism which preoccupied the Homeric translators and notably Robert Wood: how accurate did a poet need to be in depicting scenes and events. There was also the question, raised in another context by Jean Jacques Rousseau, of the relative merits of primitive and sophisticated society, which led Herder to describe naive folk poetry as expression of a nation's character. Finally there was the 'Homeric question' itself; whether the *Iliad* and the *Odyssey* were or were not compilations from a number of separate poems, and the results of deliberate editing and interpolation.

Towards the end of the eighteenth century men's eagerness to dispel old myths, to become aware of the historical roots of their culture, and, in connection with these aims, to seek the truth about Homer, had reached a point where nothing much remained to be done – except to elaborate, or to forget history for a while and especially Homer. Homer had become a myth, operating on the level of a high culture, which followed the same pattern as popular myths which exist as tales and have no author: the moment their real origin is clearly understood and they are perceived consciously as 'myths', they cease to exist as vital parts of culture and become the dead wood of the processes of learning and tradition.

The issues debated during the eighteenth century in connection with Homer overlapped, and it is not possible to discuss one without trespassing on some of the others. The work of every eighteenth-century writer on Homer has several facets; and this explains why this book deals separately with the major contributors to Homeric criticism and the themes which that criticism explored. And because the issues overlapped, the debates about them reinforced each other.

The problems presented by the existence of two obvious masterpieces in epic literature at the very beginning of recorded history came to a certain end in the eighteenth century. That is why the period deserves special attention from those interested in Homer's influence. This unmistakably rich period pursued its familiarity with the various levels of the Homeric myth to the point of making the poet a contemporary. Although there is evidence that at least the same amount of energy and motivation was spent during the fifth century B.C. and in the Italian Renaissance in order to discover Homer, and thus there is some justification in speculating that we are dealing with something like a changing fashion on a large scale, it is unlikely that, since the work of the eighteenth-century writers and scholars is done, a similar cultural meaning can again be given to Homer. Perhaps this is not a great loss, for other myths have emerged, Homer is not alone in the category of the greatest epic writers, and the nature of oral literature is well understood and is seen to belong to a particular type of society which cannot even be hoped to be artificially created. At the same time, if we are to appreciate the climactic character of the period in this context, it is necessary to realize that the issues which the eighteenth century came to discuss in detail had been raised in earlier times in some form or other. It is of some importance to look into the long and at times very quiet historical development that can perhaps be seen as culminating in the eighteenth century which learned to use its sources in an original way.

Homeric criticism begins in Graeco-Roman antiquity. If however this period is taken as a starting point of the ideas about Homer, the history of the poet is hardly a story of how an originally correct picture gradually became more and more out of focus and distorted. The Greeks were divided in their views about Homer.[1] The *Iliad* and the *Odyssey* were known to every schoolboy. They had a considerable influence on poetic diction, not only of the epic, but also of the lyric, the drama and the elegy, and the stories incorporated in the epics have found pictorial representations in the vases, wall-paintings and sculpture from archaic Greece to the Roman period. But Homer himself was a shadowy figure. Imaginary portraits of a poet believed to be Homer exist from the fifth century B.C., and indicate that the Greeks had no unanimously accepted idea of the Homeric face, even as regards age, hairstyle or apparel (which would suggest the region of his origin).[2] Lucian, the nimble-witted commentator on Greek literature and mythology, summed up the confusion of his countrymen about Homer by saying, in his *Panegyric of Demosthenes*, that there was no 'foundation of fact' on which 'to build the edifice of praise', and that nothing concerning Homer was certain but the poems which existed.[3]

Homeric criticism in antiquity sensibly enough concentrated on the poems, and we can distinguish a number of standard responses which recur in varying forms. Ancient Homeric criticism ought to be helpful to us because the Greek commentators had their language at least in common with the poet, and the Roman critics were nearly all bilingual. This leads us to expect, from the example of analogous situations, that the Homeric criticism produced in Greek and Roman antiquity would be subtle and profound; but this was not the case. The aim of ancient literary criticism was explication of obscure passages, moral commentary for educational purposes, and hagiography. Homer was the most famous of the poets whom the Greeks, especially in Athens, venerated, and whom they amply honoured in public life.

First of all, we find Homer praised for being the master of all knowledge: in philosophy and in rhetoric as well as in the practical arts. Pseudo-Plutarch's strong defence of Homer recapitulated ancient views on these heads. In order to demonstrate that Homer was the master 'in omni scientiarum et artium genere', pseudo-Plutarch's treatise, *De vita et poesi Homeri* defends the poet's knowledge of the position of the sun and the fixed stars, of minerals, earthquakes, winds, currents, in other words, of many aspects of astronomy, geology and meteorology. The fact that pseudo-Plutarch also presents Homer as a master of rhetoric who had set a standard for future writers in poetry and prose (*oratio ligata et soluta*) reflects the great importance that the Homeric epics had gained as the schoolbook from which new generations were taught to read and write.[4] Even in earlier philosophy and criticism, represented by Democritus, Gorgias and Ion of Chios, Homer is cited as an authority on the issues of metaphorical expression, inspired writing and fluency of speech. With the progress of material civilization in the Greek world, the stress on Homer's authority in practical arts diminished, but the belief that the epics furnish examples of all rhetorical devices lingered on to the times of Dionysius of Halicarnassus and the pseudo-Longinus in the first century A.D.[5]

The Athenian praise of Homer's practical knowledge is very similar to some of the eighteenth-century views which will be discussed in this book. It is tied up with the realism and the accuracy about the physical environment that was Robert Wood's thesis in his study of Homer, and with the fact that the Homeric epics gave a picture of early civilization, which was maintained by Mme Dacier, and even by Perrault and Voltaire who for other reasons belittled the value of his poems. Indeed the humanist attacks on the poet's naivety and vulgarity concentrated on the question of Homer's authority in practical matters and on the society that had produced him, and these too can be seen in the framework of the issues raised for the first time in antiquity.

The ancient world also saw Homer as the source of a true and significant picture of the moral and human universe. The generally held view that Homer was *sophos* was contested for the first time (as far as we know) by Xenophanes, who attacked Homer's misrepresentation of the gods. But such accusations were largely directed against the mode of poetry as opposed to enlightened philosophy, and when Plato lets Socrates pour scorn on Homer, it is a condemnation of poets in general who can have no vital part in teaching men the way to wisdom and to true knowledge (*episteme*). All poets can do is help people cherish their false opinions (*doxa*) of the human and divine worlds, and Homer was the prime teacher in this art. Plato's attack on Homer was also connected with his opposition to those teachers of rhetoric, such as Gorgias and Protagoras, whose sophisticated devices of expression he equated with the art of lying.[6]

But Plato's condemnation of this school did not diminish the authority which was accorded to Homer by the majority of Greek educators. Pseudo-Plutarch vigorously supported Homer's conception of the moral universe, and on the controversial issue of the gods' liberal intercourse with men he took the stand that Homer had wanted to show how 'Dii homines adiuvant.'[7] The main defence, however, came in the form of allegorical interpretations of the Homeric epic, and there are rudiments of this practice in pseudo-Plutarch's views. The Stoics, led by Zeno and Cleanthes in the third and second centuries B.C., had turned literary and historical exegesis into allegorizing. The allegorical school of interpretation wanted to see the Homeric epic as a picture of humanity where the gods represented certain moral forces, for good or bad. Porphyry, who wrote towards the end of the third century A.D., has left us testimony in his *Homerica problemata* and *The cave of the nymphs* of this method of extracting true wisdom from Homer by seeing his poetry as an allegorical representation of man's effort.

Dion of Prusa, who wrote on Homer in his *Discourses* at the end of the first century A.D., had largely rejected allegorical interpretation, but the essay on Homeric epic is significant because he explicitly condemned Homer for having produced no true hero. Ulysses was a liar, Achilles was a coward, and the expedition to Troy was a shameless Greek enterprise. The lack of a hero especially in the *Iliad* was noted already by the Greek commentators, and when the legend of Alexander began to grow in the Graeco-Roman world, the contrast appeared startling. Cicero in his *Pro archia poeta*, and Plutarch in his *Life of Alexander*, stated a case which held the field till the eighteenth century.[8]

The high regard in which Homer was nevertheless held in antiquity is perhaps most clearly exemplified in Aristotle's theory of the epic. Plato's views on the function of poetry were criticized by Aristotle, who saw poetic creation as primarily *mimesis*, a presentation of reality in the chosen medium. In the *Poetics* Aristotle raised Homer above other poets, because they 'are engaged throughout, and only rarely use *mimesis*; but Homer after a brief preface at once brings on a man' (1460 A). To imitate the world of reality by means of art is an innate human characteristic (1448 B). Homer, according to Aristotle, was the teacher of all other poets in the technique of *mimesis* (1460 A). Aristotle saw no contradiction between poetic *mimesis* and that reality which is the object of *mimesis*, so he could fully appreciate the complexity of the Homeric poems without having to resort to allegorical interpretations (1460 B).

In the numerous literary imitations of the Homeric epic in antiquity the conventional predilection for the techniques of the master is evident, although the shorter form, the epyllion, is increasingly preferred by poets from the hellenistic period onwards. Callimachus employed Homeric diction but rejected a long epic. When Virgil chose to write in the Homeric tradition, after the moderately successful attempts in the long epic form by Naevius and Ennius, he decidedly rejected the Homeric morality and conception of the hero. He chose to write a long nationalistic epic with an imperial theme and to furnish his hero, *pius Aeneas*, with such a rigorous set of qualities as would fit the task and could not be misinterpreted. Thus the real objections to Homer come from the Latins with their preference for Virgil. In Macrobius we trace a new ideal for epic stressing *decorum* and *gravitas*, and Servius, a meticulous commentator on the *Aeneid*, condemns

Achilles in favour of the Latin Aeneas. As the hellenistic poets had preferred more sophisticated forms of poetic expression, such as the epyllion, the elegy and the lyric, to the long Homeric narrative, and as it was this tradition rather than the Homeric that was transmitted to the Roman poets, so Virgil took only the outward epic form from the Homeric tradition for his essentially serious, redemptive and cosmopolitan message.

These two influential factors in the actual literary practice, supported by the Latin commentators on Virgil, survived right through the Middle Ages to the Renaissance and contributed to the decline of Homer's reputation, since Homer was increasingly considered to be provincial, ambiguous and unserious. The late Latin antiquity pushed Homer away to an obscure corner of literary learning to which geographically also he was seen to belong. The allegorical interpreters of Homer continued the efforts to understand the poet better than he himself had done, but their practice gradually moved further away from Homer, and became a general approach to literature and to mythology, exemplified in the writings of Fulgentius in the late fifth century A.D.[9] The displeasure and belittlement shown by antiquity with regard to Homer had of course started with Plato and the philosophers of the Athenian Enlightenment, and we may remember Nietzsche's conviction that with Socrates a development had originated which was to make a conscious and enlightened man for ever incapable of understanding the popular mind of Homer.[10]

The early Christian writers felt obliged to comment on the nature of the Homeric poems in formulating the principles of Christian life and education. The Church fathers had a natural distrust of paganism while they esteemed the learning that pagan antiquity could show; Clement of Alexandria and Basil of Caesarea have left us testimony of this.[11] The early Christians were led to make the objections expressed in antiquity to Homer's gods particularly their own, and they fully endorsed the views of Dion of Prusa, for example, who thought that Homer had presented the divine beings as behaving in an immoral and vile manner. But they also had a predilection for allegorical interpretation, which in pagan antiquity was separated from the criticism of Homer's gods since pagan allegorizing was intended to justify the gods. The Stoics had been concerned to explain the meaning of the myths, and the neoplatonists had wanted to create for pagan philosophy the equivalent of the Christian myth. But this pagan tradition of allegorizing again plays a prominent part in the Byzantine Christian commentators on Homer, the twelfth-century Eustathius and Tzetzes who were devoted to the poet and regarded him as the source of esoteric wisdom.[12]

The practice of allegorizing lived through the Middle Ages, when the literature of classical antiquity was freely treated to suit contemporary pedagogical aims: excerpts from famous works were bound together and retitled, poems that closely followed the subject matter, style and metre of the ancient author were added, moral and allegorical commentaries were attached as advice to the reader, and the works themselves were christianized so that Ovid, for example, was turned into a Christian writer.[13] But the occidental Middle Ages, departing from the early Christian writers as well as from the Byzantine scholars, knew the Homeric story only in Latin through Dictys Cretensis and Dares Phrygius; and knowledge of the Greek language existed only in the remote asylums of Irish monasteries and of Southern Italy.[14]

Homer re-enters the European tradition in the fourteenth century as the man behind Virgil, possibly a greater Virgil; and his champions from Petrarch to Cuperus and Kuester in the seventeenth century tend to acept him as great without specifying why, except that the allegorical tradition is brought in again to present him as a mine of esoteric wisdom.

The Renaissance, conventionally so termed, covers a series of 'renascences' which happened independently over a long period of time, and it would be outside the purpose of this introduction even to attempt an exhaustive survey of those new beginnings which gradually broke away from the latinized composure of the Middle Ages by seeking new roots in Greek antiquity. What interests us here is to establish how the Renaissance scholars attempted to rehabilitate Homer and how they were disappointed with what they were able to find in the poet.

It would be very helpful to discover exactly how well the Renaissance scholars knew their Homer, apart from the fact that they had access to manuscripts of the Greek text, thanks to the Byzantine contacts of Nicolaus Sigeros, Manuel Chrysoloras, Francesco Filelfo and Giovanni Aurispa at the end of the four-teenth century and the beginning of the fifteenth.[15] But it is difficult to settle this problem. Some evidence is provided by the

fact that improvements to the Homeric text were slow in coming,
and that the line-by-line version thrown together by Leonzio
Pilato in 1369 survived without much change until the Cambridge edition of 1689.[16] The epics were read with the help of the
more or less word-for-word interlinear Latin translations of
Pilato and P. C. Decembrio (1439–44) and the Latin prose translation of Lorenzo Valla (1440–4),[17] and this provides an interesting indication of the 'popular' knowledge of Homer, for students
and most non-experts read Homer in versions with these interlinear translations. But none of them were much good either as
Latin or in giving the sense of the Greek. On the other hand we
have Angelo Poliziano making his translation in Latin hexameters
of the second book of the *Iliad* in 1470; and we know that he and
Andronicus Callistus lectured on Homer in the 1470s and 1480s;
and this provides some evidence of a genuine interest in Homer
in the academic circles of Florence.[18]

But the fact remains that there was a note of definite disappointment with Homer. This is evident even in Petrarch's
enthusiasm for Greek poetry in his *Africa* and *Bucolicum Carmen*.
The fifteenth-century Italians were disappointed because Homer
did not emerge obviously as a greater Virgil. To some extent they
put down their unfavourable impressions to the poverty of the
translations, and that is why they call persistently for a good
verse translation. But the verse translations that were made had a
Virgilian character. The superiority of Virgil, implied in the work
of Macrobius, was implicitly recognized by translators, such as
Poliziano (1470) and Eobanus Hessus (1540), who used Virgilian
phraseology, and was explicitly stated by Angelo Decembrio in
Politia literaria (1462).[19]

The disappointment is mirrored in the relative neglect of
Homer by the scholars of the period: the poet did not attract a
major scholarly effort. The Homeric text was not improved to
any marked extent. When Demetrius Chalcondyles printed his
edition of Homer (1488) he merely used the Byzantine vulgate as
the basis of his text. The scholia minora were very gradually
brought into use after their publication by J. Lascaris in Rome
(1517);[20] they did not influence the Aldine printings of Homer
(1504, 1517, 1524). The major step forward was taken by
A. Turnebus, who utilized the recently published commentary by
Eustathius (1544–50) for his Paris edition of Homer (1554). But

again, subsequent editions, notably by H. Stephanus in Geneva (1566), made only slight improvements on Turnebus, though Stephanus's edition became the standard text of Homer and was used by Chapman for his English translation in 1611 and 1614. Commentaries were also thin on the ground, and were neither particularly illuminating nor penetrating. The tradition of allegorizing survived in the teaching of Battista Guarino and in the lectures given by A. Callistus in Florence in 1472–3.[21] J. Camerarius produced a reasonably adequate translation and commentary of the first book of the *Iliad* in 1538, but the only scholarly, full-scale commentary, by Spondanus in 1583, again gives us allegories and moralistic comment. We have to wait for the eighteenth century and Bentley before there is any further advance in Homeric scholarship.[22]

With the sixteenth century and Vida's *De arte poetica* (1527) and J. C. Scaliger's *Poetices libri septem* (1561) the disillusionment with Homer deepened into explicit condemnation. Their theories of the epic, which were based on Virgil, found no room for Homer's everyday realism and his irreverent handling of the supernatural. The main objections to Homer were his lack of *decorum* and *gravitas* and the lack of a unifying hero in the *Iliad* and the *Odyssey*, other than unchivalrous and very human characters. Homer was also attacked as an epic writer because he had chosen to describe a historically trivial conflict and had dealt with his subject without a sense of organized dramatic development.[23] Their preference for Virgil on these specific grounds can be seen as related to the debate about taste by the *modernes*. It was a direct source for d'Aubignac's and Perrault's critique of the *anciens* during the *querelle*. But on the whole these attacks must be generally regarded as less significant than the obvious neglect Homer suffered during that time at the hands of scholars and in the awareness of interested readers, what Meric Casaubon calls the *fati Homerici iniquitatem*.[24]

The dismal picture is somewhat corrected by the fact that there was a steady stream of translations first in Latin, then in the vernacular among which those of Hessus (1540), Chapman (1611, 1614) and finally Dryden (partial, 1700) were outstanding. From about 1640 onwards there was a stream of books on the Homeric background, lexica and critical commentaries, so that by the time Boileau produced his Longinus in 1674 there was a basis for a renewal of interest in Homer. This interest can to some extent be seen as connected with that work, which was known some years before it was published. For the point about 'Longinus' is that he does give good reasons for rating Homer high as a poet, and these served to counterbalance the more specific objections to him as a writer of epic. The sublimity and fire emphasized by 'Longinus' found their most powerful expressions in Vico's poetic theory and in Pope's analysis of Homer in the eighteenth century, which reassessed Homer's originality on these grounds.

The French humanists' repeated claims for the necessity of Greek learning brought about a brief revival of interest in Homer, though a taste for hellenistic poetry was far more enthusiastically maintained, and in fact agreed better with the poetic theory and practice of the Pléiade.[25] Ronsard, however, quite explicitly rejected the symbolism of his teacher, Jean Dorat, in favour of simple poetic sentiments, which he saw admirably expressed in Homer. In writing the *Franciade* (1573) he hoped to become a 'Homère français', though in his lyric poetry he still looked upon the Alexandrinian poets as models.[26] Rabelais called Homer the 'paragon de tous philologes', and while he rejected allegorical interpretations of the Homeric epic, he greatly admired Homer as a source of true wisdom in Gargantua's famous letter to his son in *Pantagruel* (1537).

During the seventeenth century the centre of interest in Homer moved decisively to France, although the story there may appear again to be one of ignorance and misunderstanding.[27] While the humanists had seen a possibility of creating a new French hellenism through a return to Greek antiquity, the seventeenth century believed in the myth of a 'grand siècle': men compared their own age with the illustrious periods of classical antiquity and saw its greatness exemplified in the art and literature of the age of Louis XIV. This is evident even in the relatively early works of Paul Pellisson (1650) and Claude Fleury (1665) on Homer. As the century drew to a close, classicism as a doctrine of the imitation of the classics crystallized round Boileau's *Art poétique* (1674); but at the beginning of the *querelle*, the problem of establishing whether in fact the French classical period had outlived this myth became an issue – whether, in other words, the obvious contemporary masterpieces had owed anything that was essential in them to the writers of antiquity, since the French classical epic that was

produced in conscious imitation of ancient models was definitely
second-rate. This conflict between the values of classical antiquity
and modern sensibility that was confident enough to express itself
in contemporary modes, the conflict between permanent and
transient, was at the heart of the *querelle* during which Homer
was again rejected.

Neoclassical criticism both in France and in England associated
the epic genre with the highest level of poetic creation, following
in this such Renaissance critics as Tasso and Scaliger. The critics
also thought that only two poets, Homer and Virgil, had truly
succeeded in epic poetry. As they considered the literature of
classical antiquity to be the model for contemporary poets, on
the grounds of continuance of esteem, they singled out Homer
and Virgil, because these two poets fulfilled another important
criterion of neoclassical criticism, namely that of universality and
scope. Although the Homeric epic was regarded as more original
in the sense that the *Iliad* and the *Odyssey* had been the first
instances of the epic genre, neoclassical critics had a clear preference for the Virgilian epic. The reasons for this preference become
obvious when we remember that neoclassical criticism defined the
epic as 'a discourse invented by art'.[28] An epic poem should
ideally be a formal treatise in poetic metre concerning those issues
that were universally valid and morally ennobling. French and
English critics agreed that Homer was the 'père de la poësie'.
But this traditional way of referring to Homer became increasingly a mere label, with little consequence to the actual content
of criticism of the epic. In the neoclassical picture of poetry as a
form invented through art and practised according to rules,
Homer stood like a giant who was visible enough but, on the
whole, unapproachable. The critics admitted the greatness of
Homer, while at the same time their critical method, which
favoured formal criteria, seemed to leave them without proper
tools for analysing the special qualities of Homeric epic.

The neoclassical attitude to Homer is best illustrated in the
comparisons with Virgil which became a critical commonplace.
The critics discovered the distinguishing marks of genius –
originality, sublimity and 'fire' – in the poems of Homer, but were
not greatly interested in these and based their discussion of such
issues on the views of pseudo-Longinus. It was in Virgil that they
found such poetic qualities as elegance, regularity, discretion,

judgment and humanity, which were in accordance with the standards of taste of their own age. Homer was valued for his invention and scope, which were included in the neoclassical criteria of the epic; but he was regarded as inferior to Virgil because great invention could result in a lack of proportion and decorum. The critics also recognized an element of vulgarity in the Homeric poems which Virgil, writing for a more sophisticated society with more highly developed conventions, had avoided. It was exactly these views about the poems of Homer and Virgil, promulgated at the time by the neoclassical critics, that provided meat for the arguments of the *modernes* that the literature of classical antiquity, created in an alien culture, was an inadequate model for contemporary poets.

But here we are already approaching the themes of this book. Homer did not suffer neglect because of the *querelle*. It can be argued that during and after the *querelle* and the Homeric war, the centre of interest in Homer moved again, and this time to England. This shift had been prepared by the strong vernacular translations of Greek epic by Chapman (1611, 1614), John Ogilby (1669), Thomas Hobbes (1676–7) and Dryden (1700). It was also helped by the major scholarly discovery of the Homeric digamma by Bentley (1699); but it happened perhaps also because of the original conclusions (or lack of them) that the English writers and critics drew from the French *querelle*. Homer entered the English eighteenth century relatively undamaged by the debate between the ancients and moderns. He was seen as a major classic, whether he was read or not: he could be studied in the Greek or with the help of translations, and his inherent interest could be, if not always appreciated, at least utilized for the purposes of literary and social theories. The objections to Homer concentrated on the fact that Homeric poems had become storehouses of epic rules which were inadmissible in contemporary practice, and that Homer was obscure and difficult to understand. But both these objections also resulted in practical efforts to overcome the obstacles they represented. The fact that Homer's epics had set a norm in different periods and different cultures could be read as evidence of his originality and scope, which were eighteenth-century preoccupations, and his obscurity could be seen as an indication of his being an authentic representative of an alien culture. Perhaps the most important point is that there was enough interest centred on Homer in the eighteenth century, and enough tension between the values of originality and the respect for tradition that is due to a classic author, to make the Homeric epics the focus of vital literary and cultural developments which will repay our attention.

PART I

ANCIENTS AND MODERNS

'Quel est donc votre père que vous cherchez? reprit la déesse. Il se nomme Ulysse – dit Télémaque – c'est un des rois qui ont, après un siège de dix ans, renversé la fameuse Troie.'

François Fénelon, *Les aventures de Télémaque* (Paris 1699), ed. J. L. Goré (Paris 1968), p. 66.

1

Ancients and moderns: the problem of cultural progress

Should modern writers copy the ancients or should they rather follow their own creative talent? That was, in its simplest form, the question debated during the *querelle des anciens et des modernes*. The issue was not a new one. It had been raised during the fourteenth century when the modernists of the early Renaissance had discussed cultural progress. But during the seventeenth-century *querelle*, Perrault and the *modernes* made certain theoretical assumptions about progress which were to prove rich in consequences. It is hardly an oversimplification to say that the *querelle* itself was the most crucial intellectual struggle in the early development of modern Europe. During the *querelle* values derived from classical antiquity were for the first time set in opposition to progress, and the late seventeenth and early eighteenth century hence marked the beginning of a new phase in the history of thought.[1]

Initially, the *querelle* represented the revolt of French and English writers against the traditional acceptance of antiquity as a linguistic, literary and artistic model. The name itself owes its origins to Charles Perrault, whose *Parallèle des anciens et des modernes* (1688–97) gives an account of the issues at stake in support of the modernist position. The origins of the linguistic and literary debate can be traced back to Jean Desmarets de Saint-Sorlin's *La comparaison de la langue et de la poësie françoise avec la grecque et la latine* (1670), where a decided attack on Homer was made. This was the most famous of the many treatises produced in the 1670s which defended the French language and thus could be considered modernist. When de Callières published his account of the *querelle* in 1688, its title, *Histoire poëtique de la guerre nouvellement déclarée entre les anciens et les modernes,* indicated the existence of a prolonged debate that had recently gained greater prominence.

In the 1680s the debate moved by slow stages to consider critical, creative, educational and cultural questions in general. Literature constituted the crucial area in which the problem of cultural values was being worked out. Perrault and his friends assumed that a literary work owed its character to the social and cultural conditions that existed at the time of its creation. Their idea that the level of cultural development determines literary productions reflected particularly badly on Homer, since the Homeric epics were the products of a primitive age. Theories implicit in the statements the *modernes* made about classical antiquity and cultural development became the dominant issues of the eighteenth century in the work of Vico and the Scottish primitivists.

During the *querelle* a new humanist concern manifested itself, and the humanistic implications of the debate are still largely with us.[2] The central questions of the *querelle* can be characterized as a series of enquiries into the meaning of culture by an age which was becoming conscious of itself and saw its relation to the past in a more detached way than the previous generation had done. The men of the 1670s and 1680s grouped around the French Academy were increasingly interested in three interconnected questions: the different standards of artistic excellence in ancient and modern culture (the *literary critical* problem), the dependence of creative genius on its culture and environment (the *creative* and *educational* problem) and the debt owed by contemporary arts and sciences to antiquity (the *cultural* problem). Two fundamentally different concepts of man were reflected in the discussion of these problems. Either man could be always the same, as La Bruyère, the supporter of the ancients, put it: 'Les hommes n'ont point changé selon le coeur et selon les passions, ils sont encore tels qu'ils étaient alors et qu'ils sont marqués de Théophraste'; or man was changing and constantly bettering himself, because man was essentially a function of his brain and intellect, not of his heart and emotions, as Fontenelle argued: 'l'homme n'est homme que par la raison, et rien n'est plus beau que d'apprendre aux autres comment ils s'en doivent servir à étudier la Nature, et à développer toutes les enigmes qu'elle nous propose'.[3]

The supporters of the ancients and the moderns, led by Boileau and Perrault respectively, differed also in their views as regards the method and the solution. The ancients saw no essential need for adopting new standards of criticism for value judgments of contemporary works, arguing, as they did, for universality; likewise they largely ignored the importance of environment as a factor in the formation of genius, and stated that a level of perfection had been attained in antiquity which contemporary literature could only imitate.

While the ancients equated classical antiquity with nature in saying that 'sed iuxta antiquos naturam imitabere pulchram', and stated that the classics should be imitated because they had imitated nature so well, the moderns viewed humanity as constantly transforming and dependent on cultural and environmental forces largely outside its control. Human phenomena, including individuals, societies and their intellectual and cultural achievements, were set in opposition to nature. Fontenelle argued for nature's continual power to mould human events; there was an abstract principle, not unlike that proposed by Newtonian physics, that was shaping humanity and its history according to natural laws. Classical antiquity represented one stage in the history of humanity that is subject to these forces of nature.[4] However, judgments concerning the individual productions of antiquity had to be rendered in relative, human terms, because the men of genius who had created these works were formed by the early environment.

In literature, the moderns argued emphatically for relative criteria. The evaluation of poetry involved in the first place an attempt to assess the period in which poetry had been produced. Descartes' anti-authoritarianism was evident in the modernist position. Cartesianism wanted to emancipate not only philosophy but also literature, and break the ties that were thought to unite antiquity and the French 'esprit' (*Discours sur la méthode*, 1637). Saint-Evremond, who through his personal contacts with England became the mediator of the relativist view to English criticism, argued in his essay 'Sur les anciens' (?1685) that the Homeric poetry could not be a guide to modern writers because between antiquity and the modern age 'tout est changé: les Dieux, la nature, la politique, les moeurs, le goût, les manières'. The moderns denied the value of classical antiquity and its literary and artistic productions as models, while nevertheless perceiving their inherent merits. Here is the crucial difference between the moderns and the ancients; and even though Saint-Evremond was relatively moderate in his arguments – he steered away from the heat of the *querelle* by staying in England – his view of the Homeric epic expressed the position maintained by the moderns until La Motte: 'Si Homère vivoit présentement, il feroit des poèmes admirables accomodez au siècle où il écrivoit: nos poëtes en font des mauvais, ajustez à celuy des anciens, et conduits par des règles qui sont tombées avec des choses que le temps a fait tomber.'[5]

The imitation of antiquity based on admiration could be positively harmful. Fontenelle, the most notable philosopher among the moderns, argued that it was exactly on this issue that the progress of human knowledge was crucially held back: 'Rien n'arrête tant le progrès des choses, rien ne borne tant des esprits, que l'admiration excessive des anciens. Parce qu'on s'était dévoué à l'autorité d'Aristôte, et qu'on ne cherchait la vérité que dans ses écrits énigmatiques, et jamais dans la nature.'[6] Fontenelle's influential essay *Digression sur les anciens et les modernes*, appended to his literary piece *Poësies pastorales* in 1688, has relevance to the discussion of human knowledge insofar as this is scientific, for in science we can meaningfully speak of progress based on accumulative knowledge. Seventeenth-century French writers worked out a new attitude to classical antiquity largely because they had to respond to the challenge presented by the progress of experimental science and scientific thought. In these fields of knowledge the superiority of the modern age was obvious even to those who were not scientists. The popularization of science had become a serious aspect of culture by the time of the *querelle*. There was not only the opposition to Aristotle's view of scientific method, expressed here by Fontenelle and maintained, on different grounds, already by Bacon; it was more generally realized that the ancient writers had believed in the Ptolemaic universe, and that even Aristotle and Lucretius had held views about natural phenomena which most educated people found preposterous. Fontenelle capitalized on these shortcomings of ancient science, and in his *Entretiens sur la pluralité des mondes* (1688), which was immediately translated into English, he demonstrated to the public the advancement of modern scientific ideas in relation to the ancient: 'The Ancients were pleasant Gentlemen, to imagine that the Celestial Bodies were in their own nature unchangeable, because they observed no change in them: but they did not live long enough to confirm their opinion by their own experience; they were Boys in comparison to Us.'[7]

Fontenelle's ideas – and those of the moderns – on natural sciences, physics, chemistry and astronomy and their methodology have only a marginal interest here; but they do have a bearing on the argument of this chapter. During the *querelle*, a confrontation between the ancients and the moderns as regards literary critical, creative, educational and cultural issues was inevitable, because the concept of man presented an infinitely more complex problem than it had done for the thinkers of previous generations. Montaigne is a representative of a century that knew its classics thoroughly and read them primarily for personal reasons and because they revealed a rich and full picture of human nature.[8] Even in the generation after Descartes, scientists could not yet adequately tackle the complexity of man's nature. There were philosophers and sensitive students of man who continued to use classical literature as their material evidence, and the need for a science was echoed by Pope some thirty years later – 'Know then thyself, presume not God to scan; / the proper study of mankind is Man' – but a science of man in the modern sense of psychological and social sciences was virtually non-existent. It was in natural sciences that the advancement from the ancient position could be clearly stated and even shown. The certainty of progress there suggested to moderns that similar development had occurred in the arts and humanities. Only it was much more difficult to prove.

The moderns argued that human nature revealed in contemporary works was in fact much richer and more complex than that in the literature of antiquity. Fontenelle pointed out in his *Digression* that centuries differ in regard to the number of people who have been able fully to realize their potentialities: 'Elle [nature] produit dans tous les siècles des hommes propres à être des grands hommes, mais les siècles ne leur permettent pas toujours d'exercer leurs talents' (*Digression*, p. 170). Perrault in his *Parallèle* (discussed in the following chapter) expressed most clearly the idea of some slow but steady development in man's intellectual capacities which better qualify him for the study of his own nature.

In the last phase of the *querelle,* at the end of the seventeenth century and the beginning of the eighteenth, the issues expanded to cover every vital aspect of culture. The scope of Perrault's *Parallèle* is evidence for this. Even in that work, though its main attack was directed against classical culture and its men of genius, there were elements which suggested that literary men and scholars alike were beginning to feel that more factual information about antiquity was needed for a proper revaluation of the classical heritage. The existing view of classical literature was dependent on a textual tradition which even the Renaissance scholars had realized to be insufficiently critical, while the physical environment of antiquity was known only through books or through impressionistic travellers' accounts. It was realized that if more factual information were available, in terms of both reliable texts and archaeological findings, the attitudes to the classics might substantially change. Perrault's generation knew its classics very badly and through translations; but it awakened to a new adventurous interest in the reality that had produced classical art and literature. A plea for a kind of imaginative archaeology was made in the *Parallèle*: 'Nous naissons au milieu de sphères et des cartes géographiques, qui nous enseignent dès nostre enfance la véritable situation de tous les pays, et nous croyons mal-à-propos qu'il en a esté de mesme du temps d'Homère.'[9]

By the time discussion of the issues of the *querelle* had spread outside the circle of the participants, and the controversy itself had ended, the division of labour between the ancients and the moderns was beginning to be settled. The moderns made the practical proposal that contemporary literature and art should proceed independently of what had gone on before, because in their eyes the fact that the classical forms of literature had survived for centuries was evidence of their adaptability and variety, not of their superiority as such. The ancients interested themselves more and more in the practical problems that emerged in the study of classical antiquity. The classical scholars of the late eighteenth century and of the nineteenth can be seen as the descendants of the ancients of the *querelle*. The eighteenth-century contribution to classical studies lay in investigating the philological accuracy of ancient texts and testing the archaeological authenticity of the classical remains; and by this development one of the issues raised during the *querelle* was brought to its material fruition.

Classical scholarship was not much help, however. The age began with the dominance of Bentley (*Dissertation on the epistles of Phalaris*, 1699), and none of his successors did more than equal him until F. A. Wolf (*Prolegomena ad Homerum*, 1795) came on the scene. In any case, the gap which had been growing since the sixteenth century between the professional scholar and the literary world had by the end of the eighteenth century become very wide indeed, and the labours of men like Gesner, Hemsterhuys, Porson and Heyne did not make an impact on the influence exerted by the classics.

Simultaneously, in literature and arts, an idealized and romantic view of antiquity, which yet had a far more solid basis in physical reality than any previous view, emerged as a creative force. Even the most fervent classicists were learning from their opponents to look upon ancient culture as separate from their own. This development was greatly helped by the abandonment of Latin as the common language of learning, which had occurred at the end of the seventeenth century; and it was helped too by the growing interest in classical art. The enthusiasm of archaeologists like Scipione Maffei (1675–1755), author of *Verona illustrata* (1731–2), and P. M. Paciaudi (1710–55), and of collectors like Cardinal Albani (1692–1779), and the Comte de Caylus (1692–1765), led to that new view of the past, the romantic classicism, which we find in the work of Winckelmann. His concept of a classicism that reduced passion to harmony had a questionable influence in the field of the fine arts where it gave birth to the chillness of J. L. David, Nollekens and Flaxman, but its inspiring effect on literature cannot be denied. With Goethe, Schiller and Hölderlin we come to a group of writers who were as devoted to antiquity as the great neoclassical masters had been. But they viewed that antiquity in a new light. They did not regard their age as part of a single unified culture existing since the days of Homer, nor did they look upon the works of the ancients as furnishing norms that they ought to follow. They admired and they were prepared to imitate, but as one admires and imitates an alien excellence.

In the meantime, the moderns were learning to modify the intransigence of their opposition. Literature could not help betraying its cultural origins, and the natural answer of the ancients had been to see the origins of contemporary writings in classical antiquity. In the controversy about literary issues, the moderns realized that their position was admittedly more ambiguous than in that about scientific questions. The cultural debate that dealt with fundamental problems of artistic creation, such as tradition and originality, and demanded clear-cut statements about them, seemed rather to hamper than to promote the creativity of those who were closely involved in the war. The masterpieces of the classical period, like the tragedies of Racine, the plays of Molière or the maxims of La Rochefoucauld, were based on ancient models, but then these authors had taken no active part in any stage of the *querelle*. And although after their time the idea that emancipation from imitation of the classics was necessary for the development of national literatures was advocated by the moderns, the fruits of this programme were not apparent.

During the eighteenth century the balance of achievement between the parties gradually altered. On the side of the ancients there were still writers who took the Greeks and Romans for models, but they were fewer than before, and their productions were no longer of the first rank. Marivaux's plays, though classical in their portrayal of stereotyped characters, only vaquely conveyed the direct comic simplicity of Plautus or Terence: and Voltaire exploited ancient classical themes for his tragedies only in order to demonstrate their adaptability for a contemporary message. The mood that had inspired Racine and Boileau was spent.

II

In both literature and literary criticism, the eighteenth century marked the beginning of an experimentation with forms which were independent of those developed by the classical writers. After their first provocative pronouncements, the moderns based their position on recognition of the classical influence on European culture, but coupled this with a critical analysis of the nature of that influence. They looked at the culture of antiquity for the first time from the standpoint of a stranger. The classics had been like a father or mother to them, and had nourished and educated them; but in their own work they were spiritually alienated from them. The moderns were prepared to recreate classical themes in a new literary context. When one looks at the great number of the themes of the classical epic – the voyage of adventure, the miraculous rescue, the hero in disguise, true love put to the test – in the novels of Fielding, Richardson, Smollett and others, one must conclude that perhaps the true heirs of the moderns were the detached novelists who utilized classical themes in what was essentially an unclassical genre.

While the creative efforts of the would-be innovators were limited to genres which antiquity had wholly or partly neglected, a work appeared which was a straightforward rereading of classical epic, and managed to satisfy both the intellectual aspirations of the moderns and the sense of tradition that characterized the best of the ancients. The case of Fénelon's *Télémaque*, which was published in 1699 and enjoyed great popularity in France and England,[10] is instructive. Fénelon admits the principles of progress and the permanence of natural forces advocated by the moderns, but he sees that antiquity was for ever in a more advantageous position than the modern age. Associating himself closely with the issues of the *querelle* and yet never giving himself completely to either party,[11] Fénelon wrote the *Télémaque* with a view to recreating the heroic universe of the classical epic in a series of prose tales united by the character of a minor Homeric hero, Telemachus. As an imitation of Homer, it satisfied the ancients; as an experiment in literary form, 'a moral poem in prose', it coincided with the views of the moderns. Its idea of literature as a philosophical and rational exercise pleased the classical critics such as Boileau, as well as Perrault and La Motte, and in its conscious attempt to correct the morality of the Homeric epic – in the Eucharis episode, the virtue of Telemachus faced with erotic temptation is fully reinstated – it proved to be a popular work, wholeheartedly of its age. In Telemachus Fénelon portrayed a young prince who loves his country (which represents his original condition), who is brave and virtuous without being pious, and who goes through experiences which constantly shape his thinking and moral outlook. A choice on personal grounds is always open to him, and in this respect he differs, as a fictional character, from both Homer's Ulysses and Virgil's Aeneas, since these two have a function outside their individual character and personal development, Ulysses in renouncing his adventures in order to relieve his people, Aeneas in learning through his experiences only to become the founder of an empire. Nevertheless, while the narrative of the *Télémaque* contains fantastic elements characteristic of novellas and fictional techniques typical of the novel, and is a conscious imitation of the Graeco-Roman epic, it is not meant to be like any of these genres in particular, and is unclassifiable. Its purpose is moral education and the cultivation of taste; while it may be said to contain ideas which inaugurate those of the Enlightenment, its structure and narrative technique are totally non-innovatory and traditional.

Before the novel came into its own, at a time when the classical epic was continued in the poor imitations that were the nationalistic and Christian epics in France and in England,[12] or in such large-scale romances of the age that had certain epic qualities, the moderns explored the possibilities of literary expression in the fable and the fairy-tale.[13] The innovatory character of these productions is easy to ignore. Perrault, Fontenelle and La Motte, while actively engaged in the *querelle* on the side of the moderns, sought new ways of communicating original European sensibility in the narrative of the fable, tale and fairy-tale. Their scholarly and artistic interest in these genres was one of the paradoxes of the controversy, because it was both a tribute to the original sources of story-telling, which they undoubtedly perceived in the *Iliad* and the *Odyssey* as well as in the minor works of antiquity, and a departure from classical models in favour of literary forms primarily associated with central European culture. It was in these genres that they first discovered alternatives to the literary forms of classical antiquity. Classical writers had, admittedly, known some form of the fable and the fairy-tale, as we can see from the work of the first-century Phaedrus who used Aesop's fables and the second-century Lucian who wrote both satirical and science-fictional tales, and from the Milesian tales retold in Petronius (first century) and in Apuleius (second century), which may be called novellas; and it is well known that there are unmistakable elements of the fairy-tale in the *Odyssey*.

But the moderns selected the tales from vernacular sources, and emphasized their European origin. Alien classical mythology was replaced by the histories of kings, queens and peasants. The questionable moral values of the classical stories did not burden the vernacular fairy-tale: the moral choices of its characters were motivated in a way that was familiar to eighteenth-century readers, and the resolution of the psychological or moral dilemma was always good or instructive. The moderns argued, therefore, that the fairy-tale was a form more natural to European culture than any literary product of classical antiquity.

Charles Perrault (1628–1703), author of the *Parallèle*, was with his brother Claude the foremost collector and writer of fairy-tales of his day.[14] Their complexity is immediately apparent. When the modern reader is confronted with these narratives written in a ponderous baroque style, he becomes aware of the web of underlying motives and intentions disguised as literature for children. Perrault in fact claimed that his sixteen-year-old son Pierre D'Armancour had been the author of *Les contes de ma Mère l'Oye*, published in January 1697. He utilized the Italian Renaissance sources of Straparole, Basile and Boccaccio, and seventeenth-century French tales collected by Mlle Bernard, Mlle Lhéritier and Mme D'Aulnoy,[15] and produced the complex universe of modern man attempting to reach to the hidden levels of his personality. Perrault gave an expression to the need for the irrational felt by a pre-eminently rational age; he set value on the irrational and the unknown and was interested in methods of approach to it.

The preface which Perrault wrote to his *Histoires ou contes de temps passé* (1697) displays, however, some of the difficulties of which the moderns were aware when presenting a new genre to their contemporaries. Fairy-tales could be regarded as trivial and simply entertaining, and were certainly without the supporting authority of a long literary tradition. Perrault therefore felt the need to argue:

Mais comme j'ai affaire à bien des gens qui ne se payent pas de raisons et qui ne se peuvent être touchés que par l'autorité et par l'exemple des Anciens, je vais les satisfaire là-dessus. Les Fables Milésiennes si célèbres parmi les Grecs, et qui ont fait les délices d'Athènes et de Rome, n'étaient pas d'une autre espèce que les Fables de ce Recueil. L'Histoire de la Matrone d'Ephèse est de la même nature que celle de Griselidis: ce sont l'une et l'autre des Nouvelles, c'est-à-dire Récits de choses qui peuvent être arrivées, et qui n'ont rien qui blesse absolument la vraisemblance.[16]

He was led into an unfortunate comparison between the tale of the matron of Ephesus and the fairy-tale of patient Griselda. The similarities do not go beyond the certain element of realism. The virtue of Griselda is tested by an accumulating series of atrocities against her roles as a bride, a wife and a mother, and is rewarded in the end. The matron of Ephesus is, like the character of the classical tales, a very different heroine, whose natural instinct leads her to make a mockery of virtue. The tale has an overt erotic element which was exploited by Boccaccio in his tale of the Marquis de Saluces, and through Petrarch's Latin translation the story became known all over Europe.[17] The sexuality of fairy-tales, such as can be found in 'Bluebeard', 'The Sleeping Beauty', 'Little Red Riding Hood' and 'Patient Griselda', operates on another level. When La Fontaine rewrote *La matrone d'Ephèse* in verse (1674), he wanted to show that 'souvent les femmes qui semblent le plus vertueuses le sont moins'. He had a better understanding of the different nature of the tales than Perrault. For in 'Griselda' Perrault seemed to be wanting to do two things: on the one hand, to explore a complex sexual relationship; on the other, to demonstrate the virtue of women, especially of those to whom public opinion had been unjustly severe. His comparison in the preface can thus be seen as an interesting misreading of his own tales.

Despite the apologetic tone by which the first full-length collection of fairy-tales was introduced to the public, the genre proved a success. Perrault's tales were translated into English in 1729, and later in the eighteenth century a forty-one-volume definitive collection of fairy-tales, *Le cabinet des fées*, was published by de Mayer (Amsterdam 1785–9) which included the slightly edited texts of Perrault's original tales and the fairy-tale 'Beauty and the Beast' by de Villeneuve. The creative resources of vernacular literature were continued in the fairy-tale of the eighteenth century, and we can regard this genre as a real discovery of the moderns.

The fable was far more dependent on classical models. Jean de La Fontaine rewrote Aesop's fables by adopting a mixture of the heroic metre, Alexandrines and heterometres, and by refashioning the moral points of the fables to suit a more sophisticated audience. Innovator though La Fontaine was, he admired the writers of antiquity above those of his own generation.

> Mon imitation n'est point un esclavage:
> Je ne prends que l'idée, et les tours, et les lois
> Que nos maîtres suivaient eux-mêmes autrefois. . .
> Mais, près de ces grands noms, notre gloire est petite.[18]

La Fontaine aimed to preserve a neutral role in the *querelle*, but in his work he paid great tribute to the classical models. His fables became immediately popular, for what he utilized in ancient writers was their essential simplicity. Antoine Houdar de La Motte, translator of the *Iliad* (1701–14) and a partisan of the moderns during the last phase of the *querelle*, was also a prolific writer of fables. But their morality was more contemporary and everyday than in La Fontaine's more universal examples. A fable of 'Homer and the deaf man' was included, which was an allegory of the 'deafness' of moribund tradition. In *One hundred new court fables*, which was translated into English in 1721, he gave his definition of the genre: 'Fable is nothing but Instruction disguised under the Allegory of an Action. It is a small Epic Poem, which is in no way inferior to a great one, but only in its smallness of Extent.'[19] It is interesting to notice the definition of the fable as the small epic poem. Not only in La Motte, but also in the criticism of Pierre Daniel Huet, the fable is understood to be, not the animal tale of the classical Aesop, but essentially a story, for which a prototype can be found in the tales of the *Odyssey*, in the episodes of Circe, Calypso, Polyphemus, the Laestrygonians and the Lotus Eaters. The comparison of the fable with the epic also showed how far the contemporary classical epic poets in France had neglected that aspect of the genre. The national and Christian epic poetry of Le Moyne, Scudéry, Chapelain, Desmarets de Saint-Sorlin, La Laboureur and Carel de Saint-Garde was founded on a narrowly formal reading of the *Iliad*, the *Aeneid* and the *Thebaid*, on a subservient study of the epic rules as well as on an anachronistic imitation of their heroic idealism. The moderns had indeed set themselves an ambitious programme, and their work had to be continued far beyond their own generation.

Finally, when it comes to deciding whether the new genres were in any way superior to the greatest achievements of classical antiquity and whether the freer experimentation with ancient models was any sign of progress, we can say that the moderns certainly offered in their work a wider scope for literary expression which their present culture necessitated. Louis Sebastian Mercier, the utopian writer of *L'an deux mille quatre cent quarante* (?1770), who thought that in future times it would be possible to have thousands of poets of the stature of Homer, also thought that Perrault's tales were more valuable than the *Iliad*.[20]

The idea was gradually recognized that in literature cultural origins are at least as much an individual matter as wider cultural dependence.

III

Voltaire, observing the situation in England in 1727, realized that in a country that had produced Shakespeare and Milton, the need to work out a distance from the ancient writers was not felt in the same way as in France. The neoclassical criticism of the epic came to England as an importation from France, and during the time it dominated English critical writing (c. 1680–1730) it retained its French characteristics. Most of the works of Boileau, Rapin, Le Bossu, Huet, André Dacier, Mme Dacier and Fontenelle on the epic were immediately translated into English and were provided with prefaces and notes in the style of the original by their English translators.[21] The terminology and syntax of the translations were largely derivative of the French text. It was in this connection that the controversy of the ancients and the moderns was introduced to England.

Saint-Evremond had close connections with the English literary scene at the end of the seventeenth century, and can be seen as a mediator between the French and English views. He enjoyed a high reputation in England, and John Dennis openly borrowed from him. He had a sensitive appreciation of literature and could understand originality. Although his main works were on classical literature, on which he wrote with some psychological perceptiveness, he stood aside from the *querelle*. His relativistic ideas were sketched in an essay 'Sur les anciens' (?1685), where the analysis of the Homeric and Virgilian epic emphasized the idea of literature's dependence on its historical background. The main point of Saint-Evremond's criticism was that the rules of poetry were created in the practice of writing and were conditioned by the particular and often individual circumstances of poetic creation. This historical view of literature had a great influence on eighteenth-century criticism in England, where the debate was mainly concerned with the question of rules and originality in epic writing.

Jean Le Clerc (known in Holland since 1684), a many-sided literary critic who had a hand in the famous *Bibliothèque univer-*

selle, was also, by his great popularity, an influence in English literary criticism of the turn of the century. His rather compilatory critical work *Parrhasiana* was translated into English in 1700; in it he argued that imitation of artificial models, whatever they were, was against the nature of art. Because of their imitation of the ancients, modern writers were inferior in all respects: ''Tis because the Moderns are sordid Imitators of the Ancients, and can pretend to nothing that is truly original, because they are only Poets by Rote and by Imitation, and have not penetrated the Principles of their Art.'[22] But he added a positive suggestion to this negative view of contemporary poetry. Le Clerc is interesting because he is one of the first critics who explicitly stated that originality could be restored to modern writing by the strong practice of the vernacular. This view characterizes English poetic criticism of the eighteenth century, but it is also related to the educational changes that were occurring everywhere in western Europe at this time – changes which favoured modern languages: 'To disengage himself from this servile Spirit of imitation, a Man ought to write in his own Mother-Tongue: By this means he will think less of the Expressions and Thoughts of the Ancients; and as he is full of modern Words and Ideas, with which he is perfectly well acquainted, he will become an Original.'[23]

The English neoclassical critics and poets, who took sides in the debate between the ancients and the moderns, were far more interested in the problem of originality versus poetic rules in composition than the French had been. This problem was related to the issues of the *querelle*, but their concern with it was indicative of their more practical and creative approach. Their writings were relatively free from the personal hostilities and the clear-cut antagonism that characterized the *querelle*. But they came no nearer than Boileau or Perrault to deciding whether the classical authors represented the natural source of inspiration or a confining strait-jacket for modern writing. Where they differed from the French, however, was in recognizing originality from the start as a particular quality of the poetic mind. Though they were unable to define its character or its place in the creative act – this became a main theme only with the Scottish primitivists in the 1760s – they certainly discussed an aspect of writing which the French did not recognize.

English critics asked whether any of the writers of classical antiquity, from Homer onwards, had been original in the sense of enjoying a total freedom from poetic rules. Sir William Temple (1628–99), who claimed to be an English 'ancient', thought in his essay 'Of poetry' (1690) that Homer at least, by dint of the calibre of his genius, had been close to total freedom.[24] The simple point Temple made about Homer's originality formed part in a long controversy about the value of classical learning; and the mini-*querelle* between Temple and William Wotton which inspired Jonathan Swift was the closest to what the English could show of the style of the French debate. It was paradoxical, however, that Temple was played into the corner of the extreme traditionalist by his clever opponent Wotton, who exploited Fontenelle's ideas of the different nature of learning in humanities and arts and in sciences.[25] The respective merits of the ancients and the moderns could be judged only in terms of whether their achievements had been literary or scientific, Wotton argued; and Temple, though he conceded this point, regarded poetry as a totally independent activity where considerations about cultural progress were virtually meaningless.

But in general, English criticism took the view that the classical authors, including Homer and Virgil, seemed to have been far more confined by poetic conventions as regards both content and expression than the native Shakespeare. Charles Gildon, who in his criticism consistently advocated the necessity of poetic rules, considered the problems this raised, and in his study of Shakespeare he came to express the idea that poetic rules need not be opposed to originality but were its complement.

'Tis my Opinion, that if *Shakespear* had had those Advantages of Learning, which the perfect Knowledge of the Ancients would have given him; so great a Genius as his would have made him a very dangerous rival in Fame to the greatest Poets of Antiquity: so far am I from seeing, how this Knowledge could either have curb'd, confin'd, or spoil'd the natural Excellence of his Writings.[26]

In the English tradition of literature, the originality and the untutored genius of the poet has been an established notion, and the prime example of this has been Shakespeare, not Homer. I am arguing here that there had been some indulgent admiration for poetic qualities which relate but dimly to the world of reality, and a lack of appreciation for visually accurate and intelligent prose. For these reasons Homer had been really valued in English criticism only by an elite minority, which had always been there. For some of his most original qualities, those of the straight-forward narrative and the visual description of detail, can only be apprehended in the Greek. But in the eighteenth century the labours of translators and a more general knowledge of the Homeric background began to open the primitive aspects of Homer's epics to the majority of educated Englishmen. And this bardic quality of Homer certainly struck a chord in England. Addison in 'The pleasures of the imagination' (1712) expressed what his readers were looking for in Homer: 'Reading the *Iliad* is like travelling through a country uninhabited, where the fancy is entertained with a thousand savage prospects of vast deserts, wide uncultivated marshes, huge forests, misshapen rocks and precipices.'[27] Such a notion of original writing the English could also find in Shakespeare, and direct comparisons between Homer and Shakespeare were made. Peter Whalley wrote about the subject in 1748: 'Shakespeare has been deservedly esteemed the *Homer*, the Father of our Dramatic Poetry, as being the most irresistible Master of the Passions: possessed of the same creative Power of Imagination, abounding with a vast Assemblage of Ideas, and a rich Redundancy of Genius and Invention.'[28] But the originality of Homer was fully appreciated in England only after the primitivists had hit upon the idea that Homer was a poet of a primitive culture who used such techniques of poetic creation as were familiar to them in native popular poetry, and Homer was relieved of his duties, for a time at least, as a strictly classical poet and the 'father of the epic rules'.

Leonard Welsted was an early example of a critic who valued this kind of originality. His criticism of poetic rules amounted to an attack against the neoclassical principles, and he had to speak in opposition to such influential critics as John Dennis. While John Dennis had claimed in *The advancement and reformation of modern poetry* (1701) that 'the Renowned Masters among the Ancients, *Homer* and *Virgil*, etc. had too much Capacity, and too much Discernment, not to see the Necessity of knowing and practicing the Rules, which Reason and Philosophy have prescrib'd to Poets',[29] Welsted thought that poetic rules were 'nothing but a pert insipid Heap of Commonplace; nor do any. . . contribute. . .towards raising or finishing a good Genius'. This was because the rules were thought to be simply part of the poetic artifice. In Welsted's opinion of poetry, the rules

> touch only the Externals or Form of the Thing, without entering into
> the Spirit of it; they play about the surface of Poetry, but never dive
> into its Depths; the Secret, the Soul of good Writing is not to be come
> at thro' such mechanic Laws; the main Graces, and the cardinal
> Beauties of this charming Art, lie too retir'd within the Bosom of
> Nature, and are too fine and subtle an Essence, to fall under the
> Discussion of Pedants, Commentators, or trading Critics.[30]

It must be emphasized that even during the dominance of neo-classical criticism in England, voices both sensible and passionate were raised in defence of originality.[31]

At a time when the term 'original' was generally used to describe something that was the first instance of its kind – the original of a translation, the original of a poetic imitation, the original from which the artist's copy was made – some discussion of the type of originality Homer and Shakespeare presented was obviously needed. The Homeric epic, by the common consent of both ancients and moderns, was original in the sense of being the first instance of its kind. It was for this reason that the neo-classical critics could accept it as a perfect model for the contemporary epic too. They were divided, however, in their views about the classical origins of English literature, partly because they lacked the close familiarity with the ancient classics on which value judgments in poetry at their best are based, and partly because the links between England and the classical world were, for obvious geographical reasons, educational rather than culturally integral. The French writers of the period were spiritually far closer to the Mediterranean world. And the critics did not travel in the way the poets may have done. Gildon was of course totally wrong about Shakespeare's ignorance of the classical authors, for Shakespeare had been in a special sense much more intimately familiar with Ovid, Plutarch, Suetonius and their world than any of the neoclassical critics had been. We can see that the dichotomy of the *querelle* between the ancients and the moderns did not quite apply to the English eighteenth-century literary scene. There was no wish to decry the achievements of antiquity as such. Rather there was the instinctive veneration of originality which sought its poetic examples either in the earliest of ancient epic poets, or in the native woodnotes of the English tradition.

2

Opposition to antiquity: Charles Perrault

'Nothing is more natural and reasonable than to have great veneration for all those things that are truly valuable in themselves and which have the additional merit of being old', begins Charles Perrault's massive four-volume analysis of the two cultures, the classical and the contemporary, his *Parallèle des anciens et des modernes* (1688–97). Considering its scope, the range of its intentions and its immediate impact, the *Parallèle* can be regarded as the culmination of the ideological controversy in which French poets and critics questioned their relation to the values and criteria of classical literature.[1] Perrault's work challenged the traditional valuation of the achievements of classical antiquity, and although its bias is thus decisively on the side of the moderns, it remains the most comprehensive ideological review that has reached us from late-seventeenth-century France.

As we know, Perrault first won notice for his views when he read a small poem entitled 'Le siècle de Louis le Grand' at the meeting of the French Academy convened to celebrate the recovery of Louis XIV from a recent illness on 27 January 1687. He could not have chosen a more propitious moment. And although this polemical exercise, intended simply to provoke, was by no means the origin of the *querelle*, the debate was considerably enlivened by it.[2] Perrault argued that classical antiquity and all the notions about it that had become part and parcel of French late-seventeenth-century culture should be taken down from their pedestal and thoroughly re-examined. He did not argue for their dismissal.

> La belle Antiquité fut toujours venerable,
> Mais je ne crus jamais qu'elle fust adorable.

37

Je voys les Anciens, sans plier les genoux,
Ils sont grands, il est vray, mais hommes comme nous.

The re-examination should start with a comparative analysis of the achievements of antiquity and the modern age: 'Et l'on peut comparer sans crainte d'être injuste, / Le siècle de Louis au beau siècle d'Auguste.' The spearhead of Perrault's criticism was thus directed against that stagnation which respect for the past, seen as an essential element in humanities, might produce in the life of a culture.

The *Parallèle* was a continuation of the line of thought first sketched in the 'Siècle', and the poem's argument served as the starting-point for it: 'Il m'a paru tant d'aveuglement dans cette prevention et tant d'ingratitude à ne pas vouloir ouvrir les yeux sur la beauté de nostre siècle, à qui le Ciel a départi mille lumières qu'il a refusées à toute l'Antiquité, que je n'ay pu m'empêcher d'en estre ému d'une véritable Indignation: ç'a esté cette Indignation qui a produit le petit poëme du siècle de Louis le Grand.'[3] The poem and the *Parallèle*, a work in a more sustained and reflective form, attacked the authority of those who maintained that the imitation of the classics was necessary for contemporary literature and arts. This was the view which Perrault regarded as inimical to him, and the indignation of which he spoke had a curious personal force.

It is ironical that the man who devoted his life to the criticism of traditional values is now considered to be a classic himself. Charles Perrault came of a distinguished family of lawyers, and his elder brothers did very well in their chosen fields, Pierre as a lawyer, Claude as a physician and architect, Nicolas as a classical scholar and theologian. Charles himself had a career apart from his literary achievements as a public administrator and academician.[4] His interest in classical literature had a long if somewhat unusual history. While still in his early twenties, he wrote in collaboration with his brothers Claude and Nicolas a burlesque epic, 'Les murs de Troie', which was a parody of Homer, and a burlesque translation of the sixth book of the *Aeneid* (?1648–9), a parody of the *ancien régime*.[5] These poems display in full the raillery that is the disturbing undercurrent of Perrault's later serious writings. All his life, he remained a mixture of an iconoclast manqué and a considerable contributor to the culture of his age. A savage critic of authority, he was at the same time interested in discovering new solutions, so that his fame rests rather on his *Contes* than on the *Parallèle* which has been one of the underestimated masterpieces of French literature.

The *Parallèle* is not an easy work. The ambiguity of Perrault's position is evident in the fact that the book was cast in the form of a literary dialogue, a classical genre made popular by Valla and Erasmus in the Renaissance. But in Perrault's hands it largely served to take the edge off his sharpest arguments, and perhaps intentionally so. There is a complexity which is clearly intended neither to prove nor to disprove. There is little that is originally Perrault's, and yet the *Parallèle* manages to convey a round and at times entertaining picture of late-seventeenth-century French life and ideas. Its conflicting arguments largely recapitulated the complex views of his eminent opponents like Boileau, Arnauld, Fénelon and Huet, who had already protested at the 'Siècle',[6] and of his modern supporters like Fontenelle, who was an active accomplice, and the Homeric scholar abbé d'Aubignac, who remained quietly behind the scenes. Despite its dramatic structure, the *Parallèle* does not achieve the artistic unity that characterizes the Platonic dialogues. It is unclassical in the special sense of being unclassifiable; but it bears the endearing stamp of search and research of time past and present, with all the ramifications that this might involve.

The *Parallèle* discusses the fields of ancient and modern poetry, rhetoric, epic literature, philosophy, mathematics, natural sciences, religion, the visual arts and architecture. It thus aims at a comprehensive panorama of culture. These topics are discussed in five dialogues held while the three participants are walking and taking the air in the garden of Versailles. They are le Président, l'Abbé and le Chevalier, each of whom represents a different element in society and a different point of view as regards antiquity. Le Président is a representative of the ancients; he appears to be fearsomely learned, especially in the classics and fine arts, but is in fact the archetypal pedant and a fool, and the perfect caricature of everything he stands for. He defends Homer as the 'prince of poets' as tradition since the Renaissance had done, and is shocked at the idea that the Homeric poems might have been compilations, as l'Abbé suggests. L'Abbé is a representative of the moderns, and thus Perrault's most obvious spokesman. He, too, is learned, but feels more at home in philosophy and the sciences than in literature, and likes to throw original ideas into the conversation. Le Chevalier is also a representative of the moderns, although his role is a mediatory one. He captures some of the French liking for 'bel esprit' that characterizes the Jesuit tradition, and his comments which support l'Abbé's more serious disquisitions often have a jovial, vivacious style. As the dialogues proceed each new topic defines the roles more closely. In the fourth dialogue the participants discuss Homer and the classical epic, and draw general conclusions about poetry and the dependence of genius on culture. It is on these issues that Perrault comes most clearly into his own and clashes with the ancients and with his arch-enemy Boileau in particular.

Nicolas Boileau was the principal target of Perrault's attack and parody. His popular *L'art poëtique* (1674) had shown him to be a reasonably flexible critic who was prepared to admit that 'poeta nascitur, non fit', or at least must learn to recognize his talent. He had maintained however that it was through imitation of the classics that the poet could achieve excellence.

> C'est en vain qu'au Parnasse un téméraire Auteur
> Pense de l'Art des Vers atteindre la hauteur.
> S'il ne sent point du Ciel l'influence secrète
> Si son Astre en naissant ne l'a formé Poëte,
> Dans son génie étroit il est toujours captif.
> Pour lui Phébus est sourd, et Pégase est rétif.[7]

The crucial difference between Boileau and Perrault was over the question of artistic excellence and originality. Boileau did not deny the value of genius and originality as artistic criteria, but unlike Perrault he saw no obvious contradiction in coupling them with the rules and patterns to be observed within literary tradition, and thus maintained primarily formal criteria in the production and evaluation of literature. The greatest works of antiquity were seen as the models and the storehouses of rules to be imitated. The superiority of Homer and Virgil was unquestioned, as Boileau stated in his 'laudatio Homeri'. Boileau also set an essential value on the continuous and general esteem and admiration that some works of classical antiquity had earned in European literary tradition. In his *Réflexions critiques* (1694) he answered Perrault's views in the first three volumes of the *Parallèle* and in the 'Siècle'.[8]

Where Boileau wanted to see excellence in the degree to which

a contemporary work of art observed universally valid forms and
the general rules of poetry, Perrault argued that all literary works,
including the classics, should be approached as products of
specific cultural situations. Herein was the true test of originality,
and thus in making value judgments the critic should look to the
poetry itself.

Si les ouvrages d'Homère étoient perdus, je serois fort curieux
d'apprendre ce qu'en auroient dit, et ce qu'en auroient pensé ceux qui
les auroient vus. Mais puisque ses ouvrages sont entre nos mains,
pourquoi nous tourmenter tant sur ce que les autres en ont jugé?
Voyons-les nous-mesmes et disons ce qui nous en semble.

C'est comme si nous disputions icy des beautés de Versailles sur les
descriptions qu'on nous en a données, au lieu d'aller nous-mesmes sur
les lieux voir ce qui en est.[9]

Though Perrault maintained from the start that there is progress
in the arts and humanities, and admitted that this progress
depends on the accumulation of ideas and forms of expression
that have been repeatedly found viable, he realized that in
literature and the arts creative achievements must be in some way
products of their culture, which he regarded as an organic unity.
No real assessments could be made without realizing that there
was an individual, as well as a specific cultural situation, behind
each classical masterpiece. Every work of art or cultural act
should be traced back to its human origins.

Hence Perrault belittled the Homeric epics for cultural, and
not for exclusively formal reasons.

Pour ce qui est du nom d'Homère, qui signifie Aveugle, ils disent que
plusieurs de ces Poëtes étoient de pauvres gens, et la plûpart aveugles,
qui alloient de maison en maison reciter leurs poëmes pour de l'argent;
et qu'à cause de cela ces sortes de petits poëmes s'appelloient com-
munément, les chansons de l'Aveugle.[10]

Perrault's thesis, that the modern age represented enlightenment
in the arts and literature as well as the sciences, and was therefore
superior to antiquity, comes out clearly in his discussion of Homer.
Homer proved to be his greatest stand-by in his battle against the
ancients. The manner of composition of the epics, in which Homer
had taken part as one of the many rhapsodists, that is as one of a
collective class of blind and poverty-stricken mercenary singers,
suggested an essentially inferior age:

ils disent que l'Iliade et l'Odyssée ne sont autre chose qu'un amas, qu'une collection de plusieurs petits Poëmes de divers Auteurs qu'on a joints ensemble.[11]

In order to demonstrate the cultural backwardness of Homer, Perrault utilized as his sources the unfavourable views on Homeric poetry which were available at that time in the work of the abbé d'Aubignac and the Renaissance scholar J. C. Scaliger. Perrault, like all the moderns, showed a keen interest in the authorship question of the Greek epic, as he perceived in it possible ways to discredit some of the most cherished notions about Homer, those of the 'prince of poets' and the 'father of epic rules'. The controversy about the authorship and authenticity of the *Iliad* and the *Odyssey*, which originated with the ancient writers Josephus, Plutarch and Aelian, became topical again at the end of the seventeenth century, partly because it was in the interests of the moderns. D'Aubignac's treatise *Conjectures académiques, ou dissertation sur l'Iliade* (written c. 1665) rose out of this background of doubts concerning the personal Homer. Their first exponent in England was Richard Bentley, who in his *Remarks upon a late discourse of free-thinking* (1713) argued that the epics had been collected together in Athens at the time of Pisistratus.[12] D'Aubignac's study was suppressed twice by the public authorities because of its 'fausse et pernicieuse' thesis. It was known to the Perrault brothers, however, as the *Parallèle* tells us, and also to a number of contemporary writers and critics through Adrien Baillet's resumé in his *Jugements des savants* in 1685, before it was eventually published in 1715.[13] D'Aubignac's argument was that the author of the *Iliad* could not have been the same person as the author of the *Odyssey*, the poems being too discordant in style and subject matter, and that Homer had been a collective name for a group of rhapsodists. This was the standard view among the moderns, and Perrault, in his eagerness to criticize the ancients, went as far as stating that 'il n'y a jamais eu au monde un homme nommé Homère'.[14]

In order to demonstrate the unsuitability of the Homeric epics for modern imitation, Perrault exploited J. C. Scaliger's famous disparagement of Homer. The points he made were in the first place related to questions of style and taste. Scaliger in *Poetices libri septem* (1561) had claimed that Virgil was superior to Homer on the ground of such qualities as *simplicitas*, *humanitas* and *dignitas*, which were Virgilian, not Homeric, characteristics. The Homeric epic was seen, by contrast, simply as a confused account of the military valour and robust heroism of the early Greeks. Scaliger rejected Homer for his puerility and his lapses of taste. Perrault echoed these views, too. Homeric epics, 'quoy qu'admirable en certains endroits, me paroissent pleins de grossiereté, de puerilité, et d'extravagance', whereas the works of Virgil 'me semblent remplis de finesse, de gravité, et de raison'.[15] Perrault maintained an idea of the epic which incorporated the values of humanity, universality and omniscience. The epic poem should be 'le chef-d'oeuvre de l'esprit humain' and should express nature perceived by the individual poetic mind.

Un Poëte et particulièrement un Poëte épique doit parler pertinemment de toutes les matières qu'il traite dans son poëme, ou bien il se mesle d'un métier dont il est indigne. Il faut qu'il connoisse les choses de la Nature.[16]

But Perrault did not see that the Homeric poems met this idea of the epic, and in this too he differed from the neoclassicists and the ancients. Perrault and the moderns, who maintained the theory of continuous progress in the arts, logically rejected everything they saw to be old and primitive. Naturally they also discarded tradition and authority as the significant shaping forces in literary production. The notion that Homer was omniscient and the father of all arts seemed to them unacceptable in modern times. The common belief that the Homeric poems contained all the rudiments of wisdom, 'qu'Homère n'a rien ignoré des choses de la Nature, et qu'il est le père de tous les Arts', was absurd because knowledge itself had had its evolution.

Visions qu'on a pu avoir dans les siècles passez, mais qui ne sont plus supportables dans le temps où nous sommes.[17]

But insofar as there was a continuity and interdependence between the ancient and modern literatures and arts – which would have been very difficult indeed to disprove – Perrault argued that contemporary literature had an undeniable advantage over classical antiquity because it was created in a far richer and more complex cultural situation. Although there were some differences in the ways arts and sciences had progressed, the modern age was superior to antiquity even in the arts and literature, since the soil in which art grows can be held to be enriched by the progress of scientific knowledge. Moreover, Perrault claimed with Fontenelle that humanity was subject to a steady progress which was reflected in all its cultural achievements.

Pourquoi voulez-vous, Monsieur le Président, que l'éloquence et la poësie n'aient pas eu besoin d'autant de siècles pour se perfectionner que la physique et l'astronomie? Le coeur de l'homme, qu'il faut connaître pour le persuader et pour lui plaire, est-il plus aisé à pénétrer que les secrets de la Nature, et n'a-t-il pas de tout temps été regardé comme le plus creux de tous les abîmes, où l'on découvre tous les jours quelque chose de nouveau?[18]

Perrault seems to have envisaged a progressive amelioration in man's potentialities; and using literature as his field of enquiry he came to grips with man's complexity more successfully than Fontenelle, who concentrated on the natural sciences. He looked at poetic imagination as the key to the individual mind, and assumed that cultural achievements could be meaningfully explained by the study of the individual. The way he thus came to look at literature and the arts is related to his interest in genius. But he saw genius as the extent to which personal endowments enable an artist to take advantage of the general level of contemporary potentialities, and certainly a genius could produce remarkable work in any age, however backward. There was no reason in principle why a culturally backward poet, such as he saw Homer to have been, should not have possessed genius and imagination and produced work that was valuable on that score. The handicap of detrimental environment should even relatively raise the merit of the individual genius. All this did not however in Perrault's view apply to Homer, as the Homeric poems had a collective authorship.

Perrault regarded literature as an activity essentially dependent on imagination; and his negative attitude to the high valuation of imitation of the ancients was related to his emphasis on poetic imagination. As a poet can give 'to airy nothing / a local habitation', it was preposterous to make literary production depend on imitating the classics. Imitation was an abuse of the rich material provided by classical writers – who ought indeed to be valued primarily for their imagination – and betrayed a narrow view of the creative act. For at the moment of writing a real poetic genius will dispense with the models. Poetry is the expression of visual images in the language.

La Poësie n'est autre chose qu'une peinture agréable, qui represente par la parole tout ce que l'imagination peut concevoir, en donnant presque toujours un corps, une âme, du sentiment et de la vie aux choses qui n'en ont point.[19]

It is a curious fact that whereas visual description, invention and poetic imagery were exactly the qualities for which the eighteenth century came to value Homer, Perrault was unable to perceive them in the Greek poet. He, too, was a product of his age and culture, and was consumed by his indignation at the antiquated robes in which he saw his contemporaries wrap themselves.

In his discussion of seventeenth-century French literature, *Les hommes illustres* (1697–1700), translated into English as *Characters historical and panegyrical of the greatest men* (1704–5), Perrault evaluated poets and authors in terms of genius. His starting point was that genius is the quality that distinguishes a great author from minor poets and imitators, and he held moreover that it is a quality that cannot be transmitted to others or imitated. 'It may even be advanc'd, that those who have thus distinguished themselves by the single force of their Genius, are more visibly the work of Heaven, than the rest of Mankind.'[20] In La Fontaine he praised originality: 'Never did a Person merit more to be looked upon as an Original, and as the first in his kind'; Malherbe, he said, had suffered from his environment, as Caën, his birthplace, had not had men of letters 'remarkable particularly for the fineness and beauty of their Genius'; and in his essay on Racine, he emphasized that genius is inborn: 'Genius is a Gift of Nature which cannot be hid, and which shews itself in Children almost as early as Reason.'[21] This appraisal of genius is related to the issues of the *Parallèle*, where Perrault attacked imitation and the uncritical acceptance of classical models. His insistence on the role of genius ran counter to the high value he placed on cultural influences. *Les hommes illustres* was intended to be a kind of dictionary of famous men of his day, and it develops the same idea as the *Parallèle*, namely the superiority of modern culture to antiquity. The apparent contradiction in the dual emphasis on individual talent and environment in Perrault's criticism can be resolved by the special meaning that he gave to genius. Genius was more than a talent or an aptitude. Whereas an individual poetic genius can appear in any age, there were certain periods that manifestly produced more men of genius.

3

The interpretation of early Greek epic: Mme Dacier and the Homeric war

On 5 April 1716 the French Academy toasted the health of Homer. The Homeric war, a tributary of the *querelle des anciens et des modernes*, had gone on for some five years, and the passion it had aroused was now spent. The immediate source of the war had been a clash of principle between two translators of Homer, Mme Dacier (1654–1720) and Antoine Houdar de La Motte (1672–1731), who had published their versions of the *Iliad* in 1711 and 1701–14 respectively.[1] The *querelle*, which used Homer merely as the obvious example, had prepared the way for the next stage, in which Homer was the protagonist. Mme Dacier had worked on her Homeric translation for nearly fifteen years: and as editor of Dictys Cretensis, Florus, Callimachus and Aurelius Victor, as translator of Anacreon, Sappho, Aristophanes, Plautus and Terence, and as wife and collaborator of the classical critic André Dacier since 1683, she had followed the *querelle* closely.[2] La Motte had published his version of the first book of the *Iliad* in 1701, as well as a collection of fables, and, as a personal friend of La Fontaine, Fontenelle and Fénelon, had been interested in the modernist contribution to the late-seventeenth-century debate.[3] By the time of the Homeric war, however, the antagonism between the ancients and the moderns had largely lost its impetus, and both Mme Dacier and La Motte thought they were raising points in the interests of Homer.

Although a great part of the battle was waged directly *ad hominem*, it raised some issues of cultural importance and produced considerations on the perennially problematic subject of the function and scope of classical translations which are universally true and valuable. The translation of Homer, a subordinate issue in the total cultural context, became the topic of a wide

46

literary debate, which was polarized between the irreconcilable views of Mme Dacier and La Motte, and in which the differences extended from the Homeric problem to such key concepts of culture as aesthetic taste and nature. The fact emerged that the translation of a major classical author involved more profound judgments about culture than had been apparent to any previous generation.[4]

Voltaire, one of the last great writers still attached to the classical world view, rejected both Mme Dacier's and La Motte's ideas of Homeric translation, but captured in his estimate of the literary controversy an essential element of the Homeric war: 'Les querelles d'auteurs sont pour le bien de la littérature, comme dans un gouvernement libre, les querelles des grands, et les clameurs des petits sont nécessaires à la liberté.'[5] The most positive aspect of the war was that it aimed at making some final judgments about culture and its current ailments, and managed to suggest some improvements. However much Mme Dacier was a *laudator temporis acti* in the worst sense when dealing with works like La Motte's Homer, she was deeply devoted to her subject and sincere in her belief that she knew the remedy for the cultural decline which she perceived. Hers was an attitude often found in fanatics but one which is certainly rare in classical scholars, who usually flee from open confrontation like mice from a cat. As for her opponents, grouped round La Motte, they were as keenly interested as she was in the cultural implications of interpretations of early Greek epic.

The main events of the Homeric war cannot rate more than a brief mention here.[6] The participants produced a great number of publications, and the controversy also figured prominently in the pages of such varied periodicals as *Le Mercure galant, Les nouvelles littéraires* and *Les nouvelles de la république des lettres.* The first blow was struck by Mme Dacier's publication of her prose translation of the *Iliad* in 1711, to which an argumentative preface and a detailed life of Homer were attached. La Motte responded to this with his own translation of the *Iliad*, an abridged and greatly adapted poetic version of the epic in twelve books, which appeared in January 1714. An essay, 'Discours sur Homère', explaining the principles of his work, was prefixed to this publication; and Mme Dacier quickly replied with her long pamphlet *Des causes de la corruption du goût* in 1714. After this first phase of the debate, which set the scene, others joined in. Defenders of both Mme Dacier and La Motte appeared, while a number of critics preferred a reconciliatory role.[7]

The abbé d'Aubignac's *Conjectures académiques* (written c. 1665), published in 1715, was more careful and profound than most of the works that appeared in the war, and its repudiation of the traditional view of Homer as the conscious artist had important consequences. La Motte then responded to Mme Dacier in his weightiest critical pamphlet, *Réflexions sur la critique* (1715). Fénelon's *Lettre sur les occupations de l'Académie française*, containing his rejection of La Motte's Homeric translation, was published after his death in 1716. Meanwhile, two rather exceptional works on Homer appeared. Jean Terrasson published his idiosyncratic views in *Dissertation critique sur l'Iliade d'Homère* (two volumes, 1715), and Père Hardouin wrote an *Apologie d'Homère* (1716), proposing a wild theory intended to show how the Anchises family recaptured Troy – to which Mme Dacier replied in a short pamphlet, *Homère defendu contre l'apologie du R. P. Hardouin ou suite des causes de la corruption du goût* (1716). Finally, Etienne Fourmont attempted a more conclusive reconciliation in his *Examen pacifique de la querelle de Madame Dacier et de Monsieur de la Motte sur Homère* in 1716. Marivaux parodied the issues of the Homeric war in his *L'Homère travesti* (1716),[8] and with this cheerful note the controversy in France came to an end.

In the arguments of Mme Dacier and La Motte not only two different conceptions of Homer, but two different world views came into collision. It is instructive to notice how the same period and more or less the same cultural milieu could have produced two such diverse translators, and to see how this is reflected in the actual text of their translations. Where Mme Dacier's prose is simple, La Motte's verse has been forced into a pompous and slightly vulgar poetic metre. We are fortunate in having not only the translations, but also lengthy statements by both writers about the nature of the Greek epic.

Mme Dacier explained her idea of epic translation in the preface to her *L'Iliade d'Homère* in 1711. Her determination from the start was to be the foremost Homeric translator of her century: 'j'ai toujours eu l'ambition de pouvoir donner à notre siècle une Traduction d'Homère, qui, en conservant les principaux traits de ce grand Poëte, pût faire revenir la plupart des gens du monde du préjugé désavantageux, que leur ont donné des copies difformes qu'on en a faites'.[9] Even before the accomplishment of her task she had been convinced that she had a sympathetic rapport with the 'veritable goût du Poëme épique'. She felt a natural sympathy with the Homeric epic, found the *Iliad* especially congenial and thought that her translation would reveal to her contemporaries the early origins of the epic as they had really been, without the distortions of later interpretations. She emphasized the need to keep in mind the conditions of the age in which a work was originally produced: 'En un mot le poëme imite ce qui est, et non pas ce qui n'a été qu'après lui. Homère ne pouvait pas se conformer aux usages des siècles suivants; et c'est aux siècles suivants à remonter aux usages de son siècle. C'est un des premiers préceptes de l'art poétique de bien marquer les moeurs.'[10] In practical terms, the project of translating an early epic entailed a certain amount of research into the customs of the age in which the poem was written; and this idea was apparent in the serious, though somewhat unpenetrating, studies and notes attached to the actual translation.

The rendering of Homer for contemporary audiences involved special difficulties which Mme Dacier discussed under five headings. First, she explained, there were the difficulties inherent in poetry in general, when the poem had been created in a distant past and in a historical and literary context totally different from our own. The difficulty of the translator was in bridging the imaginative gap between two worlds of fantasy and imagination. Second, the beauty of the Homeric epic lay essentially in the richness of its myth and fable, which could yield an infinite number of interpretations, and were opaque elements hard to recapture when the original context was lost. Third, contemporary society had great difficulty in sympathizing with Homer, partly because of its reluctance to understand the spirit and morality of a heroic age. The *Iliad*'s straightforward morality of war and necessity appeared too simple and crude to the people of the early eighteenth century who had been used to peace and valued subtlety and sophistication in their human interactions.

The last two problems concerned the formal aspects of the epics. The narrative of the *Iliad* and the *Odyssey* was simple, but also took liberties in terms of flash-backs, repetitions and improbabilities. Homer in his day had been free to surpass the limits of probability and verisimilitude, since this was part of the technique of a poet writing of a common heroic past. But the fantastic and miraculous features of his poetry violated the laws laid down in the neoclassical criticism of fiction and might thus be objectionable to Mme Dacier's contemporaries. The final difficulty of the Homeric translator was that he had to be able to reproduce the grandeur, nobility and harmony of Homeric Greek in a modern language. Mme Dacier confessed that it was the Homeric language more than any other element of the Greek epic that was perhaps beyond her powers as a translator. The problem was brought about by the nature of modern French which was rational and insonorous.[11] And although Mme Dacier had some understanding of the subtle relationship of poetry and language, she avoided the problem by choosing prose as her medium.

La Motte's conception of the translator's task had very little of the care, determination and impetus of Mme Dacier's. His work, the translation of the *Iliad* which he called an imitation – evoking by this term a series of confusions inherent in eighteenth-century ideas of classical translation – was a rationalized and mutilated adaptation of the *Iliad* rendered into twelve books of French heroic couplets.[12] Its success can be explained by the fact that large numbers of the reading public were not primarily interested in authenticity.[13] And why should they have been? The sixteen-page version of Milton's *Paradise Lost* or the rewritten Shakespeare plays no doubt also fulfilled an important function in eighteenth-century England; and the genre represented by such works as *Trojan tales, related by Ulysses, Helenus, Hector etc.* (1714), *The new history of the Trojan wars* and *The siege of Troy, a tragi-comedy*, remained popular among contemporary readers.

Yet La Motte did not lack a certain idealism in his work. He realized the educational value of antiquity and favoured the imitation of the classics as a kind of informal apprenticeship of the poet. In the 'Discours sur Homère' appended to his version of the *Iliad* (1714) he emphasized the point that the modern writers should learn to select what was best in the past and to dismiss the rest without further concern.

En regardant les Anciens comme nos Maîtres, on peut croire que plusieurs de leurs disciples ont été plus loin qu'eux, sans même avoir été d'aussi grands hommes; qu'il faut enfin les étudier les uns et les autres, sentir et apprécier le beau par tout où il se trouve, sans que le respect de l'Antiquité nous le surfasse, ou que pour être plus voisin de nous et même notre contemporain, nous rebattions rien de son prix.[14]

The best of antiquity could be extracted from its context if the best had a universally valid meaning. The task of the translator was, then, to iron out the obscurities and to render the essential meanings of the translated work relevant to the contemporary audience.

La Motte was aware of his shortcomings, as becomes apparent from his 'Discours', but he defended his translation of the *Iliad* by the argument that a new work of art is created in each act of translation. In the translation everything is changed and must be re-established in the new context: 'Ainsi, j'ai changé sans scrupule toutes ces circonstances, pour rétablir la gloire des deux Héros de l'Iliade.'[15] In practice, La Motte's words can be read to mean that the classical heritage could be exploited freely to one's own ends, and that its historical character had no value in itself, in the antiquarian or ethnographical sense. The view of translation as an act of communication was directly opposed to Mme Dacier's idea, which regarded the original text as the perfect copy for the translation, save for the different language. La Motte treated Achilles and Hector as universal heroic types whose humanity had been obscured by the imperfect poetic language of Homer and the unfortunately crude moral code of their age. La Motte's main argument was that the original context may be sacrificed for a contemporary message.[16]

But La Motte's view also indicated a certain distrust of the people for whom he was writing. Mme Dacier had an unfailing faith in her readers; and even though she was aware that they knew no Greek, she believed them to share her own high scholarly and moral standards. She saw her task as a service to her readers, but unlike La Motte, she conceived the service as necessary only as regards the linguistic transposition; she did not translate 'pour ceux qui le lisent en sa langue'.[17]

Mme Dacier skilfully defended her prose translation by the argument that the first loyalty of the translator should be to the original meaning, and she did not see that the meaning was dependent on the poetic form. This assumption betrays a degree of unsophisticated thinking on her part, because poetic meaning is an interrelationship of form and content and cannot be adequately conveyed by the sheer narrative. But because of the simplicity and clarity of her prose she established her place in one tradition of classical translation, in what one might call the prosaic line.

Un traducteur peut dire en prose tout ce qu'Homère a dit; c'est ce qu'il ne peut jamais faire en vers, surtout en nostre langue, où il faut nécessairement qu'il change, qu'il retranche, qu'il adjouste. Or ce qu'Homère a pensé et dit, quoyque rendu plus simplement et moins poétiquement qu'il ne l'a dit, vaut certainement mieux que tout ce qu'on est forcé de lui prester en le traduisant en vers.[18]

One might say that Mme Dacier and La Motte were writing for two completely different types of reader, and in that sense there need not have been a collision. Mme Dacier chose prose because she thought her translation might lead the reader to the Greek Homer; La Motte regarded his poetic version as a substitute for the original. But the inevitable clash of opinions between Mme Dacier and La Motte may be explained by their different backgrounds. Mme Dacier was versed in Greek and classical literature from childhood, and her family background partly accounts for the rare fact that a woman in seventeenth-century France could have risen to such prominence as a cultural authority. La Motte knew Greek very badly if at all. He came to the field of classical literature somewhat as an outsider, having tackled a number of literary tasks before. This was unacceptable to Mme Dacier who was thoroughly at home with the classics and the problems of epic translation and indeed had no other field in which to express her literary talents.

The antagonism between the ancients and the moderns did not however quite apply to the positions of Mme Dacier and La Motte; their difference lay rather in their social responses. La Motte had a genuine respect for Homeric poetry and the classics. In his own way he was a defender of the ancients and denied the value of a total break from the past. His main target was the vanity of those who uncritically worshipped the figure of Homer.[19] Ideologically very far from Perrault and Fontenelle, he saw himself as a propagandist of the ancient culture, even though he must have realized that he lacked the judgment necessary for such a task. The more severe criticism of his standpoint is that he seemed clearly unable to grasp the meaning of a great work of art.

The fundamental difference between Mme Dacier and La

Motte seems to have been the one which French society established between 'les habiles' and 'les demi-habiles', or 'les doctes'
and 'les gens du monde'.[20] As products of these two different
worlds of discourse, Mme Dacier and La Motte had different
views of their task as translators of Homer and propagandists of
classical values.

In *Des causes de la corruption du goût* (1714) Mme Dacier
developed her views on the formative influences of culture, and
looked at the Homeric epic from this point of view. The *Corruption du goût* was written as a learned essay, but it did not, as a
piece of literature, rise to the standard of her prefaces to the
Iliad and the *Odyssey*. Previously there had been no need to
justify in public her life-long convictions and her sincere devotion
to Homer; but now the critical moment had come. Her 'cult
fanatique pour Homère' had been treated as evidence of a lack of
mature literary judgment, and a rebuttal had to be made. She
had to win support for her views, and this proved a considerably
difficult task for such a secluded idealist. Hence the style of the
Corruption du goût is enthusiastic and spontaneous, but it has also
an ironic and vindictive tone. Mme Dacier was fighting for a
lost cause, and she sensed this. The clash with La Motte's ideas
was unusually fierce on her part, as she realized that La Motte's
world was gaining the upper hand, even if only temporarily, and
even though La Motte himself was not a particularly well-armed
warrior.

The value of the *Corruption du goût* lies however in Mme
Dacier's account of the reasons that lead to cultural crises.
Although she concentrated on a single target, La Motte, whom
she saw as an epitome of the factors that bring cultural and
intellectual values to ruin, she managed to rise above the merely
personal.

La Motte's approach to Homer and his ideas of classical translation were indicative of his overall attitude to literature and
culture, as has been explained above. Mme Dacier stated bluntly
the worthlessness of her enemy: 'Car il ne s'est pas contenté de
critiquer ce Poëte dans un Discours qu'il a fait contre lui, sans
l'avoir jamais lu et sans connoître sa Langue: il a encore estropié
toute sa Poësie, et il l'a tellement défiguré, qu'il n'est plus recon-
noissable.'[21] La Motte, and everything La Motte represented, was

corruption: ignorance, carelessness and misjudgment. These were the individual symptoms of low standards, and would be uninteresting as such; but Mme Dacier gave some general reasons for the corruption of that more abstract expression of the human spirit, *goût*. There were current theatre performances and public spectacles that violated common decency and intruded into the privacy of the individual as a kind of spiritual pollution; there were also frivolous adaptations of the epic and romantic novels simply meant for entertainment and intentionally misrepresenting antiquity. Thus she came to criticize not only La Motte's literary activities but characteristics that are common in affluent society, and to imply that sophisticated social life is in general in bad taste.

Mme Dacier offered, however, one single reason for the corruption of taste, and that was the licentious use of the original. Good taste was formed by the imitation of masterpieces which were repeatedly and generally valued. But she argued, moreover, that the earlier the original was, the better it necessarily must be. In *Homère défendu* (1716) she again claimed that Homer was the best model: 'la principale cause de cette corruption vient du mauvais usage que l'on fait de ces excellents Originaux, et qu'en matière de Poësie surtout, le goût n'est jamais si faux ni si corrompu, que quand on s'éloigne de l'esprit et des idées d'Homère'.[22] The educational problem was closely related to the fact that Homer had been misused and misunderstood. The corruption of eloquence and rhetoric – these included literature in general – was caused by bad education, by the ignorance of teachers and by the negligence of students. The actual causes of the corruption of taste could be corrected by starting from the educators and the youth of the nation and by establishing a new code of good taste which would be based on the earliest and best examples of literature.[23] Mme Dacier thus realized the immense value of poetry in society and its development.

But what did Mme Dacier mean by *goût*? We look in vain for a definition. Her use of the word was intuitive rather than philosophical. She made the distinction between good taste and bad taste; but then she allowed the notion of *goût* in itself without qualification to carry the meaning of something good, and used it at times as a criterion when making value judgments. Literary works have *goût* or do not have it and are good or bad respectively. But *goût* was not to her an aesthetic norm in the sense the English eighteenth-century philosophers, notably Shaftesbury, Hutcheson and Hume, spoke of the standard of taste.[24] Neither was it simply a substitute for 'morality', though she frequently discussed these two concepts together. Rather *goût* seemed to be a kind of vehicle through which the human spirit positively expressed itself. She thought that *goût* was an inborn quality, which individual people, groups of people or nations either had or did not have, or had in lesser or greater degree. It was an innately correct response to the culture that represented the sum total of men's imaginative and intellectual activity.

Mme Dacier noted first of all the difficulty of discovering the factors contributing to the formation of taste. Taste was as manifest as it was intangible, and the evidence of the earliest ages consisted only of their literary and artistic remains: 'Il seroit bien difficile de dire comment le bon goût s'est formé parmi les Nations qui ont été les plus célèbres par leur politesse et par leur esprit.'[25] The importance of the environment, including climate and historical circumstances, was emphasized, and in this she relied on Montaigne. She asserted the superiority of early Greek civilization over the Hebraic and the Egyptian.[26] This argument was meant to prove that Homer mirrored the Greek *goût* and culture in the most perfect way, and not only mirrored, but assimilated a culture that was conceivably the best in the history of civilization. 'Je vois un Poëte, qui...joint à la gloire de l'invention celle de la perfection; et qui nous donne une sorte de Poëme dont il n'avait jamais vu de modelle, qu'il n'avoit imité de personne, et que personne n'a pu imiter depuis.'[27] The idealization of Homer was thus intricately related to her idea of cultural progress. Greek culture, because it was the earliest in the development of contemporary European culture, had originality and an absolute value. What is earliest is best; and her *goût* was a concept which illustrated this original, uncorrupted state of civilization where moral and intellectual values were self-evident and where the individual could, without models, give expression to the imaginative activities of his age. When attacking the bad taste of her contemporary culture, Mme Dacier concentrated on those aspects that indicated sophistication, complexity and intellectual redundancy; and she imagined the possibility of an educational system in which methods of going back to the great originals of literature would be taught. Her concept of *goût* thus expressed the absolute value which she attached to an initial and original state of society. She saw civilization as declining in a continuous line from archaic Greece through the Renaissance to her own period. Homer was the representative of the ideal early culture, an ideal poet who reflected the ideal conditions of his early society.

Mme Dacier's aims were thus evidently more far-reaching than just an attack on La Motte. The Homeric war had urged her to a project in which she, from the position of the scholar, translator and critic of Homer, attempted to become a cultural critic and guide. Her initial stance was, however, not a very fortunate one. She had to remain the defender of her idea of the classical values. She was too deeply immersed in the classical past, and failed to communicate with any effect what she had absorbed. Even in her diatribes she basically retained the defensive position, and in her translations she worked with piety and caution, being careful not to transgress neoclassical sentiment and decorum.

La Motte was in many ways better placed. He worked with the conviction that the classics could be made relevant to contemporary readers who had no first-hand knowledge of ancient literature. But unfortunately this basically sound idea led him to believe that popularization consisted in explaining away obscurities and crudely transforming values whenever these were likely to be alien to the average contemporary audience; and for these reasons his writings have little lasting merit.

In the final analysis, we can see that the Homeric war was a necessary episode during which the issues of the relevance of classical translations were discussed, and the traditional views about antiquity were questioned. Neither Homer nor the Homeric epic were studied with a serious historical or philological method, but there was a certain shift from the mythical view of Homer towards a greater understanding of the historical poet. This was evident even in Mme Dacier's idealization of him as the poet of the earliest European culture, the Greek.

4

Pope's view of Homer: 'fire' and invention

The picture of Homer in the eighteenth century has been described so far in the context of the French *querelle*, during which the notions derived from the seventeenth century were questioned for the first time. Perrault's programmatic opposition to the values of classical antiquity made him evaluate Homer as a poet from an inferior age. Mme Dacier's eulogy of Homer was bound up with her idea of *goût*, and she saw perfection of taste reflected in the works of the first poet of western civilization. Pope was a contemporary of Mme Dacier, and a translator of Homer, as she had been, but his Homeric criticism represented a new departure for the eighteenth century. This was mainly because he explained the power of Homeric verse in terms of poetic fire and brought the concept of originality into the field of contemporary poetics.

Pope's translations of the *Iliad* (1715–20) and the *Odyssey* (1725–6) played a seminal role in the critical debates of the century. Like La Motte, but with much more respect for his source, Pope set himself the task of adapting a work produced by an alien culture to the understanding and taste of his contemporaries. This involved his making a number of choices in language, style and metre, which could not be made without a preliminary interpretation of the culture he was seeking to mirror and without some assessment of the value of the conventions of his day. Furthermore, the epics he was translating occupied a very special place in the critical tradition of his contemporaries. Both England and France in the eighteenth century derived much of their critical terminology and theory from antiquity and in the Graeco-Roman world Homer stood as the first and best of poets, the basis of education and a model for later writers. Any attempt to analyse and evaluate him was bound to implicate a great many fundamental assumptions about literature and culture. It is not surprising, therefore, that Pope's translations inspired a controversy that touched upon most of the topics of early-eighteenth-century criticism.

Pope's view of Homer was formed during a life-long attachment to the Greek poet; and even after he had expended so much labour and research on his translations that he expressed the fear of getting cured of the 'itch of poetry' which Homer had given him, there still remained some element of a childhood love affair.[1] The warmth with which he spoke of Homer in his preface to the *Iliad* (1715) is unmistakable, as it is in the far more conventional references to the poet in his early work, the *Essay on criticism* (1711). By the time he was launched on his project of translating Homer in English verse, he had become fully aware of the debt he owed to the previous translators, as well as of the competition he had to face in the work of contemporaries like Mme Dacier, Thomas Tickell and William Broome. He was acquainted with the issues of the French *querelle* and knew Mme Dacier's translation, whose principles and solutions he rejected.[2] He was well read in the neoclassical criticism of the epic by André Dacier, Boileau, Rapin and Le Bossu, and the number of his actual collaborators was large. Most of these, like John Jortin, William Broome and Thomas Parnell, were Greek scholars who could advise him in the field in which he knew himself to be at his weakest.[3]

The psychological background of Pope's Homeric enterprise had the complexity of that of a work of art. He attempted to lift the status of translation to the level of an original work, giving it a large measure of autonomy with regard to the original. He chose to take considerable liberties with the Homeric text, and to use the poetic language and form which he and his contemporaries found the most congenial, namely the heroic couplet. The eighteenth century in England was especially productive in translations and imitations of classical masterpieces,[4] but Pope regarded Homer in the first place as the object of his personal creative impetus. Homer was to him the 'what' of his dictum 'what oft was thought, but ne'er so well expressed': he thought of Homer as often read, imitated and translated, but never so well as he hoped to do it. The fact that his *Iliad* and *Odyssey* established not only a type of poetic diction but also the ethos of epic poetry for nearly three generations stands as evidence that he had succeeded in making an original poetic statement which, quite apart from the work translated, coincided with the aspirations of the age. Those who rejected his interpretation of Homer (apart from his enemies in Grub Street), notably Richard Bentley and John Dennis, were either devoted classical scholars or critics brought up in the rigorous Aristotelian tradition, who, as men of the past, belittled the artistic element in Pope's intentions.

It was the purpose of the preface, attached to the first part of the *Iliad* in 1715, to justify the translation and to indicate the essential spirit of Homer that this sought to preserve. The essay has a place in the history of aesthetics as well as in the history of Homeric criticism, and Pope's single-minded originality is more apparent in it than in the copious 'Observations' which were added to the latter part of the work. Whereas the 'Observations' include a commentary on Homeric antiquities, translated from Eustathius, discussions on some aspects of Homeric Greek, derived largely from the notes of William Broome and Ralph Bridges, comments on the interpretation of the Homeric epic which were also unoriginal, and an analysis of the description of the shield of Achilles, the preface is an interesting personal view of the poetic qualities of Homer and of Homeric translation with special reference to the work of Pope's predecessors in the field, Chapman, Hobbes and Mme Dacier. The revisions that were made to the preface before its publication indicate that Pope gradually came to rely less and less on the opinions of other contributors to the Homeric tradition.[5]

As the key concepts by which Pope revaluated Homer were those of 'fire', 'invention' and 'judgment', it will be convenient to start by analysing Pope's assessment of Chapman's translation (1598–1614), which embodied the poetic concept of the English Renaissance and advocated in particular its doctrine of inspiration. It was to be Chapman's Homer that spoke to the Romantics, rather than Pope's. Chapman saw in Homer the divinely inspired poet whose gift of poetry had been given him by the Muses. The translator would in the act of translation enter this secret sphere of poetic inspiration so that the translation itself would be poetry divinely inspired. The basis of Chapman's Homeric poetics

was 'with Poesie to open Poesie', which was a method for capturing the spirit of the original work.[6] He repudiated the principles
of his predecessors, Lorenzo Valla (prose, 1474), Hessus (verse,
1540) and Spondanus (literal prose, 1583), though he relied
greatly on Spondanus's Latin renderings.[7] Chapman's achievement can be located in the fact that he seemed to have devised
for himself a special technique of inspired translation which
enabled him to produce an initial draft of the *Iliad* in a few
weeks; as he could not be a translator with a cultural mission he
wanted to be the divinely inspired poet. Despite its many obvious
mistakes and crude interpolations – in one place he makes twenty
lines out of two of the *Odyssey* – his work remained among the
translations of Homer as a statement of the freedom and inven-
tiveness of the poet.

Pope seems to have understood the essence of Chapman's
Homer; in his view its merits overruled its confusion and poetic
licence. As a source and reference for his own translations he
found it disappointing, as he did the other English renderings by
Hobbes and Ogilby, but he was interested in its arrogance and
enthusiasm. He admitted that Chapman had accomplished an
exceptional Homeric translation by his individual method. The
main criticism which could be levelled against it was that the
method was unrepeatable and clearly could not serve as a model
any longer – a judgment which conformed with his view that a
poetic translation should express the age in which it was written.
Nor did his primary poetic concern with expression in language
mean that he did not feel a certain sympathy with Chapman's
method. His argument that Chapman shows 'a daring fiery Spirit
that animates his Translation, which is something like what one
might expect *Homer* himself would have writ before he arriv'd to
Years of Discretion', was, furthermore, an appreciation of a poet
by a poet who set greater store by inspiration than by the imitation theory.[8]

The notions of 'fire' (*ignis*) and 'invention' (*inventio*) were
concepts that the Renaissance had derived from antiquity and
that had survived with changing emphases in meaning up to the
early eighteenth century. 'Fire' was associated with the notion of
furor poeticus, which was originally the central concept of Plato's
theory of poetic inspiration as set out in the *Ion* and the *Phaedrus*.[9]
In neoclassical criticism the notion of 'fire' had come to be

dissociated from the idea of poetic inspiration and had been reduced to mean merely an elevated, impassionate style. *Inventio*, on the other hand, was traditionally the finding of material and had nothing to do with originality. It had been a key term of rhetorical and literary doctrines throughout the entire period from Cicero to the eighteenth century, and the shift in meaning that had started with the sixteenth century was concluded during the eighteenth.[10] By the time Pope came to use them in his discussion of Homer, both 'fire' and 'invention' had acquired such a variety of meanings as to be open to redefinition. 'Fire' could again be used to describe an aspect of poetic creativity, and we see Pope wanting to use it in this sense, while 'invention' had come increasingly to approximate to the sense in which imagination was used by the Romantics in the nineteenth century.[11] Pope certainly regarded these two notions as the cornerstones of his conception of epic poetry, where reason is not the ruling element.

Though Pope had no great interest in the formal aspects of aesthetic evaluation, he made his meaning reasonably clear as he related the terms 'fire', 'invention' and 'judgment' to his analysis of Homer. First of all, 'invention' and 'judgment' were used as contrasting, yet interdependent terms, the emphasis being on invention as the primary faculty which may in some instances be qualified by judgment. Both were applicable to the creative poet and to the work created.

It is the Invention that in different degrees distinguishes all great Genius's: The utmost Stretch of human Study, Learning, and Industry, which master everything besides, can never attain to this. It furnishes Art with all her Materials, and without it, Judgment itself can at best but *steal wisely*.[12]

In Pope's picture of poetic creativity, Homer had the greatest power of invention, and Virgil, admirable judgment. Virgil had based the *Aeneid* on the Homeric model, but in doing that he had been using merely his judgment, 'stealing wisely' from another work what fitted his own purposes, and therefore 'Homer was the greater Genius, Virgil the better Artist.'[13] For invention was, in Pope's view, the ability to come up with original solutions to any given task. More specifically, in poetry, invention stood for the talent of the poet to create something that did not exist before. Invention was a mark of originality and directly opposed to

imitation, which was an activity of the reason. Great inventive-
ness, a 'strong and ruling Faculty', constituted the poetic imagination that creates 'a world for himself', the unity of the work of art.
Pope argued that invention should display its variety, versatility
and unexpectedness in a work of art: there should be scope, but
not a preconceived order. It was in this sense that Homer's epics
were 'a wild Paradise' and not 'an order'd Garden', to be valued
the more highly because they were wild.

In his discussion of the element of 'fire' which we can find in
Homer, Pope showed himself to favour the inspiration theory and
expressed ideas that connect with the mystical views of Plato and
the Renaissance neoplatonists. The neoplatonists had attached
certain theological implications to their notion of *furor*, but Pope
discussed these aspects in a thoroughly secular and human context. His interest in the poetic faculty of 'fire' was also related to
his role as translator, since he was faced with the difficulty of
capturing the essence of Homer's poetry in a different language.

Pope offered 'fire', first of all, as a concept which could explain
the mystery of the relationship between the poet and the reader.
He spoke in several instances of the 'Rapture and Fire, which
carries you away with' Homer, and offered the great force of
'fire' as a distinctive mark of his work. The critic could analyse
other aspects of poetry. He could study the way the poems are
created. He could lay down rules so that the poetic forms could,
in some ways, be repeated. But 'fire' was that element that was
unrepeatable and inexplicable. Yet its presence was obvious and
could be intuitively perceived whenever it occurred.

It is to the Strength of his amazing Invention we are to attribute that
unequall'd Fire and Rapture, which is so forcible in *Homer*, that no
Man of a true Poetical Spirit is Master of himself when he reads him.
What he writes is of the most animated Nature imaginable; every thing
moves, every thing lives, and is put in action.[14]

In analysing 'fire' in such serious and sincere terms Pope
attempted to come to grips with a very genuine poetic experience.
He used the term 'fire' to describe what happened in the act of
reading and hearing poetry, and linked this with the poet's experience of the act of creation. He likened the power of poetic fancy
and invention to a chariot-wheel that catches fire by its own
rapidity – a conventional characterization of the poetic experience
which resembles the numerous bee-metaphors of Pindar about the

same topic. In a huge poetic metaphor Pindar compares himself with the bee who infuses his listeners with divine fury by his rhythm and song;[15] Pope merely thought that the poet can convey sensations in poetry with the vividness of life. But he also discussed the aspect of poetic experience in which the poet's inspiration can indeed become the experience of the reader: 'the Reader is hurry'd out of himself by the Force of the Poet's Imagination, and turns in one place to a Hearer, in another to a Spectator'.[16] The translator thus faced his severest problem in attempting to communicate the 'fire' of the original text. If translation was regarded as an imitation of the original poem, it was the inimitable elements of poetry that the translator should imitate in the first place. The secret was to create an equivalence for the original text in the new context. Pope insisted that the Homeric translator should see as his most important task the rendering of the Homeric fire, that elusive and inimitable element, a compound of rhythm, sound values and meanings which so affected him in his role as reader that he was carried away.[17]

From the whole body of classical and modern authors, Homer emerged as the poet whose writings contained the greatest amount of 'fire'. It logically followed that he was the most difficult of authors to translate, while he gave the most pleasure and reward to his readers.

This *Fire* is discern'd in *Virgil*, but discern'd as through a Glass, reflected from Homer, more shining than fierce, but every where equal and constant: in *Lucan* and *Statius*, it bursts out in sudden, short, and interrupted Flashes: in *Milton*, it glows like a Furnace kept up to an uncommon ardor by the Force of Art: in *Shakespear*, it strikes before we are aware, like an accidental Fire from Heaven: But in *Homer*, and in him only, it burns every where clearly, and every where irresistibly.[18]

Homer was the first and Milton, perhaps, the last in this volcanic canon of poets. For Milton's 'fire' was the result of 'the force of art', which was an unacceptable source in Pope's view of poetic creation.

The weakness of 'fire' as an aesthetic term is that it is a metaphor, and, when used in the evaluation of a poet's work, can only suggest the sort of ideas it stands for. Pope used the term in the way that later eighteenth-century poets and philosophers, notably the primitivists Brown, Duff and Ferguson, came to use the word 'genius', meaning by it the innate forces of man.

'Let thy genius rise', said Edward Young in 1759. Pope's relation to the inspiration theory has now become clear: he believed in an uprush of human force that had effects similar to those of external inspiration, for the force of 'fire', like that of genius, could make the reader feel as if he were inspired. Pope restricted the term for the purposes of literary analysis and used it as a touchstone to characterize a whole series of classical and English masterpieces. His analysis of Homer's 'fire' nevertheless indicates that he had a conception of some internal force that manifested itself in the Homeric epics.

For the term 'fire' derives strength as well as weakness from being a metaphor. With the term 'invention' Pope expressed his idea of the originality and imagination of the poet. In the attempt to explain the genius of the poet, a metaphor like 'fire' seemed more appropriate and communicative. By the use of 'fire' Pope wanted to emphasize two interconnected ideas which he held about epic poetry: firstly, that poetic fire was an innate force which showed itself in varying degrees in poets, and secondly, that it had certain inspirational effects which ranged from mild pleasure to a total acceptance of the poet's portrayal of life.

Voltaire and the poetry of the primitive age

Homer had never before enjoyed such popularity in France as came his way during the Homeric war, but it was a popularity that did not last, and Voltaire provides evidence of this decline. Intellectually and emotionally detached from classical antiquity, he looked on the Homeric poems as records of the past, as mere stones and marbles from the ruins of a vanished civilization. He saw in them the most primitive examples of the epic genre; and whereas this was a decisive proof of the poet's merit to Mme Dacier, Pope, Blackwell and the primitivists, Voltaire argued that such ancient poetry could not possibly compete with the artistic complexity and interest of later works. It must be emphasized, however, that these ideas of his stand in isolation among the eighteenth-century discussions of Homer. So far from being an addition to the Homeric tradition of the period, his views were a criticism of it. They constituted a reasoned expression of the doubtful value of ancient works.

Voltaire's 'Essay on epick poetry' was written during his eighteen months' stay in England, where Homer had, thanks to Pope's translation, become part of the national literature; and many of its conclusions can be seen to have resulted from his experience of English literature, London literary and political circles and the country's climate and food during his visit. The essay formed part of a larger work called *An essay upon the civil wars of France extracted from curious manuscripts, and also upon the epick poetry of the European nations from Homer down to Milton* (1727). It was translated into French by Desfontaines in 1728, and in 1733 Voltaire himself rewrote it in French. The differences between the English and the French versions occurred mainly in the accounts they gave of Homer. Biographical information about the Greek poet was provided for the benefit of the French reading public, and, what is more important, the French chapter on Homer seemed to indicate a greater familiarity than the English with the Greek text of the epics.[1] Voltaire's main concern in the 'Essay' was the poor standard of contemporary epic in French as compared with the English achievements of Milton and Pope, and he saw the French poets' imitation of the classical models as the main factor contributing to its plight.

The view of Homer that emerges from the 'Essay' is somewhat negative and fragmented. Voltaire seems willing to withhold any final estimate of his merit. It may simply be that he did not know his Homer well and so did not want to betray his opinions or take sides after the manner of the Homeric war.[2] What interested him was the intellectual history of his subject. He realized that La Motte was wrong to have tried to 'donner de l'esprit' to Homer, and that Mme Dacier was wrong to have gone to such extremes in trying to justify Homer's superiority. Perhaps Voltaire's negative view of Homer in the 'Essay' should be compared with his rather reserved assessment of Sophocles in the 'Lettres sur Oedipe' (1719), where he is clearly putting forward his idea that classical authors should be adapted to suit contemporary taste and customs.[3] But the Homeric section of the 'Essay' is also concerned with a particular question: what were the reasons for the fact that a poet of a remote time and place, called Homer, was regarded in modern times as an authority on a variety of issues, from the theory of the epic to the moral values an epic should embody? And the way this question was framed was characteristic of Voltaire.

Voltaire's irony was not expended directly on Homer or on the ancient writers, but rather on the poets, critics and common readers who had let themselves be deceived by a myth. He disagreed with the view of Boileau that the esteem people have for the great poets of antiquity is a genuine part of their merit. 'Ceux qui ne lisent que les anciens sont des enfants qui ne veulent parler jamais qu'à leurs nourrices', Voltaire had written in his notebooks. Homer was an instance of an ancient writer whose authority had produced a virtual standstill in the contemporary epic. There was an artificially created Homeric tradition which now took the form of fixed rules for the genre:

The greatest Part of the Critics have fetch'd the Rules of *Epick* Poetry from the Books of *Homer*, according to the Custom, or rather, to the Weakness of Men, who mistake commonly the beginning of an Art, for the Principles of the Art itself, and are apt to believe, that everything must be by its own Nature, what it was, when contriv'd at first.[4]

It was the critics of earlier generations that Voltaire held to be principally responsible for much of the weakness of French epic writing. He did not blame Homer. He attacked Le Bossu, who in his influential *Traité du poëme épique* (1675) had looked at the Homeric poems as a mine of epic rules. He points out that to form such rules men did not even have to go back to the original source, but had merely to read what Aristotle and his commentators had said about Homer. The actual practice of writing was founded on precepts which on the one hand had lost their validity for the contemporary situation, and on the other hand did not always have a foundation in the original text to which they claimed to refer. Le Bossu had insisted that the *Iliad* and the *Odyssey* thoroughly accorded with his idea of the epic as a moral lesson and a thematic and narrative unity within a great structure.[5] Voltaire argued that this was not the case: 'But as *Homer* wrote two Poems of a quite different Nature, and as the *Eneid* of *Virgil* partakes of the *Iliad*, and of the *Odissey*, the Commentators were forc'd to establish different Rules to reconcile *Homer* with himself, and other new Rules again to make *Virgil* agree with *Homer*.'[6] Homer belonged to the past. The rule-hunting of the neoclassical critics seemed absurd to Voltaire, who maintained that the *Iliad*, the *Odyssey* and the *Aeneid* were each the product of historical circumstances which defined both their content and their form. The classical epics were created by individual poets in a cultural situation essentially different from ours and one that was lost for ever. They were determined by as complex a set of factors as determined any modern work of art, but these factors were not necessarily rules. Voltaire's idea of the creative adaptation of Greek literature, namely that classical works should be reinterpreted for contemporary audiences, was based on a view of literature in which convention and historical circumstances were the determining factors rather than poetic rules.

Nevertheless, if there was to be a rational discussion of literature, certain criteria remained indispensable. Some agreed principles were needed, even though prescriptive rules were for those who could never write themselves. It needs to be emphasized that Voltaire realized the power of convention in the production and criticism of literature, since he employed the terms 'custom' and 'use'. The Homeric poems had become the source of rules 'according to the Custom'; and the epic was termed so because of 'Use', although originally there had been scope for great freedom and variety in long narrative poems. Convention had restricted the name of epic to poems that related a great action. Voltaire realized that the central theme of the Odyssey was not one great action but a series of adventures linked by one hero, and that the central theme of the *Iliad* was a moral dilemma which remained unsolved. Both are narratives which have great variety and freedom of form and could be appropriately described as 'Discourses in Verse'.[7] The differences between the classical and the modern epic lay in the intentions of the writers, and it was evident that different things needed to be said in different ages. Voltaire's emphasis on judgment and imagination as the epic poet's most important assets clearly illustrates this point. Epic rules as such can give no guidance to the poet. When writing *La Henriade* Voltaire had Homer in mind, though in detail his poem owes nothing appreciable to Homer.

Voltaire rejected the neoclassical position, as he saw that the historical circumstances of the poet were a more vital factor in the production of literature than universal poetic rules. The main part of the 'Essay on epick poetry' concentrated on the question of the relationship between ancient and modern literatures, and on the relationship between the literatures of different nations; and the literature of classical antiquity was treated for the first time in a dispassionate manner as one of the national literatures. Voltaire argued that the enormous differences between the classical and the modern world in language, customs, religion and concepts of the universe made the literature of antiquity an artificial model for the contemporary epic. New departures should be sought, and these were to be found in the works of the foreign writers of the period. 'Our just Respect for the Ancients, proves a meer Superstition, if it betrays us into a rash Contempt of our Neighbours and Countrymen.'[8]

Voltaire in England could look at the contemporary French scene from the outside. Critics in England had never exercised the authority over poetic practice that critics had in France, even

though John Dennis and Charles Gildon earnestly tried, by copying and translating the French models, to exert a similar influence.
During and after his visit to England, Voltaire became an advocate of English literature and ideas, which he found congenial.
He praised Milton, Addison and Pope, as well as Locke, Boyle
and Newton, for the freedom of their thought and genius. But
although he was also the man mainly responsible for introducing
Shakespeare to the French reading public, he basically distrusted
the type of genius Shakespeare represented,[9] just as he distrusted
Homer and Sophocles. In Shakespeare's, Homer's and Sophocles'
poetry there was the undisciplined genius of nature which the
cultured genius of Voltaire abhorred. He was sufficiently confident
to condemn what he did not understand – a feature which was
exemplified in his treatment of the best achievements of ancient
and modern literature.

Voltaire was himself actively engaged in writing an epic poem
and dramatic pieces based on Greek themes, and perhaps for
that reason he concentrated his criticism on the French epics and
their critics. It is true that they had erred in taking Homer as
their exclusive model and in imitating poetic expressions and
moral values that belonged to a different social situation. Voltaire
quite rightly saw that literature that was artificially created
without regard for its cultural and national context and in
imitation of an alien culture was nonsense. He emphasized
the importance of a more varied literary stimulus, but did
not suggest that the purpose of wide reading was the search
for literary models. Wide reading, he held, would merely enhance
the reader's understanding of the principles of art, based on a
study of individual works, each of which uniquely represented its
environment. Voltaire himself believed that he at least could be
such a polymath, and could penetrate the original conditions of
works of art in whatever culture he found them. Knowledge for
him was a means and not an end, and he had contempt for those
compilers of facts whom he, nevertheless, greatly relied upon.
The traditional view of how Greek culture should be used was
static. Voltaire's use of its achievements was intended to be
dynamic and creative, as he claimed in fact that all existing
literatures could be used selectively so as to fit some immediate
purpose. Some at least of his weaknesses as a critic were due to
this belief that knowledge was there to be exploited, and that it

was possible to grasp literature by a process of intellectual selection.

His suggestion that French writers should disregard the ancients was merely a practical measure. It was not Voltaire's intention to construct a system of poetics on the basis of such a negation of poetic imitation and rules. Rather he thought that imitation in epic poetry was the natural outcome of certain continuities in culture and poetic convention. It could not be deliberately practised. To the critics who had argued that Virgil's *Aeneid* was a successful epic poem based on the imitation of a single model, he replied that most of Virgil's imitation resulted from a natural cultural dependence. The Graeco-Roman world formed a cultural unity which was reflected in its art. Virgil, Voltaire said, 'could not avoid introducing the Gods of *Homer*, who were the *Roman* Gods, too, nor talking of the siege of *Troy*, since *Aeneas* was a Trojan Hero'.[10] He rejected the argument that the continuity that had existed between Greece and Rome existed also between classical antiquity and modern Europe. No new epic could be evolved by choosing contemporary or national themes, if the style and ethos of epic writing could not depart from the Aristotelian poetics which were based on Greek examples.

It is obvious from the 'Essay on epick poetry' that Voltaire intended to do to Virgil what he considered Virgil to have done to Homer: in *La Henriade* he felt free to correct the excesses and faults in the action of the classical model so as to make it more reasonable and more acceptable to contemporary taste. He felt free to change the subject matter to fit French historical tradition, and to make whatever borrowings were appropriate. In the *Essai sur les moeurs* (1756) his ideas on literature, which the 'Essay on epick poetry' only hinted at in a didactic manner, were developed more clearly towards a view that saw the epic primarily as historical evidence for the culture that had produced it.[11]

The unsatisfactory character of Voltaire's essay on Homer is due to the fact that he studied Homer mainly to show that the Greek poet had not been worthy of the cult offered to him by later generations. The reading public had been brainwashed by the critics, for it lacked a critical understanding of its own: 'the Common Part of Mankind is aw'd with the Fame of *Homer*, rather than struck with his Beauties'.[12] Homer had become a poet whose name was often repeated but whose poetry was not read, save from a desire to appear cultured. Voltaire wanted to challenge the honesty of the contemporary reader, with whom he now, by a sudden change of emphasis, identified himself. The reader must discover no doubt that his actual reading experience of the *Iliad* was impersonal, that he remained the dutiful and uninspired schoolboy when faced with a text like Homer's: 'Notwithstanding the Veneration due, and paid to *Homer*, it is very strange, yet true, that among the most learn'd, and the greatest Admirers of Antiquity, there is scarce one to be found, who ever read the *Iliad*, with that Eagerness and Rapture, which a Woman feels when she reads the Novel of *Zaida*.'[13] The actual reading experience is admittedly the crucial test of literature. If this experience is meaningless, if there is a failure at this vital point, as Voltaire claimed there was in the case of the *Iliad*, the literary work is hardly more than a lifeless artefact. The pleasure of the reading experience depends on the ease with which the reader can absorb the intentions of the author on the written page. But what is the point of pretending to like literature that does not give pleasure? The provocative element in Voltaire's essay was his assumption that the pleasure value of Homer was very little: 'very few have command enough over their own Prejudices, and can transport themselves far enough into such remote Antiquity, as to become the contemporaries of *Homer* when they read him'.[14] Most of the essential meaning of the epics was lost beyond recovery.

There was the problem of the Homeric language, in the first place. Mme Dacier's scholarly rendering of the *Iliad* and the *Odyssey* was a poor substitute for the original, and those French readers who knew no Greek had no assistance from La Motte's rationalized version. The situation was better in England, where the English reading public had Pope's Homer, and Voltaire fully recognized the merit of Pope's translation. It is debatable how well Voltaire himself was acquainted with Homer in the original when he wrote the English version of the 'Essay on epick poetry'. He probably did not know very much Greek then, and throughout his life his understanding of that language could not have been more than superficial. This can be seen as part of the reason for his unfavourable opinion of Homer.

Voltaire's main criticism of the *Iliad* was, however, that the poem did not seem to be a good epic by the standards of modern sensibility, and that it was quite simply uninteresting for the modern reader. It was too long. Its narrative was incoherent. Homer's eulogized mythological conception was hardly worth serious attention. 'His Gods are perhaps at once absurd and entertaining', Voltaire stated. The ill-conceived characters of the *Iliad* constituted a graver epic fault. Homer lacked the capacity of a great poet to evoke pity and sympathy for his heroes; and with the possible exception of Hector, Voltaire thought them trivial and inhuman. Where these features of the epic were concerned, Virgil surpassed Homer, who belonged to a primitive age and was its simple poet. The *Iliad* reflected the primitive values of Homeric society, its vulgarity and unrefined emotions, and for this reason it was to be condemned.

The more positive outcome of Voltaire's discussion of Homer was the point that it was the task of literary criticism to focus on literature itself rather than on the person of the poet. The method by which the false assumptions of a literary tradition could be eliminated was to go back to the original. The Homeric epics contained important information both about their historical background and about the poetic techniques characteristic of their period. But the *Iliad* was a mere compilation of independent 'rapsodies', which one would expect in an epic of a primitive age. It was the absence of the conscious individual artist that finally deprived the epics of merit and made them unfit as models of modern epic writing.

Voltaire was generations ahead of his time in his insistence that the Homeric epics were just one work of literature among many, both ancient and modern. To the question of why Homer still continued to hold such an authoritative place in epic literature and in the minds of men, he offered an unsentimental and cynical answer. He looked at Homer as the myth created and employed by those culturally conscious poets and critics to whom literary production had come to mean the preservation of certain continuities in culture. Men need myths, however, and when one such myth had been recognized as invalid, new myths will emerge. Obviously Voltaire stands in the modernist tradition of La Motte and Pope. The main effect of his argument is, however, to emphasize the primitive character of the Homeric epics and the fact that they are the product of a certain culture in the past. Personally he regarded them as bad because they were primitive, but he nevertheless understood some of the essential features of the poetry produced in the early stages of civilization. His 'Essay of epick poetry' therefore leads up to Blackwell and the primitivists, who established the case for that particular culture more firmly than Mme Dacier had done.

PART II

PRIMITIVISM AND REALISM

'And there we are, right at the heart of the problem! Supposing we had a new Homer...Let us ask ourselves with complete candour whether we would be capable of listening to him at all. I think we must answer in the negative. We have not got him because we do not deserve him!...If we need him, we should have him! For in the last resort nothing negative happens in history. What therefore can be the meaning of the fact that we transpose all that is truly great and essential into the past?'

> Robert Musil, *Der Mann ohne Eigenschaften* (1930–43), trans. E. Wilkins and E. Kaiser, *The man without qualities* (New York 1953), vol. i, pp. 232–3.

6

Epic genius:
the departure from the neoclassical model

When we examine eighteenth-century ideas on Homer as the first epic poet, we can trace a development from an initially neoclassical approach, that was popular about 1700, to a critical analysis sixty years later that emphasized the poet's originality and his debt to his cultural background. This development seems to have been the consequence of a general growth of interest in the historical causes underlying the production of works of art. The discussion of epic genius reflected contemporary trends in the field of critical theory whereby convention gradually replaced poetic rules as the principle governing literary production.

This shift of emphasis can be followed in English criticism of the epic from the neoclassicists to Johnson who, though rejecting the neoclassical principle of the normative value of classical literature, was occupied, as the neoclassicists had been, in finding the universal criteria for lasting works of art. At the same time, the theory that the Homeric epics represented a literary version of a collection of original rhapsodies was gaining wider acceptance, and interest in the epic shifted to the creation of these supposed originals. The classical form of the epic lost ground as a living genre and was used for the most part only by second- and third-rate poets like Richard Glover (*Leonidas*, 1737, *Athenaid*, 1767), Robert Southey (*Joan of Arc*, 1797) and Henry Pye (Alfred, 1801). And when the primitivists worked round to the idea that all poetry is culturally dependent and that a particular type of society brings the genius of the poet to its full perfection, the specific conditions for originality were seen in the epic of Homer.

Various reasons can be suggested for this change from a normative to a culturally conditioned view of the epic.

Firstly, there was the realization that the literatures of classical antiquity belonged to a particular period of cultural development and could be understood only if that period was rendered intelligible in its own terms. Since the circumstances governing the production of contemporary literature were not the same as those that had prevailed in ancient times – language and taste, the two influential factors shaping modern literature, having both taken on new forms – the models provided by the ancient authors were seen as inadequate.

Secondly, the ideas of the early Enlightenment were making an impact on the field of literature. Their anti-authoritarian bias was teaching men to look at the most cherished notions embodied in the classical tradition as problematic. It was coming to be realized that the answers to literary problems could be found through rational and systematic enquiry; and by the 1730s we see examples of this radical method being applied to classical works.

Thirdly, from the end of the seventeenth century there was a growing interest in the popular poetry of Europe, and its unique character was emphasized from the start. This interest developed from an amateurish and sporadic collecting to an effort to build up a picture of folk poetry that would reveal the nature of popular imagination as essentially different from the sophisticated and self-conscious outlook that had produced the literature of classical times.

Fourthly, by the 1760s there was more material available concerning ancient and geographically remote cultures, and its quality and reliability had improved. Discoveries and travelogues added the important dimension of realism to the understanding of literature. It was realism of this sort that was looked for in both the study and the description of societies and individuals and that found expression in the novels of Defoe and Fielding, who wrote about contemporary England. A realism that rendered the author's view of the world as accurately as possible was seen as a mark of originality, and attention came to centre on the fact that the Homeric epic gave a realistic description of the life and society of its time.

The complex development I am tracing in eighteenth-century ideas of Homer's genius is related to these several overlapping developments. As I pointed out earlier in this study, interest in the originality of the epic genius had manifested itself even at the time when neoclassical criticism was dominant both in England and in France. It is true that Perrault had criticized the cultural backwardness of Homer, but he did so mainly because of his opposition to the ancients in the French *querelle* and because of his eagerness to question the value of classical culture in general. He was prepared to discuss literature as a product of culture and could appreciate a genius like Homer, whom he considered an exceptional individual set above the general cultural level of his age. Mme Dacier, in her eulogy of Homer, represented his epics as interesting and valuable in their own right because they were the product of an early Greek poet and of the first poet of European civilization. She singled out the *Iliad* for praise because she felt it depicted the moral values and customs of an early culture in the most perfect manner. Voltaire, who represented the modernist view, thanks to his feeling for contemporary taste, also emphasized the fact that the Homeric poems were records of a primitive age. But whereas Voltaire set only a minor historical importance on the epics and denied their literary value, Mme Dacier esteemed them principally because they gave a picture of early Greek culture, and this view prepared the ground for the Scottish thinkers of the 1760s who went a step further in their evaluation of the Homeric society, regarding the primitiveness of Homer as his chief merit.

The third exponent before the 1760s of the idea that there were some unique and specific qualities to be discovered in Homer's genius was Pope, who took the view that 'fire' was an essential element of poetic genius, and that Homer possessed the greatest degree of it. By combining 'invention' and 'fire' in his concept of poetic genius, Pope gave a fuller analysis of Homer's special quality than any earlier critic. It is noteworthy that this appraisal of the importance of 'fire', which was to indicate a decisive change in poetic taste, came from a poet who as translator of Homer claimed a place in the Graeco-Roman tradition. The concept of individual genius as an inner fire finding expression through the imagination, which we associate more with the Romantic movement, found isolated heralds in the early part of the eighteenth century also in the work of Shaftesbury and Blackwell, and during the latter part of the century in the writings of the primitivists, who came to emphasize this particular aspect of poetic genius as they studied the Homeric epics.

Perhaps we should ask why the concept of Homeric genius yielded such a variety of interpretations even during the relatively short period of history we are considering. Literary history has developed in such a way that it provides room for only a few writers of exceptional merit; and it seems that whenever standards of excellence are to be sought and redefined in literature, we always refer to the same handful of examples. In literary practice, examples are more effective than rules, and it is the writings of the few that are found to contain such literary principles as have proved useful. Criticism of the epic has been able to state quite legitimately that Homer is good, Virgil not so good, or vice versa, since Homer and Virgil stand for certain agreed notions in the literary tradition that rests on Graeco-Roman foundations. As it is difficult to define standards of excellence in other than the most obvious and simplistic terms, the agreed masterpieces of western literature have come to serve as a kind of shorthand for a multitude of critical notions; and periods, such as the eighteenth century, which interpret these labels in a greater number of ways than other ages, also indicate a more rapidly diminishing consensus as regards accepted standards. Investigations into the nature of the classical epic on which definitions of poetic excellence were based resulted in two kinds of answers: modern literature had produced no epic genius either because there was a disregard and ignorance of the standards set in the classical epic, or because these standards were too rigorously observed, so that in place of original creations only imitations of alien models could be found. The latter view became more pronounced as the century advanced. Byron's comment that 'an Irish peasant with a little whisky in his head will imagine and invent more than would furnish forth a modern poem'[1] expresses one opinion of the difficulty of finding a suitable middle course between the two answers. We can say that the eighteenth century was extremely well suited to discussing literary questions and defining literary norms because of its anguished preoccupation with its own genius, which it was always comparing with what it saw in the classics.

The notion of genius was associated primarily with the epic, since this was held to be the genre best fitted for the expression of noble ideas. The epic was supposed to encourage the unfolding of the capacities of a great poet, which would have been wasted in the restricting medium of the lyric or dissipated in the violence of tragedy. The epic, wrote the anonymous English editor of *Verdicts of the learned* (1697), a compilation of the sayings of the French neoclassicists, is 'the noblest and most important Work of the Mind' (p. 1). Tragedy was classified as a near equal to the epic in the canon of literary genres. It manifested examples of genius such as Aeschylus and Shakespeare, but although their originality was extolled, they were seen to have serious short-comings because of the poetic liberties they took. Admittedly the critics regarded originality as the crucial element of genius, although their arguments did not substantially add to those given by 'Longinus' on the sublime, and although their assessment carried the qualification that originality may result in a lack of elegance and art. Nature and art, on the other hand, could be combined in the epic genius.[2]

Most neoclassical critics maintained, however, that the Greek and Latin epic poets had owed most of their genius to their observance of the rules. The epic was a product of art. René Le Bossu's influential manual *Traité du poëme épique* (1675) defined the epic as 'a Discourse invented by Art'. His definition serves to illustrate the rather hopeless state of stagnation that the neo-classical critics were led into: 'The Epopea is a Discourse invented by Art, to form the Manners by such Instructions as are disguis'd under the Allegories of some one important Action, which is related in Verse, after a probable, diverting, and surprising Manner.'[3] Charles Gildon's criticism of the epic maintained a rigorously formal position similar to Le Bossu's and to most neo-classical critics. He warned his contemporaries against writing without knowledge of the rules under the false pretext of original-ity: 'the Rules of Art are to shew us what Nature is, and how to distinguish its Lineaments from the unruly and preposterous Sallies and Flights of an irregular, and uninstructed Fancy'.[4] Furthermore, Gildon explicitly associated poetic rules with stan-dards of poetic excellence. According to this view, the most successful modern poet would have been the critic himself. He also maintained that the more ancient these rules were in their origin, the more obvious was their correctness: 'no Modern has any Merit but what he owes to the Rules and Precedents of the

Ancients: we are asserting the Necessity and Use of the Rules of Art established by the Ancients'.[5] In this neoclassical picture of a genre created by art and practised by rules, Homer was, not surprisingly, regarded as the source of epic rules. This was true insofar as the formal criteria were concerned, namely the epic unities analysed by Aristotle and interpreted by André Dacier (*L'art poëtique*, 1692). Originality in epic could be achieved by imitating the Homeric model, with the help of rules drawn from these poems by critics.

The critics generally agreed that Homer was the father of poetry and the greatest epic poet. This was a constant and mono-chrome picture from which no detailed Homeric criticism could have emerged. The narrow and unimaginative formalism that characterized neoclassical criticism of the epic was to provoke a strong reaction in England. This development coincided with the arrival of the new criticism of the epic elsewhere in Europe. In particular, two Italian early-eighteenth-century philosophers deserve attention, Gian Vincenzo Gravina and Giambattista Vico. In their criticism of the Homeric epic the lines of development which we have followed in the first half of this book, the problems of individual genius versus culture and of primitive versus sophisticated society, were given a new formulation which was to prove rich in consequences.

II

Neoclassical criticism produced, however, some ideas about literary tradition and the epic which remained useful after the period of its dominance. During the time of neoclassical criticism, critics of the epic arrived at many of their most characteristic results by comparing Homer and Virgil, and it is in this con-nection that we find some analysis of Homer's work. In these comparisons of Homer and Virgil, the differences between the periods and societies which had produced the two poets were noted. The idea that an epic poem is a product of its culture was put forward in an elementary form. There was also the suggestion that the moral values of a people are reflected in its literary products, although morality can improve independently of litera-ture and the arts. René Rapin, from whom the standard passages come, praises 'Homer's Method, who to appear wonderful in every part, wou'd do evertyhing by ways and means Extraordinary', and points out that Homer's shortcomings in the moral field may have been due to the age in which he lived:

We must pardon this Weakness in *Homer*, who wrote in a time when the precepts of Morality were scarce form'd. The World was as yet too young, to have learnt the Principles of true Honesty. Morality was more accomplish'd, and the Precepts of it better known in *Virgil's* time, in whom we shall find them less defective than in Homer.[6]

Rapin uses the standard neoclassical criteria in comparing the works of these two great men of genius, and admits that Homer should be preferred because Virgil had derived his structure and ideas from the Homeric poems.

Invention, which is one of the most essential qualities of a Poet, is in the Number of those Advantages, upon the Score of which, *Homer* deserves the preference to *Virgil*. For he is the Model and Original by which *Virgil* form'd his whole Design.[7]

But when it came to making the final choice, contemporary taste proved decisive. Rapin, as well as the other neoclassical critics, preferred the Latin epic to the Greek.

Homer, has more Spirit and *Virgil*, more Judgment; and shou'd I chuse to have been *Homer*, rather than *Virgil*; I shou'd at the same time, much rather wish to have writ the *Aeneid*, than the *Iliad* and *Odyssey*.[8]

Richard Blackmore, who wrote two unsuccessful epic poems, *Prince Arthur* (1695) and *King Arthur* (1697), follows this line of comparison, but observes that 'Homer and Virgil are two different Genius's.' Their poetry should therefore be approached with different literary criteria. Homer and Virgil stand at the beginning of two mainstreams of epic writing, and represent two possible lines of development for the later epic. Blackmore wrote in 1697:

Homer excells in Genius, Virgil in Judgment. Homer as conscious of his great Riches and Fullness entertains the Reader with great Splendor and Magnificent Profusion. Virgil's Dishes are well chosen, and tho' not Rich and Numerous, yet serv'd up in great Order and Decency. Homer's Imagination is Strong, Vast and Boundless, an unexhausted Treasure of all kinds of Images; which made his Admirers and Commentators in all Ages affirm, that all sorts of Learning are to be found in his Poems. Virgil's Imagination is not so capacious, tho' his Ideas are Clear, Noble, and of great Conformity to their Objects. Homer has more of the Poetical Inspiration. His Fire burns with extraordinary Heat and Vehemence, and often breaks out in Flashes.[9]

On the whole, neoclassical critics were agreed on the fact that the classical epic was *useful* for modern epic writing, but that different things could be gleaned from Homer and Virgil. The ancients were regarded as teachers of the modern poets on the technical aspects of epic writing as well as on the study of human nature. The cultural difference was understood, but was not regarded as a hindrance to imitation. Anthony Blackwall explained in his *An introduction to the classics* (1718):

> The Ancients. . .had good natural Parts, and apply'd them right; they understood their own Strength, and were Masters of the Subject they undertook; they had a rich Genius carefully cultivated: In their Writings you have Nature without Wildness, and Art without Ostentation. For 'tis vain to talk of Nature and Genius, without Care and diligent Application to refine and improve 'em.[10]

Neoclassical critics held that differences in culture and moral values were made unimportant by the fact that the classical epic expressed universal truths about humanity and nature. Moreover, they took the approbation of centuries of men and poets as a proof of the relevance of the classics in a contemporary situation. They saw antiquity as continuing in an unbroken line to the eighteenth century; the only difficulties were matters of interpretation resulting from ignorance of the classical background.

Finally, we can say that neoclassical emphasis on the universal relevance of classical literature in general and of Homer in particular contributed to the development of the ideas that we find in later English criticism, in Hume and Johnson for example. Hume maintained (in 1741) that causes of a general kind govern the literary and creative activities of men, for which reason individual poets should not be the object of literary criticism.

> The question, therefore, concerning the rise and progress of the arts and sciences is not altogether a question concerning the taste, genius, and spirit of a few, but concerning those of a whole people, and may therefore be accounted for, in some measure, by general causes and principles. I grant that a man, who should inquire why such a particular poet, as Homer, for instance, existed at such a place, in such a time, would throw himself headlong into chimera, and could never treat of such a subject without a multitude of false subtilities and refinements.[11]

The neoclassical view was taken a step forward by Hume, who stressed that literary criticism can get to the root of individual works of genius by the study of general causes and principles which manifest themselves in the life of a people and its culture.

III

Samuel Johnson bears witness to the survival of neoclassical criticism in England. His ideas on literary tradition and the epic are contained in their most compact form in his 'Preface to Shakespeare' (1765) and his 'Life of Milton' (1779),[12] while definitions of such key eighteenth-century terms as 'enthusiasm', 'fire', 'genius', 'invention', 'judgment', 'nature' and 'original' appear in his *Dictionary* (1755).[13] That he was a classicist critic is shown by his insistence that the true test of literary excellence is 'length of duration' and 'continuance of esteem'; and the authority of his opinion was backed by the fact that he selected for consideration only the finest products of the classical writers. But he was not blind to the merits of national and contemporary literature, and his criticism can be seen as an attempt to construct a system by which a literary critic can recognize and evaluate universally excellent qualities even in writings that are relatively new.

Homer and Shakespeare were Johnson's examples of poets on whose merit mankind was agreed. This agreement was the result of a long-continued process of analysis, comparison and selection by successive generations. 'Continuance of esteem' was a valid criterion of excellence because literary works of the highest standard contain 'just representations of general nature', and if large numbers of individuals had responded to 'those general passions and principles' of human nature, a literary critic could safely rely on their evaluations.

Johnson's purpose went beyond just giving advice to ignorant critics on how to avoid serious misjudgments. What he had in mind was that general truths about human nature serve as a basis for literary conventions, and although these conventions may be modified from age to age, from culture to culture, in the final analysis they stay essentially unchanged. The study of the greatest works of art should result therefore in uncovering the principles that govern literary productions: 'what has been longest known has been most considered, and what is most considered is best understood'. The idea that the masterpieces of literature represent general nature does not mean that they can be produced by observing certain rules of composition, but rather that there are certain agreed notions and principles about the representation of human nature, which should manifest themselves in literature: 'the poems of *Homer* we yet know not to transcend the common limits of human intelligence, but by remarking that nation after nation, and century after century, has been able to do little more than transpose his incidents, new name his characters, and paraphrase his sentiments'.[14]

Moreover, each literary work conforms to the conventions of the genre in which the poet writes, be it epic, drama or lyric poetry, and even works of obviously great merit cannot be properly esteemed as such until a comparative analysis has proved that they are good within their genre: 'in the productions of genius, nothing can be stiled excellent till it has been compared with other works of the same kind'.

Johnson's views on epic genius are expressed in his 'Life of Milton'. He agrees with the neoclassical critics that the epic represents the greatest form of poetic creation: 'By the general consent of criticks, the first praise of genius is due to the writer of an epick poem, as it requires an assemblage of all the powers which are singly sufficient for other compositions.'[15] Johnson, however, diverges considerably from the neoclassical position, or at any rate from the narrow and didactic view taken of the epic by its English advocates. Neoclassical critics had concentrated on formal criteria and the poetical effects of the epic; Johnson is interested in the subject matter and in narrative methods which could serve either prose or poetry. An epic, he tells us, 'relates some great event in the most affecting manner'. *Paradise Lost* represented the greatest event of history, namely the fall of man; but in general the subject matter of the epic was good enough if it had a broad human importance. 'An imagination capable of painting nature, and realizing fiction' is a necessary requirement in an epic poet since such a poet describes the world of reality and narrates the reality in the context of fiction. Johnson, basing his ideas on the example of Homer, emphasized the fictional nature of the epic in order to make it sufficiently clear that the need to narrate a great event should not lead poets to the reproduction of philosophical discourses or raw chunks of national history. He related the capacity of 'realizing fiction' to the notion of invention. Johnson had reservations about Milton's inventive powers and for this reason gave him second place after Homer. For, as Johnson writes, 'the highest praise of genius is original invention'. We see therefore that the ability to represent human nature and to create fiction were revaluated in mid-eighteenth-century criticism, and Johnson's 'original invention' was to prove useful in assessing Homer as well as contemporary novels.

IV

Eighteenth-century criticism gradually moved towards the view that an epic poem is a product of its culture, a successful epic poet being one who gives his culture a poetic expression; and in this respect we witness a complete reversal of the neoclassical position. It was realized that the Homeric epics were the product of a particular area in a particular epoch; whether they were by one poet or by many did not much matter; they were recognized to have features that were highly characteristic of primitive societies. As early as 1715, Thomas Parnell had expressed the view that Homer's poems 'are now no longer the scheme of a living religion, but become the register of one of former times' – though his comment was mainly intended to counter seventeenth-century criticisms of Homer's mythology.[16] It was in mid-eighteenth-century England that the primitivists hit most clearly upon the idea of the relativity of cultures, largely through their studies of the Homeric and Virgilian epic, and through their researches into the Hebrew scriptures, Lapland songs and Scots, runic and Welsh poetry under the general concept of natural or primitive literature; and it was in this context that the special relationship of early societies to creative modes of thought was being worked out.

The idea was not new, however. An important precursor both to Vico and Blackwell (whose ideas are discussed in the following chapter) and to the primitivists was the Italian lawyer, philosopher and poetic theorist Gian Vincenzo Gravina (1664–1718), whose ideas on originality and poetry were characterized by Platonic idealism.[17] Gravina held that the conditions of early societies, such as we find described in Homer, encouraged creative modes of thought. His discussion of the Homeric epic, in his major work on poetry, *Della ragion poetica* (1708), bore the stamp of primitivist views. The scope of his work is enormous; and it is not futile to speculate that had Gravina been English or French, he would now be regarded as one of the leading figures in the early history of aesthetics.[18] The *Della ragion poetica* was known to Blackwell, who praised it, and it is an open question to what extent Vico owed his ideas to Gravina.[19] Montesquieu thought highly of Gravina, in his *L'esprit des lois* (I, 3). There is no doubt that Gravina was an innovatory and pioneering thinker of the calibre of Locke, Montesquieu and Vico in poetic theory and jurisprudence. And to have shown the misunderstood Homer in a new light, to have given a more correct point of view on the Homeric epic, stands as additional proof of his greatness as an aesthetic philosopher.

Gravina's poetic theory was based on the idea that the creative act is primary and forms the rules and structures that can be derived from the work created. He stated the purpose of his treatise as follows: 'la *Ragion Poetica*, che noi trattiamo, secondo la quale i Greci poeti e le regole loro rivochiamo ad un'idea eterna Natura, può concorrere ancore alla formazion d'altre regole, sopra esempi e poemi diversi'.[20] Gravina used classical material, as the neoclassical critics did, but not, as they did, in order to demonstrate the dependence of contemporary literature on the rules established in antiquity or the universal validity of ancient forms. Gravina's poetics penetrated to the original Greek situation because he thought it was there that evidence for the origins of poetry could be found. It was in ancient Greece that the three genres of poetry were formed, epic, dramatic and lyric, which were then continued in European literature. He believed that he could demonstrate the nature of poetic art by searching for its historical roots to the very earliest stages where gestures, mute expressions and cries formed the essential part of poetic content and technique. The logic that can be discovered in these earliest productions of poetry reveals at the same time the nature of creativity in primitive society. Poetry does not need to follow absolute precepts, but it is an imitation of the totality of reality ('di tutti il vero'); and this imitation acquires a special meaning in the context of early poetry.

Gravina made a detailed study of the Homeric epic, in order to prove his idea that poetic imagination and creative modes of thought were enhanced by the conditions of life in early societies. Poets and artists were the first civilizers of mankind, implanting the seeds of reason in their fables. Gravina regarded Homer as the most important sage and philosopher of mankind: 'Omero perciò è il mago più potente e l'incantatore più sagace, poichè si serve delle parole, non tanto a compiacenza degli orecchi, quanto ad uso dell'immaginazione e dalla cosa, volgendo tutta la industria all' espressione del naturale.'[21] The origins of poetry were incorporated in ritual and in mysteries, the former representing the social aspects of poetic creation, its significance, from the start, for the formation of culture, and the latter the essentially individual nature of the creative act. The ancient poets 'con un medesimo colore esprimevano sentimenti teologici, fisici, e morali'.[22] The myth and the fable contained the most lasting elements of poetry. 'Onde fu la poesia introdotta per favella misteriosa in cui s'ascondeano in fonti d'ogni sapienza'[23] was Gravina's argument for the cogency of a matrix of myths and fables in poetic tradition. The similarity of Gravina's ideas on poetry and society to those of Vico and the primitivists is particularly apparent in his attempt to use examples of the Homeric and other ancient lyric and dramatic literature to show the originality of the poetic act in relation to its culture, which, he held, it was the task of poets to shape.

7

Vico's discovery of the true Homer

After the first quarter of the eighteenth century the issues of the *querelle* gradually but decisively began to lose their force, and a new approach to the culture of classical antiquity was on the way. The *modernes*, those who insisted on contemporary taste and values, came to dominate the literature and criticism of the time. A certain detachment from classical antiquity was apparent even in Voltaire's 'Essay on epick poetry' (1727), which sought to demonstrate the unacceptablity of the Homeric model for contemporary writing; and after 1730 we find neither the irate attacks on the epics nor the committed treatises about their merit that characterized the discussion of Homer at the time of the *querelle*. Rather we find studies which concentrate on one or other aspect of the Homeric problem or which merely use Homer as a peg on which to hang some social, psychological or literary idea. This was the point when Vico's treatise appeared (1730), and his idea that the Homeric epics represented the collective mind of the Greek peoples can be seen as a more crucial turning point in the development we are considering. From this time, even though knowledge of the classical world was increasing, the neoclassical world view belonged to the past.

The primitivism which was to flourish in Scotland during the second half of the eighteenth century had its roots in ideas promulgated on the Continent during the early years of the Enlightenment; and the most seminal work those years produced was Vico's magnum opus, *La scienza nuova seconda* (Naples 1730). 'Della discoverta del vero Omero' forms part of the argument of this larger work. Vico held that to create a new science, which would place knowledge on a firm foundation, we must first of all identify and then re-examine the bases of our present knowledge; and, furthermore, that Homer provided one of these bases. The Homer of tradition was a myth embodying vague assumptions and false beliefs, but Vico was convinced that a myth could be subjected to a systematic analysis. The analysis from which the truth about the poet would emerge he called the discovery of the true Homer, and the method he used in this investigation was the philological practice of a return to the original sources.[1]

In the earlier version of his philosophical work, generally known as *La scienza nuova prima* (Naples 1725), Vico had discussed Homer only in passing, though references to the Homeric epics occur frequently throughout the treatise; and it was when he came to rewrite and rearrange the general principles of *La scienza* in *La scienza nuova seconda* that the few paragraphs on Homer were expanded into a lengthy book.[2] During that interval Vico had clarified for himself the meaning of the Homeric section in *La scienza* and its relation to the rest, and this had involved him in making a more systematic study of the problem than before. Vico realized the significance of the discovery of the true Homer in the total system of his philosophy of poetry and history after he had laid down the outlines of that system. It was the most important new achievement of *La scienza nuova seconda*.[3] The philosophic, scientific and poetic wisdom epitomized by the Homeric tradition stands out in the edition of 1730 as our best evidence for the unreliable nature of our fundamental assumptions, and the book therefore has a claim to be considered independently of its context.

The nature of Vico's philosophy is such that it yields a number of interpretations. Relatively unknown in his own times, he has been rediscovered by modern scholarship and has come to be regarded as the father of many sciences: the rudiments of materialist philosophy, comparative history, sociology of the humanistic bent, anthropology, pedagogy and aesthetics have been found in his works. More particularly, and without much justification, he has been seen as the forerunner of Marxist thought and the Hegelian philosophy of history. But his work deserves to be called seminal, even though it is questionable how original he was in the use of his sources (mainly classical and Jewish), and though his borrowings from Bacon, who in his time had argued for a similarly new system of science,[4] remain a largely unstudied problem. Vico's influence on poets and philosophers in Italy, England, Germany, France and Russia has been considerable and has generally crossed the boundaries of schools of thought.

Vico wrote at a time when the classical foundations of European culture were still unshaken and were protected by the Roman Church. His writings may not be fully intelligible unless one bears in mind that the Inquisition was active in Naples throughout his lifetime.[5] In order to avoid the attentions of the authorities, who were likely to interpret any questioning of the accepted world view and of the nature of the ancient texts as disbelief and an attack against themselves, Vico took considerable pains to disguise his principles in obscure language and under a veil of irony.

Our understanding of Vico's thought depends to a large extent on our acquaintance with its classical background, and this is especially true of the book on Homer. It can admittedly be argued that Vico's use of classical material for the purpose of his philosophy is of secondary importance, since his aim was to replace rather than develop ancient modes of thought. But the fact remains that the authority of the classics in early-eighteenth-century Italy gave a special slant to his work on the new science of humanity. When a great system of thought has to be built, it is helpful if another such system has to be cleared away first: and in no part of the *Scienza nuova* is this so evident as in the third book, 'Della discoverta del vero Omero', where he directly applies his critical method to classical antiquity.

In the preceding second book, 'Della sapienza poetica', Vico had discussed the nature of poetic wisdom and had maintained, as he did throughout his work, that the nature of a thing cannot be understood without knowing its origins. The methodological postulate of the *Scienza nuova* is that theorizing must begin when the matter it treats of begins. Poetic wisdom must therefore be seen essentially as 'the vulgar wisdom of the peoples of Greece, who were first theological and later heroic poets'.[6] Poetic wisdom was, moreover, the foundation of civilized life and could be traced everywhere in the origins of those varied activities and institutions that characterize human societies: 'the wisdom of the ancients made its wise men, by a single inspiration, equally great as philosophers, lawmakers, captains, historians, orators, and poets, on which account it has been so greatly sought after'.[7] Poetic wisdom was expressed in the form of fables, and our knowledge of these very early stages of human history is based on the accumulated tradition of interpretation and clarification involved in the continuous retelling of the fables. It is based therefore largely on inference.

But in fact it made or rather sketched them such as we have found them in fables. For in these, as in embryos or matrices, we have discovered the outlines of all esoteric wisdom. And it may be said that in the fables the nations have in a rough way and in the language of the human senses described the beginnings of this world of sciences, which the specialized studies of scholars have since clarified for us by reasoning and generalisations. From all this we may conclude what we set out to show in this [second] book: that the theological poets were the sense and the philosophers the intellect of human wisdom.[8]

But this was not the nature of the Homeric epics. In his criticism of the traditional sources of knowledge Vico denied that Homer had been either a theologian, that is, a 'divinely inspired' poet, or a philosopher. The tradition that regarded Homer as one of the original founders of human wisdom had confused him with that genuine type of the divinely inspired poet, the magic man and priest, that had actually existed in ancient Greece during the archaic period.[9] This false view of Homer had been maintained by the neoplatonists of the Italian Renaissance, who had interpreted many of Plato's and his followers' statements about the poet for the purposes of their own philosophy,[10] and it was this tradition that regarded Homer as the source of esoteric wisdom which was available to Vico, and which he wanted to renounce.[11]

The false Homer that Vico first examined was the sum total of the ideas that the literary and philosophical tradition had assembled about Homer's divine origins, omniscience and esoteric wisdom. The engraving that Vico attached as the frontispiece to the 1730 edition of the *Scienza nuova* was meant to illustrate this point. Homer, the false Homer, stands on a cracked base and his half-revealed body is hit by light coming from the breast of metaphysical wisdom personified. We are now in the position to understand the importance that Vico attached to his discovery of the true Homer.

The ray that is reflected from the breast of metaphysic onto the statue of Homer is the proper light which is given to poetic wisdom in the second book, and by which the true Homer is elucidated in the third book. By 'The Discovery of the True Homer' everything that makes up this world of nations is clarified, proceeding from their origins according to the order in which the hieroglyphs come forth into the light of the true Homer.[12]

Vico's conclusion that any esoteric wisdom must be denied to Homer was thus a statement directed against the whole of the previous tradition of learning and philosophy.[13] The discovery of the true Homer and the systematic exposure of the specific set of false assumptions which were current about him was an essential part of the total idea of the *Scienza nuova*. The discovery concerned Homer, but it also concerned any existing system of belief that Vico saw as erroneous and separated from its human origins. In the book on the discovery of the true Homer Vico demonstrated his general method by which large-scale fallacies can be explained.

Vico spoke of 'the doubts that put us under the necessity of seeking out the true Homer'. The primary considerations I have mentioned led to a systematic investigation of the epics themselves, of the poetry of other nations and of the lives of Homer. Finally, Vico divided the proofs for his discovery into two categories, philosophical and philological, the former comprising arguments on the nature of primitive poetry in general, the latter comprising arguments about the nature of the Homeric text.

The *Iliad* and the *Odyssey* spoke for themselves explicitly enough. Anyone who read them without the obtuseness that great poetry usually imposes on people was bound to realize that the values and intentions which they embodied were not those of a philosopher, as was currently believed in the Italian academies. The function of the poet who was a philosopher would have been to teach those who had been endowed with lesser mental abilities, but Homer had sought rather to arouse the admiration of the vulgar:

if the purpose of poetry is to tame the ferocity of the vulgar whose teachers the poets are, it was not the part of a wise man, versed in such fierce sensibilities and customs, to arouse the admiration of them in the vulgar in order that they should take pleasure in them and be confirmed in them by that pleasure.[14]

Homer depicted his heroes as engaging in worthless and stupid actions, the gods as behaving in a trivial and indecent manner. Achilles who fretted like a child, Agamemnon who made half-witted speeches, Ulysses who got drunk, Athene and Artemis who punched each other in anger, Ares who called Artemis a dog-fly, were hardly suitable examples of good behaviour, but resembled rather the lowest characters in a popular burlesque. Vico argued that the ethical attitudes found in the Homeric poems were those that characterize undeveloped minds, children, primitive peoples and women.

Such crude, coarse, wild, savage, volatile, unreasonably obstinate, frivolous and foolish customs as we set forth in the second book in the Corollaries on the Heroic Nature, can pertain only to men who are like children in the weakness of their minds, like women in the vigor of their imaginations and like violent youths in the turbulence of their passions.[15]

For these obvious reasons, Vico concluded, 'we must deny to Homer any kind of esoteric wisdom'. He then gave an ironic account of the origins of the supposedly personal Homer, which were as obscure as they are well known. After a detailed and comparative examination of the household rules and the customs, such as burials, feasting, food, clothing and rituals of cleanliness and purity, that the *Iliad* and the *Odyssey* describe, he offered a preliminary answer: 'The complete absence of philosophy which we have shown in Homer, and our discoveries concerning his fatherland and his age, arouse in us a strong suspicion that he may perhaps have been quite simply a man of the people.'[16] The answer is not surprising when one remembers that this idea had been current since antiquity, and that the debate as to whether Homer was a court poet or a popular singer had been largely caused by the different ethos of the *Iliad* and the *Odyssey*. By the early eighteenth century, thanks to the studies of d'Aubignac and the views of Perrault, the question of the authorship of the Homeric epics had gradually become current outside a scholarly minority, and educated people throughout Europe could look at the epics as compilatory works. The discovery of the true Homer may thus appear to have brought new information to the problem of the epics, if Vico's point were simply taken to mean that he supported the idea of his having been a popular singer. But the argument had been intentionally carried first of all to this intermediate conclusion that Homer may have been 'a man of the people', for this was Vico's methodological practice, and the final statement of the nature of the true Homer was now ripe to be divulged.

There was a considerable gap in time between the age when the events in the poems actually occurred and the age when they were narrated. Homer's epics, as we have them, were created in the manner that characterizes the oral traditions of a primitive culture. 'The fables, which at their birth had come forth direct and proper, reached Homer distorted and perverted. As may be seen throughout the Poetic Wisdom above set forth, they were all at first true histories, which were gradually altered and corrupted, and in their corrupt form finally came down to Homer.'[17] Homer emerges as the repository of popular poetry of the Greek heroic age. That poetry was based on actual history which had been expressed and preserved in poetic form. The Homeric epics, distant as they were from the historic past they related, had been gradually transformed into their present form by the creative work of generations of Greek popular poets. In this fact lay their powerful imaginative impact. The *Iliad* and the *Odyssey* demonstrated the essential properties of primitive folk poetry.[18] Poetic imagination and charisma, Vico held, can be found in their purest form in the poetry of the common people, who gradually learn to model their lives and customs by the examples given them in the work of their greatest creative artists.

The philosophical basis for these conclusions about Homer had been prepared in the section called 'The establishment of principles' in the first book of the *Scienza nuova*. The first principle was that 'men are naturally impelled to preserve the memories of the laws and orders that bind them in their societies'.[19] The second principle was that 'all barbarian histories have fabulous beginnings'.[20] The third principle can be found in the section called 'The ideas of the work', where the fundamental notion of Vico's new science of humanity was first sketched: 'the first gentile peoples, by a demonstrated necessity of nature, were poets who spoke in poetic characters'.[21]

In 'Della discoverta del vero Omero' these arguments were taken up again, and were related more closely to the 'discovery': 'The poetic characters, in which the essence of the fables consists, were born of the need of a nature incapable of abstracting forms and properties from subjects. Consequently there must have been the manner of thinking of entire peoples, who had been placed under this natural necessity in the times of their great barbarism.'[22] The important fact which Vico emphasized here is that one can legitimately speak of a manner of thinking common to an entire people. The mode of thought that the *Iliad* and the *Odyssey* represented indicated that their genesis must have been other than if they had been the work of a self-conscious artist. Even such famous critics as Aristotle, Horace, Scaliger and Castelvetro had not properly understood the nature of the Homeric epic.

In the *Scienza nuova* Vico tried to demonstrate the essential discontinuity between the two modes in which the human mind thinks and imagines, and that these are the modes of thought characteristic of poetry and philosophy. The Homeric epics embodied the poetic mode. Their content showed the sublimity of the poetic mind that could not think logically, and their poetic expression concentrated on particulars which the philosophical mind avoids as it naturally expresses itself in universals.

In the Homeric epic the poet's mind, the heroic lays of poetry and the popular will had coalesced in the most perfect way. Homer's poems documented the origins and the first developmental stages of the rational mind and of civilized society. Vico went even further. Homer could be regarded as the original authority in all those spheres of men's creative activity that build and maintain societies. We will discover in the Homeric epics 'the organiser of Greek polity or civilization', 'the father of all poets', 'the source of all Greek philosophies' and 'the first historian of the entire gentile world who has come down to us'.[23] Only poetry can have such creative potentiality in history, because it uses language. It expresses and preserves in language those areas of human experience which would otherwise be forgotten in dreams and action.

This Homer was not an individual poet of genius, but could be found anywhere if circumstances sufficiently similar to the Greek heroic age occurred. A people that had created the heroic epic had by this fact also created its thought, its social institutions, its leaders and its entire history. Homer's poems were the myths of their people and their ways of understanding and reacting to the world and the age they lived in; and in a rigorous sense they were fully intelligible only to those who had created and used them. The true Homer was a conglomerate of the myths of the Greek people, an expression in language of their dreams and actions: 'Homer was an idea or a heroic character of Grecian men insofar as they told their history in song.'[24] And Vico's more crucial discovery, implicit in this idea of Homer, was that languages and linguistic forms are the key to the minds of those who use words, and constitute the most profound evidence available of the mental, social and cultural life of human societies.

Vico's work thus represents a considerably sophisticated stage in the complex development of eighteenth-century notions about Homer. It was not only the absence of the conscious artist but the idea that an entire people can claim the authorship of poetic works that he wanted to show as the essential value of the Homeric poems. His analysis of Homer pertained to a variety of issues in the field of the human sciences, and its particular contribution to the development of the ideas about the epic cannot be overestimated. The way the primitivists and thinkers on the Continent, such as Herder, learned to look at the epic was essentially Vico's, but their emphasis on the creative forces buried in the poetic activity of the people led to the formulation of a practical programme which had not been Vico's original idea.

1 F. de Callières, *Histoire poëtique de la guerre nouvellement declarée entre les anciens et les modernes* (Paris 1688), frontispiece

2   John Dryden, *Fables, ancient and modern* (London 1700, edition of 1713), frontispiece

3 T. Blackwell, *An enquiry into the life and writings of Homer* (London 1735), plate XI, p. 216

A HEAD OF *HOMER*.

From the Collection of Lyde Browne Esq.

4 R. Wood, *An essay on the original genius and writings of Homer* (London 1775), frontispiece

8

Thomas Blackwell:
the problem of Homer's genius

As the eighteenth century advanced, its changing conception of Homer became ever more intricately related to parallel changes in the general climate of thought. With each decade it became more difficult to incapsulate the Homeric issue in the ivory tower of classical learning. Vico's, Blackwell's and Wood's treatises and the Ossianic controversy certainly added to the contemporary understanding of Greek epic, but they also played an important part in the general development of ideas. As the men of the eighteenth century became increasingly interested in the problem of genius, so their attention was increasingly attracted to Homer, in whose works they discovered evidence to support their diverse views, and by the time Blackwell came to write his book in 1735, the problem of Homer's genius had become an issue that could awaken the curiosity of a large part of the educated public.

Early Enlightenment thought, which forms the backcloth to Blackwell's work on classical antiquity, was characterized by the idea that there are natural causes for all phenomena in the physical and in the human world. The philosophers of that period rejected from the start the explanation that phenomena could be caused by divine influence, and in their effort to discover the truth about man and nature had hard battles to fight against the intellectual barriers set up by religious authorities.[1] During the early Enlightenment Europe was the scene of a long-drawn-out struggle for liberty of speech and opinion waged by thinkers in the fields of science and philosophy, who derived their principles largely from the study of ancient texts (as Spinoza and Vico did, for example), and who aimed to modify the ways in which men interpreted the universe and conceived of the nature of historical development.[2]

99

Although writing the biography of an ancient poet may not appear a particularly apposite task for an enlightened thinker, Thomas Blackwell's *Enquiry into the life and writings of Homer* (1735) clearly bears the stamp of Enlightenment thought. Blackwell claimed that the problem of Homer's genius became an interesting and valid question in any real sense only after the nonsense about his heavenly origins had been dismissed. This was in the true spirit of that love of free enquiry which held that no problems should be so alien or so sacred as to remain beyond the reach of critical examination. The links between Blackwell and the Continental Enlightenment become obvious when we consider the nature of the questions he posed, the manner of his answers and the spirit in which his enquiries were carried out. Scotland had suffered a great deal from religious oppression during the seventeenth century, but with the Act of Security (1706), which guaranteed in perpetuity the leading position of the Presbyterian Church, and with the ascendancy of the moderate party in that Church, the country enjoyed an unusual measure of liberty, so that Blackwell could speak of 'the happy Change that has been since wrought upon the face of religious affairs', which gave him 'Liberty to be of the contrary Opinion'[3] and to demonstrate that the author of the Homeric epics could be studied as a historical individual.

Blackwell is reticent about his personal situation, but the reference to the 'happy Change', as well as the fact that the *Enquiry* came to be viewed with suspicion by High Church men in England,[4] who considered the book as an attack on their views, throws some light on the historical circumstances in which Blackwell wrote. It was not only the disturbed affairs of the Scottish Church, with which he had a special involvement through his progressive theologian father, but also the resentful attitude shown by the dominant High Church party in England that Blackwell had to take into account when presenting his learned treatise to the public in Aberdeen and London.

Among the eighteenth-century discussions of Homer considered here, Blackwell's *Enquiry* is the one that time has treated most unkindly; but in eighteenth-century thought it had a special place. The fruit of many years of discussion in the literary and philosophical circles of London and Aberdeen,[5] it was immediately popular among the general educated reading public in

England, so that a second edition was printed in 1736.[6] It had good reviews in the leading literary periodicals of England and France,[7] and its general popularity extended to Germany, Italy and Holland, where it was enthusiastically received by the leading literary figures of the time. Parts were translated into German by J. J. Bodmer in 1743,[8] and Herder spoke of it in affectionate terms, calling it 'a key' to Homer.[9] Why then did this impassioned, badly written book, loaded with abstruse speculation and scholarship that was antiquated even by the standards of the time, enjoy the favourable opinion of the best of Blackwell's contemporaries? Why was it not only immediately popular, but also directly influential for primitivist thought of the 1770s, and what was the secret of its appeal to men who were neither classicists nor philosophers after the manner of the Enlightenment but were primarily romantics?

The explanation is of two kinds. In the first place Blackwell was well equipped for his task, both by his natural talents and by his education. The son of a Scottish minister, and the foremost Greek scholar in Scotland,[10] he was by no means an orthodox classicist. Contemporary accounts show him to have been something of an eccentric, as well as an inspired teacher, many of whose pupils became distinguished philosophers and literary men.[11] His works on classical antiquity cannot be classed either as histories or as literary or textual criticism, and cannot be regarded as contributions to classical scholarship in the strict sense. While showing a profound familiarity with the life and letters of antiquity, his books, the *Enquiry* (1735), *Proofs of the enquiry* (1747), *Letters concerning mythology* (1748) and the *Memoirs of the court of Augustus* (1753–5, 1763),[12] all treat classical sources in the interest of general problems concerning human nature, culture and myth. And for that very reason they made a strong appeal to non-specialists.

In the second place, the question Blackwell set himself to answer in the *Enquiry* was an extremely clear and simple one: 'By what Fate or Disposition of things it has happened, that None have equalled him [i.e. Homer] in *Epic-Poetry* for two thousand seven hundred Years, the Time since he wrote; nor any, that we know, ever surpassed him before.'[13] And the problem it presented was treated in a way that must be regarded as original. Although neoclassical critics had earlier discussed the lasting value of Homeric poetry and the reasons for the excellence of the two Homeric epics, their approach had been exclusively literary. Blackwell's interest can best be described as psychological and analytic. By re-examining the ancient sources that tell us about Homer, he tried to reconstruct Homer's biography and give a plausible account of him as a historical person of exceptional genius. In doing this, he far surpassed both the imaginary lives of Homer current in antiquity and the near-contemporary life of Homer by Thomas Parnell (1715), which had been published with Pope's translation of the *Iliad*, and had merely recapitulated ancient views.[14]

Two interesting facts throw light on the central question of Blackwell's *Enquiry*. Firstly, as the address to his patron, Lord Lisle, suggests, the problem of Homer's genius had been discussed among the friends that Blackwell frequented while in London,[15] and there is evidence that similar issues had been talked about in his own university, Marischal College, and in the circles that later became the Aberdeen Philosophical Society.[16] Secondly, the tone of his questions indicates that Blackwell regarded his enterprise as somehow irreverent. He frequently refers to the boldness of the *Enquiry* while remaining reticent about its actual target. These two points can be seen to be interconnected.

In carrying out his preliminary task, which was to refute the notions of Homer's divine origin, Blackwell clearly identified himself with the opposition to the High Church men of the Anglican persuasion. This may sound preposterous, which it is, but a theological interest does seem to have provided the critical impetus behind the *Enquiry*.[17] Questioning Homer's divinity was somehow associated in Blackwell's mind with the examination of the fundamentals of religion. Homer was the favourite miracle, as it were, of the classically educated. His genius had been admired, venerated and taken for granted by generations of learned men, and yet no one had bothered either to enquire how this genius had been formed or to study the elements that went to its making. Like Perrault, Pope, Voltaire and Vico, Blackwell in his own way challenged the authoritarianism and the refusal to revaluate classical antiquity that prevailed in the early eighteenth century:

were we really of the same Opinion, as the Ancients, that *Homer* was inspired from Heaven; that he sung, and wrote as the *Prophet* and

Interpreter of the Gods, we should hardly be apt to wonder...We shou'd expect no less, considering whence it came: And *That* I take to have been the Reason, why none of the Ancients have attempted to account for this Prodigy. They acquiesced, it is probable, in the Pretensions, which the Poet [i.e. Homer] constantly makes to celestial Instruction, and seem to have been of *Tacitus*'s Opinion, 'That it is more pious and respectful to believe, than to enquire into the works of the Gods'.[18]

We can see from this that he intended to explain the problem of Homer's genius in a seemingly scientific fashion. He organized his material as follows. First he formulated his problem (premises), then he stated a possible answer (hypothesis), then he displayed his evidence (discussion), and finally he gave his conclusion (result). This method was later employed by the Aberdeen Philosophical Society in their discussion of such problems as genius, the influence of climate and the origins of language;[19] and if we allow the fact that some of Blackwell's evidence cannot be substantiated, the method seems to have worked well.

The *Enquiry* was not a formal treatise, however, and much of its essential quality is lost if Blackwell's personal enthusiasm for Homer and classical antiquity is disregarded. The discussion of Homer's genius was conducted in a vein of inspired involvement. For these reasons, the *Enquiry* has been placed, perhaps incorrectly, in the line of English writings on poetry that ultimately led to the rise of the Romantic movement. The link with Shaftesbury, the main precursor of Romanticism, has often been pointed out,[20] and it is true that Scottish primitivist writers on poetic genius, such as John Brown and William Duff, took up the ideas of Shaftesbury as well as those of Blackwell. But these primitivists were also familiar with the actual practices of Scots popular poetry, and this was to give a completely new dimension to their work which neither Shaftesbury nor Blackwell could share. The resemblances of Blackwell's *Enquiry* to primitivist and pre-romantic literature were, however, more in its manner than in its intentions, and to understand the *Enquiry* correctly we must view it in the context of the early Enlightenment.

Blackwell's aim was to give a historical explanation of Homer's genius. He set out to write a precursor to John Livingston Lowes's *The road to Xanadu*, that is, a work which would account for poetic achievement in the light of a poet's sources. He held that the genius of Homer had remained inexplicable because the admiration of generations of men had hindered rational enquiry about historically valid information. Once the information was in our hands, the problem could be solved. Genius appeared miraculous and surprising only while we considered it from the wrong point of view; and he wanted to change the emphasis from the mysterious to the rational in his study of Homer. He thus gave a hypothetical answer: 'That Homer's Poems are of *Human Composition*; inspired by no other Power than his own natural Faculties, and the Chances of his Education: In a word, That a *Concourse* of *natural* Causes, conspired to produce and cultivate that mighty Genius, and gave him the noblest Field to exercise it in, that ever fell to the share of a Poet.'[21] Blackwell's hypothesis stated two important ideas that had appeared since ancient times and had transformed the manner in which genius was discussed. Firstly, he stressed the element of coincidence in the formation of genius. He posited a combination of hereditary factors, 'natural Faculties', with other formative elements, which he called 'Chances', and claimed that they account in one single stroke for the sublimity and stature that are associated with the notion of genius. Secondly, he recognized the influence of environment, which he understood in the widest possible sense as the totality of childhood experiences, education, the climatic conditions of the poet's country, and the influence of the society and the times in which the poet developed. He considered that genius must be 'cultivated'. Though he avoided taking a clear position between environmentalist and hereditarian theories, he set a slightly greater emphasis on the environmental factors, or at least wanted to look at the problem of genius in the total context of 'la race, le milieu, et le moment' (Taine). We are reminded here of Mme Dacier's discussion of the formation of *goût*, which was influenced by Montaigne, and of the fifth-century B.C. Greek physician Hippocrates, who was the first source of this line of theory. Blackwell in his discussion of Homer's genius idealized, as Mme Dacier had done, the conditions of early Greek civilization.

We may compare Blackwell's ideas with those of Shaftesbury to see where his originality lies. Shaftesbury discussed the nature of poetry in his 'Soliloquy, or advice to an author' (1710), which placed Homer among the poets of the primitive age.

'Tis no wonder that the primitive poets were esteemed such sages in their times, since it appears they were such well-practised dialoguists. . . For poetry itself was defined an imitation chiefly of men and manners; and was that in an exalted and noble degree which in a low one we call mimicry. 'Tis in this that the great mimographer [i.e. Homer], the father and prince of poets, excells so highly; his characters being wrought to a likeness beyond what any succeeding masters were able to describe.[22]

Shaftesbury claimed that the freedom primitive societies allowed the individual was an essential factor in promoting great artistic achievement. Primitive societies had a natural respect for the creative individuals amongst them, whom they regarded as useful and important for the life of their society in general.

Hence it is that those arts have been delivered to us in such perfection by free nations, who from the nature of their government, as from a proper soil, produced the generous plants; whilst the mightiest bodies and vastest empires, governed by force and a despotic power, could, after ages of peace and leisure, produce no other than what was deformed and barbarous of the kind.[23]

Shaftesbury, being a lover of all that is sublime in the world, seized on the primitive poet as his example of this sublimity. He even considered the influence of political order on artistic creation. His position was bound up with ideas of man's natural goodness, and he interpreted Homer's poetic ability in the frame of this general, idealized picture of early society.

Blackwell, being a Greek scholar, was better able to analyse the nature of Homer's genius and to estimate his individuality within the framework of Greek society. The *Enquiry* shows the realization that a poet's circumstances provide the material for his poems. Beyond this theoretical position Blackwell did not venture. The *Iliad* told of the poet's experience of war, the *Odyssey* of that of sea voyages in the Mediterranean. The genius of Homer was the result of the variety of his experience, which is not a necessary feature of all primitive societies. What Blackwell did regard as important was the fact that early Greek civilization had relatively free and flexible social systems, agreeing on this point with Shaftesbury, and that it favoured travel and art.

Furthermore, he pointed out that Homer was not an exceptional individual, the isolated star that literary tradition had taken him to be. Homer had been just as exposed in his lifetime to the vicissitudes of his environment as any man could have been at any age. But in Blackwell's view environment, important as it was, did not count for everything.

Men moving, like your Lordship [Lord Lisle], in the higher Spheres of Life, are well acquainted with the Effects of *Culture* and *Education*. They know the Changes they are able to produce; and are not surprised to find them, as it were, new moulding human Creatures, and transforming them more than *Urganda* or *Circe*. The influence of Example and Discipline is, in effect, so extensive, that some very acute Writers have mistaken it for the only Source of our Morals: tho' their Root lies deeper, and is more interwoven with our *Original* Frame.[24]

Blackwell maintained that in each individual case genius provides the matrix, the 'original frame' which can profit in varying degrees from cultural and social influences. Not all man's intellectual condition can be attributed to environment. Only the weakest minds can be regarded as wholly the products of their culture and education. The fact that Homer had written two masterpieces meant, Blackwell claimed, that the stuff that had gone into their making was far more excellent, far more surprising than that of any other poetic work. This was his idea of 'a Concourse of natural Causes' that he frequently referred to in the *Enquiry*.

The discussion of Homer's genius examines the poet's life from three points of view, in an attempt to explain it as 'a Concourse of natural Causes'. Blackwell first considered his 'public advantages', that is, the influence of the climate in Greece and Asia Minor, the manners of his age, Greek customs, and the state of Greek language at the time when the epics were written. Secondly, he discussed Homer's 'personal Good-fortune', by which he meant Homer's opportunities for extensive travel, encounters with wise teachers in Egypt, Asia Minor and Phoenicia, the poverty which obliged him to become a wandering poet, and his chance to visit the sites of the Trojan war and to be an eye-witness of many similar battle scenes. Thirdly, he instanced the themes of the *Iliad* and the *Odyssey* as 'the noblest Subject' that a poet could ever have chosen for himself. History had come to the poet's aid; the subjects chose the poet, as is often the case in the life of a creative genius.

Such propitious conditions as Homer had known had possibly concurred in many a poet's life in the time after the Trojan wars, and yet there was only one Homer. Here was a problem which

Blackwell thought it necessary to solve. 'How have we but one *Homer?* Cou'd a Space of two or three hundred Years, when Greece, and the coast of *Asia,* was in a proper Temperament for such Formations, bring forth but *one?*'[25] A beneficial environment may be a necessity, but it is not the only precondition of genius; and Blackwell certainly did not envisage the possibility of a social utopia where everyone would be a Homer. In the last analysis he recognized the value of a kind of intellectual superiority which, he thought, develops into moral superiority as well. He spoke of 'an universal and elevated Genius' as a quality that is possessed by some rare individuals and has an element of mystery in it.

It is perhaps the fate of the *Enquiry* to remain in the oblivion into which it passed after the eighteenth century. Though it raised interesting points, much of the discussion was conducted in an impressionistic manner and was based on speculation. A large part of the facts Blackwell cited will not stand up to critical scholarship. For example, he took ancient historians such as Herodotus and Plutarch as authorities on Homer's 'private Education,'[26] although he interpreted their information. He did not properly realize the chronological distance between the Trojan war and the *Iliad*, and took Homer to have been far closer to the Greek expedition than modern scholarship has established.[27] He was also too idealistic about the expressive richness of Homeric Greek, and argued erroneously, as Mme Dacier had done, that the Greek language in its highest state of perfection was just waiting for Homer to appear and use it.[28] Nor did Blackwell clearly understand the oral nature of the Homeric epics. Though he was acquainted with the work of Vico and Gravina, he pictured Homer as an individual and 'a Blind stroling Bard' who profited from the fact that Greek society held its blind poets in high esteem. Oral tradition with its laws and conventions was an unknown concept to him, as it was to his contemporaries, and he did not rate a 'folk poet' very highly. The value that the primitivists were to attach to the oral poet and the interest that Robert Wood was to show in oral tradition were not inspired by Blackwell's enquiries. He also discarded the old idea that the Homeric poems had been a compilation by later scholars from the songs of many wandering poets, as the argument of the *Enquiry* was not related to the Homeric question.

9

Notions of poetry and society in the controversy about Ossian

The view that folk poetry and popular culture have an interest of their own and are worthy of serious attention gained acceptance during the middle years of the eighteenth century. Scholars hunted for genuine folk epics. They looked for evidence for the workings of the spontaneous genius of simple peoples, not only in the past productions of northern nations, but also in the earliest works of classical antiquity.[1] The prevalent eagerness to find evidence for certain theoretical presuppositions about early stages of civilization, an eagerness most marked in Scotland, can partly explain the fact that the inauthenticity of the Ossianic poems was not immediately realized. Ossian, Homer and the Bible were utilized almost indiscriminately as evidence by the primitivists when they formulated their theories of man and society; and this meant, in the first place, that Homer had come to attract notice as a representative of the primitive poets.

James Macpherson established his poetic reputation with *The Poems of Ossian* (1760–73) and with his prose translation of the *Iliad* (1773). The primary problem about the poetry of the third-century Gaelic poet Ossian, the son of Fingal, King of Morven, is admittedly its inauthenticity. To say this is not to deny the existence of authentic Highland poetry, some of which had survived orally for several centuries,[2] but what Macpherson did was to claim the veracity of a translation for poems which were largely the offspring of his own imagination. Among educated Englishmen, he commonly passes for an audacious imposter who published his own compositions as the work of an ancient writer. Knowledge of the existence of authentic Gaelic poetry on the one hand, and knowledge about the northern parts of Europe that had been gradually accumulating since the sixteenth century on the other,[3] certainly helped the success of Macpherson's publications, but the impact of Ossian's poems in England, Scotland and then all over Europe must be understood, in the final analysis, in the context of a moment when the influence of Graeco-Roman culture was temporarily spent, and the ideas of the Enlightenment were being transformed into those which we associate with Romanticism. For the interesting fact from the point of view of literary history is that the body of literature attributed to Ossian, Orran, Ullin and other ancient Scots bards succeeded in arousing the interest and admiration of the best eighteenth-century minds throughout Europe, and it is relevant to ask if Ossian would have aroused this interest, had his work appeared in its genuine form. Macpherson's achievement was to have linked the primitivist interest with a keen awareness of contemporary taste as it was exemplified during the century in the ideas of the *modernes*.[4]

James Macpherson (1736–96) was born of an old Highland family of the clan of Macpherson (Celtic Mac Mhuirich), who inhabited the southern parts of the county of Inverness.[5] In his early youth he saw the rising of 1745. His education was by no means exceptional, but was as good as a boy whose native tongue was Gaelic was likely to receive at that time. He entered King's College, Aberdeen, in 1752, where he benefited from the teaching of Thomas Reid, the philosopher, and Thomas Blackwell. But he took no degree there, moved later to Marischal College, and then spent a year at the University of Edinburgh in 1755–6. Having written from a very early age verses which were of a mediocre and imitative kind, he came into contact with popular Gaelic poetry and began to translate it while he was a schoolmaster at Ruthven, and a lucky encounter with John Home brought early specimens of his translations to the notice of the Edinburgh literati. Macpherson's motives in publishing translations of his Gaelic 'ancestors' must be regarded as patriotic and political. He believed in the existence of a complete Scottish epic, and his extremely free adaptations of some authentic manuscripts expanded, in the course of continuing success, into the ambitious project of producing a large body of ancient Scottish literature in order to demonstrate the glory of Highland culture.

The translations appeared between 1760 and 1773 in Edinburgh and London.[6] While unreserved enthusiasm was shown in Scotland by Blair, Ferguson and others, they were viewed with suspicion by such eminent contemporaries as David Hume and Dr Johnson. Hume, basing his arguments on the nature of oral tradition deemed them inauthentic,[7] and Dr Johnson's rational mind could not appreciate nationalistic poetry, which he regarded as downright silly.[8] Later, Wordsworth, although he had a taste for the productions of 'the philosophical peasants', expressed the opinion that the natural sentiment of Ossian's poems rang false and contrived.[9] The diversity of opinion led to impartial research, and the poems were conclusively proved inauthentic in the course of an examination undertaken by the Highland Society of Scotland in 1805, a view which modern scholarship has reaffirmed.[10]

But what was the nature of the poetry that struck a chord in the hearts of men throughout Europe? An excerpt from Ossian's poems from the *Songs of Selma,* which was translated into German by Goethe, will suffice as illustration.

When bards are removed to their place; when the harps are hung in Selma's hall; then comes a voice to Ossian, and awakes his soul! It is the voice of years that are gone! they roll before me, with all their deeds!...Roll on, ye dark-brown years; ye bring no joy on your course! Let the tomb open to Ossian, for his strength has failed. The sons of song are gone to rest. My voice remains, like a blast that roars, lonely, on a sea-surrounded rock after the winds are laid. The dark moss whistles there; the distant mariner sees the waving trees!

The imagery is banal, while the pathetic fallacy, nature echoing the personal feelings of the poet, is obvious. The sentences are extremely simple and the narrator uses only a few crude descriptive techniques to produce the impression of a poet unrolling his song at the moment of inspiration. The appeal is to the emotions, not to the intellect, of the reader.

When the Ossianic poems spread, directly or through translations, to Europe, they aroused an enthusiasm that far surpassed the impact they had made in England, where their reception remained moderately cool. Taken out of their cultural and linguistic context, the poems more immediately yielded their essential message, conveying a natural sentiment and a genuine feeling which had been lacking from the literary productions of the early eighteenth century. Contemporary taste found its expression in Ossian. If we try to determine why we still continue to read Homer, Goethe or Wordsworth, whereas the poems of Ossian strike us as virtually unreadable, we are bound to raise the issue of aesthetic taste. It is unlikely that the taste that was prevalent at the time of the Ossianic movement was so unusual that it cannot be understood by any other age. But the taste for Ossian was something of an excess and was backed by evident intellectual factors present in Europe at that time.

In Germany, which proved the most receptive ground for Macpherson's inventions, four complete and 34 partial translations were published between 1762 and 1800, and nine complete and 22 partial translations between 1800 and 1868. Ossianic poetry was admired by Klopstock, Voss, Schiller and Goethe. The *Sturm und Drang* movement owed its origins largely to Ossian. Herder utilized Ossianic poetry for his theories of the epic as an expression of national spirit.[11] Schiller, in his essay *Über das Erhabene*, spoke of Ossian, declaring that a truer inspiration lay in the misty mountains of Scotland than in the fairest of meadows and gardens. Goethe, initiated into Ossian by Herder in Strasbourg in 1770–1, included his translation of the *Songs of Selma* and a passage of 'Berrathon' in *Werther*. In France too, Ossian enjoyed both popularity and serious attention. A translation appeared almost immediately after Macpherson's publication of 'Two fragments of ancient poetry' in 1760.[12] Minds as diverse as the Marquis de Saint-Simon, Diderot, Voltaire, Chateaubriand, Napoleon, Mme de Staël and Lamartine were interested in Ossianic poetry. Mme de Staël gave expression to the popular view in saying that in Ossian were contained all the essential characteristics of northern literature;[13] and it is well known that Ossian was the favourite reading of Napoleon during his military campaigns.[14] Elsewhere, in Scandinavia, in Italy and in Spain, the repercussions, either through translations such as Cesarotti's Italian version or through imitations, remained largely poetical and sentimental,[15] and Europe's infatuation with Ossian was echoed in nineteenth-century art and music.

Philosophical preoccupations characterized the reception of the poems in Scotland, France and Germany. The discovery of Ossian's poems and the Ossianic movement can be seen as an inevitable outcome of the interest in the origins and nature of poetry and the epic in Scotland in the middle of the eighteenth century. It is not entirely cynical to say that if the poems of Ossian had not existed, it would have been necessary to invent them. Documentary evidence about the early stages of poetry was welcome to theorists who had begun to realize that the existing examples provided by classical antiquity did not fit into the current conceptions of the primitive. The genuineness of the texts attributed to Homer's predecessors, such as the half-mythical poets Orpheus and Musaeus, was already much in doubt.[16] The Homeric epics themselves, especially the *Odyssey*, when carefully read, could be seen to portray a society of considerable complexity and refinement, and the moral values of the *Iliad* were thought to be barbaric and applicable merely to a war situation. Moreover, the language of Homer was beginning to reveal to scholars layers of poetic composition, and the text itself was understood to have undergone several changes from its first appearance at the time of Pisistratus to the considerable revisions suggested by the Alexandrian scholars. The eighteenth century had reappraised Homer and had largely rejected the neoclassical view that he was the father of epic rules; but he appeared to many to have possessed a kind of artistic sophistication that was alien to a truly primitive poet who, they thought, had also existed.

The theoretical assumption that poetry is an authentic record of its society and that it has a historical meaning which may surpass in importance the primarily poetic content, marks a decisive departure in eighteenth-century thought. Isolated expressions of the idea can be found in French writers like the abbé Dubos, Saint-Evremond and Mme Dacier, but not until the primitivists began to work on what they believed to be native material offered by their own popular poetry were its methodological implications fully developed in practice.

Macpherson had been influenced by the ideas current in primitivist circles in the 1750s and 1760s, but his own arguments, it must be remembered, remained naively non-theoretical. He was influenced by a genuine and life-long enthusiasm for the Scots cause and had a certain poetic sensibility. He translated Homer with the conviction that the simplicity which he had found in the popular poetry of his own ancestors was also the primary virtue of the Greek poet, and that there existed in the histories of Greece and Scotland an analogous cultural level of which their bards had given a record. Consequently, in his translation of the *Iliad* (1773), he replaced Homer's concrete and vivid descriptions with the same vague and high-sounding phrases that he had previously employed in the old Highland ballads; and in fact his Homeric translation illustrates not a little his practice in dealing with the Ossianic poems.

The preface to his translation of the *Iliad* makes two points. First, we are told that Homer was the greatest of poets because of his simplicity and ease of style, which was the result both of his individual genius and of his being conditioned by the age and society in which he wrote.[17] Second, we are to bear in mind that Homer could be translated with the original simplicity, but this meant essentially that considerable liberties had to be taken with the text. The translation had to be in prose instead of verse, the hexameter was certainly barred; and the characteristic Homeric language had to be translated so as to fit an analogous cultural level in the history of an English-speaking audience.[18]

Macpherson's idea that Homer was a poet who had lived and worked in a society similar to the third-century Ossian's was derived from his own experience as a translator of early Gaelic poetry rather than from study or understanding of the nature of the Homeric epic. Although the translation of the *Iliad* was inspired by the current enthusiasm for Homer and by a conviction of the similarity of Ossian and Homer, it also reveals the cynicism and depravity of the author. The energy Macpherson spent on his forgery and on his poor translation of Homer has few parallels in literary history, and it shows how easily fashionable literary issues can be exploited by someone who is responsive to the interests of his day but wishes only to play his solitary game with them.

Macpherson regarded his Homeric enterprise as a side issue; his poetic talents were better suited to the production of Ossian's poems, and his historical and political interests were focused on his *History of Great Britain and Ireland* (1771–3). In this work he delineated the society that he conceived to have been Ossian's: an original, uncorrupted state of humanity where social norms were created spontaneously because man had a natural will to imitate virtue, not vice.

The ancient British nations heard their poems with such rapture and enthusiasm, that they formed their character and manners upon the model of the virtues which the Bards recommended in their songs. In an age unacquainted with science men became disinterested, generous, noble, as individuals...(A publication which the Author of the Introduction has already given to the world establishes the justness of the above observation...)[19]

Macpherson's contemporaries preferred Ossian to Homer exactly because he was thought to represent an older and more primitive, hence more virtuous and original, stage of social development. He had sung about heroism without military glory. John Gordon came to Macpherson's support for these reasons: 'Ossian's skill was superior to *Homer*'s; as the great simplicity and attention to nature in them [i.e. his poems] shew...they were written in a period of greater antiquity, than the *Iliad*...I mean in an earlier state of civilization; before art had reached that height, to which it had attained in *Homer*'s time.'[20] The artlessness, the straightforward imperfection of Ossianic poetry was to the eighteenth-century English critics, at home with verse composed on rigorous neoclassical principles, a mark of originality in itself. By many the age was felt to have lost contact with originality because the classics had imposed a model for imitation in the genres of epic, lyric and drama. The curious fact about the Ossianic poetry was that the critics could not come to an agreement even as regards its genre.[21] Hence we find in England, side by side with the major trends of Augustan and neoclassical literature, a counter-movement that called for the exercise of individual genius even at the expense of reason. Ossian was 'a complete instance of first poetry' and corresponded to the ideal of those literary men who saw that poetry 'ought to give raptures' and not merely please.[22] It was this condition of immediacy and spontaneity, supposedly characteristic of primitive poetry, that Macpherson offered to his contemporaries.

Was then the enthusiasm with which these poetic fakes were received, especially in France and Germany, an indication of a greater malaise with the achievements of western civilization than has so far been realized by historians of eighteenth-century culture? The ideas we associate with the Enlightenment, which were based on the great scientific advances of the seventeenth and early eighteenth centuries, were felt to be insufficient by many who were searching for the principles of that unattainable condition, happiness in the world of here and now. Spinoza's motto, 'non ridere, non lugere, neque detestari, sed intelligere', appealed little to those who thought that man, as an individual and as a social being, need not only apply his reason but also laugh, grieve and feel delight and disgust, as an integral part of his human happiness. Moreover, despite the similarities between the Homeric epics

and the Ossianic poetry, Ossian seemed to offer a better model of
the ideal poet because he was entirely free from the burden of
tradition. The Homeric text had come to us weighed down with
commentaries and the poems had close associations with later
Greek culture, which could not be regarded as spontaneous or as
representing the infancy of mankind. Ossian, on the other hand,
corresponded to men's nostalgia for paradisiac spontaneity; and
he depicted the sort of simple heroic behaviour that could be seen
as a viable attitude in the fight against the evils of civilization.
Macpherson had hit upon a telling formula: he offered a poetry
that had an air of historical authenticity, that was easy, even
insipid by all aesthetic standards, and that yet carried with it the
promise of salvation through a new individual and collective
heroism.

The idea that a primitive society represented a state of perfection, which refinement, prosperity and scientific advance could
only make worse, runs through Macpherson's writings. Moreover,
like the poetic theorists of his time, he thought that primitive
societies which were relatively free despite the ritual organization
of their way of life were the best possible matrices of creativity.
William Duff stated that in early periods of society 'original
Poetic Genius will in general be exerted in its utmost vigour'.[23]
Macpherson argued that the era of Ossian was such an instance of
an ideal ancient society: 'The nobler passions of the mind never
shoot forth more free and unrestrained than in the times we call
barbarous. That irregular manner of life, and those manly pursuits
from which barbarity takes its name, are highly favourable to a
strength of mind unknown in polished times. In advanced society
the characters of men are more uniform and disguised.'[24] Macpherson's direct support in Scotland came from Hugh Blair, a
theorist with a speculative interest in the origins of folk literature.
He regarded Ossian as a poet without parallel either among the
classical authors or among the Hebrew prophets because the
Gaelic bard was unhampered by any form of sophisticated reasoning, and because the Celtic tribes naturally accorded great importance to poetry in their primitive environment.

Irregular and unpolished we may expect the productions of uncultivated ages to be; but abounding, at the same time, with that enthusiasm,
that vehemence and fire, which are the soul of poetry. For many
circumstances of those poetic times which we call barbarous, are

favourable to the poetical spirit. That state, in which human nature shoots wild and free, though unfit for other improvements, certainly encourages the high exertions of fancy and passion.[25]

Like Macpherson, Blair claimed that primitive society creates a totally satisfying environment because it is an environment coherent in its values – it combines the great achievements of poetry with virtues such as magnanimity and heroism; and this harmony between aesthetic and moral excellence was thought to be the natural state of man.

These ideas found a response not only in England and Scotland, in the numerous writings of Macpherson's contemporaries, but also in France. In vain did Voltaire try to remind men that early ages of civilization undoubtedly represented barbarism, vileness and moral degradation, and that progress was in every sense humanity's imperative. In vain also did he try to ridicule the Ossianic poems.[26] The primitivist arguments found their way to the Continent in connection with Ossianism. Ancient Scotland was held to represent a historically verifiable model of an ideal society, and England, together with the rest of Europe, was classed among civilization's malcontents.

An indication of the way primitivist thinking spread in France can be found in an essay by the translator of *Temora*, the Marquis de Saint-Simon.[27] He evaluates Ossianic poetry and the Highland societies at a universal level and sees their parallels in ancient Greece; he argues without hesitation that the 'Scottish Homer' has found in Macpherson its Pisistratus. The present age has exhausted its poetic genius and spent its force: 'Notre génie actuel s'épuise en vain, et n'a rien produit de semblable. Notre siècle n'a point donné de rivaux à Homère, Virgile et Milton, entre lesquels Ossian n'est point déplacé.[28] He goes on to maintain that the secret of Ossian's greatness lay in the ancient society that had produced him. There was a radical difference between that primitive state of natural freedom and the confining existence that modern civilization had brought in its course: 'L'état des Calédoniens sous le règne de Fingal doit être regardé comme celui de la pure nature; en conséquence on peut librement exercer son génie, et s'abandonner aux spéculations philosophiques, à l'aide desquelles on se flatte de pénétrer dans l'âme de ceux qui n'ont point reçu les vices et la corruption des siècles suivants.[29] Saint-Simon emphatically took the view that civilization in its higher forms had resulted in a dichotomy of theory and practice: though philosophers preached virtue, its natural vitality in society had been lost. The opposition between ignorance and self-awareness, between the primitive and the civilized state of man, could not be resolved, for once humanity opted for progress it also opted for alienation. Saint-Simon had none of the optimism that characterized Rousseau's redemptive programmes. But the poems of Ossian seemed to offer mankind useful lessons, and he was convinced that Macpherson's pioneering work had a lasting value as material evidence on which a philosophical theory could be based.

C'est au sein d'un tel peuple, dénué de toutes les sciences raisonnées, et de presque tous les arts, qu'il est consolant pour l'humanité de trouver toutes les vertus, tout l'héroisme, et tous les grands sentiments que peuvent donner la meilleure éducation et la meilleure religion. Les Calédoniens pratiquaient cette belle philosophie, que prêchent les sages de notre siècle. Ils étaient vertueux et faisaient le bien. La nature gravait dans chaque coeur les vertus de chaque état.[30]

Moreover, it was exactly Ossian's paganism that appealed to enlightened thinkers on the Continent such as Saint-Simon. Unlike the Scots philosophers who had close ties with the Church and were influenced by the Protestant climate of their country, men on the Continent felt free to stress Ossian's lack of religion. The Ossianic poetry portrayed a ritualistic and myth-centred society liberally governed by its Druids and poets, but one that seemed completely to lack a clerical hierarchy and dogma. The antireligious argument drew its evidence from the historical fact that the third-century Ossian wrote before the arrival of Christianity, and this was additional proof of the purity and virtue of his society. A pagan society had been capable of producing poetry that equalled in sublimity the works of the Hebrew prophets and surpassed in vigour those of the present century. In this way the Ossianic poetry served thinkers with a far more radical programme than young Macpherson could have envisaged.

In conclusion, we must consider the basic issues to which the Ossianic controversy gave expression. Ossian's poetry instigated men's opposition to ideas which they felt to be outdated, the dead wood of the preceding centuries, and also inspired them to discover some new solutions to current problems. It is ironical that these records of ancient poetry should have proved to be inauthentic. But to cite a parallel case, what is the degree of genuineness of the poems collected by Lönnrot for the Finnish national epic *Kalevala* – poems which are to be held responsible for the spiritual revival of a whole people?

During the Ossianic controversy there appeared to be four main clusters of ideas on which criticism was focused. First, there was a clearly expressed opposition to civilization as it existed. The grandeur of ancient poetry served men as proof of the inherent virtues of a primitive, uncultivated age. Secondly, there was the opposition to war and military glory with their false heroic ideals. The Ossianic poems seemed to advocate a natural vitality of a basically pacifist kind. Thirdly, where Ossian was compared with Homer, the opposition to the values of classical antiquity, perpetuated through the classical tradition in contemporary literature with its servile imitation of the classics, became more pronounced. And lastly, where Ossian was compared with the Bible, men discovered that sublimity could be found in a totally pagan and non-clerical context – a fact which provided further evidence for the anti-religious philosophers of the Enlightenment.

Some of the new sentiments and ideas that Ossian inaugurated can be seen to have provided a foretaste of Romanticism. The interest in the past and in ancient cultures that explains much of the preoccupation with Homer and the Bible shown by eighteenth-century poets and critics was transformed, in connection with Ossian, into an enthusiasm for the remote and the exotic that had a distinctly Romantic colour. Ossian seemed to have provided an archetypal model of the Romantic poet who could give free expression to the nature of his environment and to the history of his people; he was not merely the creative genius of a primitive society such as the primitivist thinkers wanted him to have been, but also a type of poetic genius that appealed to contemporary taste. For the body of lyrical and imitative poetry that Ossian inspired all over Europe can be understood in the context of Goethe's *Werther*: it was no coincidence, perhaps, that the poet who inspired the social utopias of sophisticated thinkers was also the favourite of all those sensitive young men whose vision proved their own destruction.

10

The primitivists and the primitive bard

The eighteenth century's original contributions to the Homeric debate can be seen emerging when writers begin gradually to look at Homer as a poet from a primitive culture or as one whose work gave poetic expression to Greek popular thought. These writers made the theoretical assumption that what they were considering in Homer were manifestations of reality; and their new theory reflected the general view of culture that was gaining acceptance in the middle of the eighteenth century.

The criticism of Homer that was to produce the most extensive consequences was contained in the writings of the Scottish primitivists. The thesis that creativity and originality are in essential ways dependent on a certain type of society was formulated by the primitivists. They studied the primitive bard both in a general sense and with the support of specific examples. They saw him as an individual poet who was the product of a particular type of ancient society. This society expected him to exercise his poetic talents to the utmost, but left him unrestricted by the norms that guided the lives of his fellow beings. The primitivists denied the value of poetic rules, because they saw that the modes of poetic expression (language, dance and music) were embedded in the poet's society. When they looked at the example of Homer they came, however, to emphasize that an individual genius could transcend his immediate surroundings. They were thus led to set a high value on the individuality of the creative mind in the sense that it was through the free realization of individuality that societies were built up, were maintained and made progress. But the freedom given to genius was given to a being whose character was already shaped in many respects by his environment. Poetic genius had to stand in a close relation to the poet's society if it was to be viable and meaningful; and this, too, they argued, had been the case with Homer.

The work of the Italian philosopher Gravina made a profound impact on Blackwell, who had also read Vico. Blackwell, uninterested as he was in poetic theory as such, attempted to delineate a society where popular myths and fables were readily available within the social framework. He believed that Homer had lived in a society that was at such a stage of its development. He characterized the ideal state of culture for poetic creation, which had been known to Homer in his early youth, as follows:

In most of the *Greek* Cities, *Policy* and *Laws* were but just forming, when *Homer* came into the World. The first Sketches of them were extremely simple; generally prohibitions from Violence, or such Regulations of Manners as we should think unnecessary or barbarous. The Tribes were but beginning to live secure within the Walls of their new-fenced Towns, and had as yet neither Time nor Skill to frame a Domestick Policy, or Municipal Laws; and far less to think of publick Methods of training up their Citizens: *They lived naturally*, and were governed by the *natural Poise* of the Passions, as it is settled in every human Breast. This made them speak and act, without other Restraint than their own native Apprehensions of *Good* and *Evil*, *Just* and *Unjust*, each as he was prompted *within*. These Manners afford the most natural Pictures, and proper Words to paint them.[1]

The primitivists proper then stated that Homer was a bard, a poet of an early society which allowed the expression of poetry in all its naturalness, force and inspiration. Homer was an original genius because he had recited and depicted the thoughts and customs current in early Greek culture, not because he was the founder of epic poetry. Homer's originality lay in the way in which he had perceived his immediate surroundings and then given them a poetic form; and such originality, the primitivists argued, could be found in any time and place provided that the cultural norms were loose enough to allow spontaneity to find expression.

We can follow the dissemination of Gravina's ideas of poetry in England, where they gained currency even before they were finally developed and expressed in the form of theory by the primitivists. The writers who made use of them, notably Manwaring, Lowth, Hurd and Beattie, were far more interested in the act of poetic creation than Blackwell was, although they were his contemporaries.

Edward Manwaring based his view of poetry on the study of the Homeric epic. He wrote:

The Matter of Poetry is Fiction, Things divine, natural, historical, moral and artificial. The first Poets were Masters of Music, and the efficient Cause of Poetry was Happiness of Genius, with a Facility of expressing the Conceptions of the Mind according to the Natural Ideas of Things, and the different Kinds of Poetry were produc'd from Diversity of Ingenuity and Temper.[2]

Robert Lowth, in *Lectures on the sacred poetry of the Hebrews* (Latin 1753, English 1787),[3] the first enquiry in England to treat the Bible from a historical and literary point of view, compared the Homeric epic and the Hebrew scriptures and argued for the ritual and religious origins of poetry:

if the actual origin of Poetry be inquired after, it must of necessity be referred to Religion; and since it appears to be an art derived from nature alone, peculiar to no age or nation, and only at an advanced period of society conformed to rule and method, it must be wholly attributed to the more violent affections of the heart, the nature of which is to express themselves in an animated and lofty tone, with a vehemence of expression far remote from vulgar use.[4]

Lowth maintained that poetry was created in 'sacred places' and that 'her original occupation was in the temple and the altar'.[5] Homer, 'divinus ille genius' (his 'divinus' was translated into English as 'sublime'), had given the perfect expression to epic poetry: 'Such is the real purpose of heroic poetry; such is the noble effect produced by the perusal of Homer. And who so thoughtless, or so callous, as not to feel incredible pleasure in that most agreeable occupation; who is not moved, astonished, enraptured by the inspiration of that most sublime genius?'[6] Richard Hurd looked for the manifestations of the primitive in English poetic history. Early English literature is regarded for the first time by Hurd as the product of the romantic and supernaturally orientated world of the Middle Ages. In *Letters on chivalry and romance* (1762) he called for a reassessment of 'these barbarities of their forefathers': 'may there not be something in the Gothic Romance peculiarly suited to the views of a genius, and to the ends of poetry?'[7] Hurd's ideas on Homer were similar to the primitivist views, although in practice he did not collaborate with the Scots: 'tho' the manners of Homer are perhaps as different from ours, as those of Chivalry itself, yet as we know that such manners always belong to rude and simple ages, such as Homer paints; and actually subsist at this day in countries that are under the like circumstances of barbarity, we readily agree to call them *natural*'.[8] James Beattie reflects many of Gravina's ideas in his *Essays* (1776). He argued that poetry can be studied as a rational discipline, but that its functions and structures are formed in the poet's creative act.

For frequently it happens, that fashion and philosophy coincide; and that an artist gives the law in his profession, whose principles are as just as his performance is excellent. Such has been the fate of *poetry* in particular. *Homer*, whom we consider as the founder of this art, because we have none more ancient to refer to, appears, in the structure of his two poems, to have proceeded upon a view of things equally comprehensive and rational.[9]

Beattie seems to have attempted to settle the question of the authority of Homer which had puzzled the generation that debated the superiority of the ancients or the moderns. This authority depended, in Beattie's view, on a kind of creative originality which characterized the individual poet, and thus 'an artist gives the law in his profession'. But there was no reason to suppose that 'fashion and philosophy' would similarly coincide, should Homer happen to be the lawgiver for contemporary poets. It is illuminating to recall Joseph Warton's influential condemnation of Pope's poetry on the grounds that it was insufficiently sublime; and his equally authoritative eulogy of the *Iliad* because of its 'rough' sublimity.[10] The problem was exactly there: as the eighteenth-century critics quite justly realized that their age lacked a Homer, that Pope had failed in the task and that the poets who most eagerly imitated some prophetic qualities of the ancients were appallingly second-rate, they had to reread their Homer and try to rescue the remains of their own native popular poetry and culture in order to create a supposedly natural matrix for new poetic development.

But who were the primitivists? The Scots primitivists were a minority group in the second half of the eighteenth century who worked in relative intellectual isolation and whose main concern was to investigate the workings of human creativity, and more particularly the creativity of primitive man. They worked in two groups, one in Aberdeen, chiefly at Marischal College where its prime mover had been Thomas Blackwell, and the other in Edinburgh. The objectives of their enquiries were philosophical and general, rather than literary and particular. But it is obvious from their published works that they had a thorough knowledge of ancient literature and of the Homeric epic.

The Aberdeen Philosophical Society (1758–73) was formed by Blackwell's pupils, Thomas Reid, James Dunbar, John Gregory, George Campbell, James Beattie and others. The purpose of the society was stated as follows:

The subjects of the discourses and questions shall be philosophical; all grammatical, historical, and philological discussions being conceived to be foreign to the design of this society. And philosophical matters are understood to comprehend every principle of science, which may be deduced by just and careful induction from the phenomena either of the human mind, or of the material world; all observations and experiments that may furnish materials for such inductions; the examination of false schemes of philosophy and false methods of philosophizing; the subserviency of philosophy to arts, the principles they borrow from it, and the means of carrying them to their perfection.[11]

The topics discussed by the society thus ranged far and wide. They included a great number of questions related to poetic genius, such as 'In the perfection of what faculty does genius consist? Or if in a combination of faculties, what are they?' (Mr Farquhar, 22 April 1758); 'Whether there is any degeneracy of genius in the moderns?' (Mr Gordon, 26 March 1765); 'Whether any account can be given of the causes why great geniuses have arisen at periods which have been most remarkable for them, and why they have frequently arisen in clusters?' (Dr Gerard, 12 December 1769); and 'Whether national characters depend upon physical and moral causes, or whether they are influenced by both?' (Dr Gerard, 26 February 1771). The treatment of these questions proceeded in the following manner. The speaker made the problem known to his colleagues well in advance, in the form of an open question; he then started his actual discourse by stating his own view; then he discussed the problem at length, and at this stage others could participate in the discussion; finally the speaker summarized the views presented and gave a conclusive answer, which was usually the one he had stated earlier. The actual proceedings were not published, but the topics provided themes for individual treatises published by members of the society.

The theme of the originality of the epic genius runs through the writings of all the Scots primitivist thinkers. Its immediate sources can be found in Blackwell's *Enquiry* (1735). Blackwell emphasized in this work that the Phaeacian Demodocus, 'Homer's blind Bard' and a representative of a class of singers, sang 'by meer Inspiration, and that the talent of the ancient poets was spontaneous and 'truly natural': 'the Ancients of early Times, as *Nature* gave Powers and a Genius, so they fought, or plowed, or merchandized, or sung; Wars, or Loves, or Morals, ὡς ἡ Μοῦσα ἐδίδου just as their Muse or Genius gave Permission'.[12] John Brown, another early primitivist, valued simplicity as 'the only universal Characteristic of just Writing',[13] and took Homer, Aeschylus and Ossian as his prime examples of original genius in poetry. William Duff, a generation later, found in their poetry 'irregular greatness, wildness, and enthusiasm of imagination'.[14] Brown thought that some of the factual blunders in Homer's poems could be attributed to the poet's circumstances: Homer 'is not blameable: He painted what he saw, and painted truly. The Fault lay in the Opinions and Manners of the Times: In the Defects of an early and barbarous Legislation, which had but half-civilized Mankind'.[15] When comparing Homer and Aeschylus, Brown discovered in the Greek tragedian an even better example of 'the rude Genius of early Periods': his

imagery and Sentiments are great; his Style rugged and abrupt; and of a Cast so totally different from that of *Homer*, that it is astonishing to hear the Critics, one after another, affirming that *Homer* was his Model. His Writings present to us all the Characters of a sublime, original, and uncultivated Genius, which scorned any other Tutoress than Nature.[16]

The point is, however, that whatever examples of poetic genius the primitivist writers chose, they emphasized the same qualities of originality, simplicity, wildness, sublimity and invention.

Alexander Gerard, a notable contributor to eighteenth-century ideas on genius, discussed at length Homer's 'rich and original invention' and related the faculties which had made it possible to the conditions that had prevailed in Homeric society. Homer, he said, 'lived in times of ignorance, when poetry remained almost in its first rudeness; that he had no model, by which he could receive so much as a hint of his grand designs; and that he notwithstanding, merely by the force of his own abilities, brought the noblest

species of poetry all at once to its just perfection'.[17] Gerard took
the view that there is in genius an element which is essentially
inborn. His argument was directed against those who had con-
founded genius with other faculties of the human mind – 'with
mere Capacity'.[18] He discusses the concept of genius under four
heads: its components are *associating power, comprehensiveness
of imagination, regularity* and *activity of imagination*,[19] and lastly
there is an element essentially related to these, though it cannot
be classed as a component: 'the fire of genius, like a divine
impulse, raises the mind above itself'.[20] Homer and Shakespeare
were Gerard's examples of genius throughout the essay. His poetic
hierarchy in terms of genius was Homer, Shakespeare, Milton and
Virgil.

Gerard's discussion also presents arguments on the relation of
imitation and genius. Though he admitted that poetry might be
called an imitation in the sense that it describes what might have
been and what is probable, yet poetry should always copy real
things in exactness and relate what the poet has seen. He argued
that poetry was called imitation only because its 'subject itself is
an imitation of some part of real nature'.[21] Here we see Gerard
coming close to Johnson's ideas: the conception of the subject
matter requires 'invention', the capacity of 'realizing fiction'. For
these reasons Virgil is a poetic genius inferior to Homer: 'The
Eneid is perhaps more correct and faultless than the *Iliad*; but few
have pretended that Virgil is a greater poet. He does not show
such copious and boundless invention, as his master. Besides,
Virgil derives from imitation, many things for which Homer is
indebted solely to his own penetration.'[22] This leads to the statement that in real instances of genius no artificial model of imitation is present, because of the great element of associative power
in the poet, and because the original of the poetic genius is only
nature, the external reality:

a poet of real genius will always draw his images from that state and
face of nature which occurs in the places he is acquainted with, and
those objects and appearances which he himself has had occasion to
observe: and by this means he often distinguishes himself from
imitators, who not having genius sufficient for observing the great
original, Nature, the real appearance of things exhibited to themselves,
describe them as they have been already described by others in situations totally different.[23]

William Duff, another active member of the Aberdeen circle,

represents a considerably 'deeper' level of primitivism than
Gerard. In his *Essay on original genius* (1767) he condemned
imitation as a principle which was inimical to all stages of poetic
creation: 'Imitation indeed, of every kind, except that of nature,
has a tendency to cramp the inventive powers of the mind, which,
if indulged in their excursions, might discover new mines of intellectual ore, that lie hid only from those who are incapable or
unwilling to dive into the recesses in which it lies buried.'[24] Duff
was not as sophisticated a thinker as Gerard, but it is in his
writings that we find some of the most straightforward eulogies of
primitive and original genius. First of all, he seems to think of
original genius not so much as an inborn faculty, but as a power
that manifests itself in some individuals, superimposed on their
personalities, in the way the Greeks thought of the δαίμων, the
godly spirit: 'A Poet...who is possessed of original Genius, feels in
the strongest manner every impression made upon the mind, by
the influence of external objects on the senses, or by reflection on
those ideas which are treasured up in the repository of memory,
and is consequently qualified to express the vivacity and strength
of his own feelings.'[25] Duff speaks of 'that enthusiasm of Imagination which is 'an essential characteristic of original Genius' and is
'indispensably necessary to the enraptured Bard'.[26] He thus makes
a clear association between the notions of enthusiasm and original
genius. One can be a genius without enthusiasm, but not an
original genius. Consequently, he also distinguishes between two
types of men of genius, the philosophic and the poetic: the latter is
capable of enthusiasm.[27] By introducing the concept of enthusiasm
in his discussion of poetic genius Duff had to argue, however,
against a century of theologians who had written about enthusiasm as demonic possession,[28] thus corrupting the original Greek
sense of ἐνθουσιασμός, 'to be filled with divine power'. Duff
wanted to re-establish the older and more positive meaning of the
word:

the Word *enthusiasm*, which is almost universally taken in a bad
sense: and, being conceived to proceed from overheated and dis-
tempered imagination, is supposed to imply weakness, superstition,
and madness. *Enthusiasm*, in this modern sense, is in no respect a
qualification for a Poet; in the ancient sense, which implies a kind of
divine *Inspiration* or an ardor of Fancy wrought up to Transport, we
not only admit it, but claim it an Essential one.[29]

Homer and Ossian represented for Duff the ideal poetic genius of the primitive age. He stated explicitly that they had an original genius because they were primitive poets. The principal argument of the *Essay* was that 'in the early periods of society, original Poetic Genius will in general be exerted in its utmost vigour'.[30] His explicit evidence was Homer and Ossian, who had been originators in their field of poetic art.[31] His preoccupation with the freedom that characterizes genius and with the sublimity of nature produced a eulogy of the primitive poet which in its unreality and beauty may well be called the primitivist thesis.

Happily exempted from that tormenting ambition, and those vexatious desires, which trouble the current of modern life, he wanders with a serene, contented heart, through walks and groves consecrated to the Muses; or, indulging a sublime, pensive, and sweetly-soothing melancholy, strays with a slow and solemn step, through the unfrequented desert, along the naked beach, or the bleak and barren heath. In such a situation, every theme is a source of inspiration, whether he describes the beauties of nature, which he surveys with transport; or the peaceful innocence of those happy times, which are so wonderfully soothing and pleasing to the imagination.[32]

Other representatives of the primitivist school, Lord Kames (Henry Home), Lord Monboddo (James Burnet), James Beattie, Hugh Blair, Adam Ferguson and James Dunbar put forward largely similar ideas about the primitive poet, and emphasized various aspects of primitive society in each case. Lord Monboddo was interested in the origin of language, Hugh Blair and Lord Kames in the origin of poetry and the early development of critical thought, James Beattie in the origin of artistic expression, and Adam Ferguson and James Dunbar in the origin of social institutions such as law and religion in the early ages of civilization. Their examples of poetic genius were also Homer and Ossian, and they emphasized that a simple and rude society promotes originality and creativity. Lord Kames wrote in his *Sketches of the history of man* (1774):

Homer lived in a rude age, little advanced in useful arts, and still less in civilization and enlarged benevolence... In such times literature could not be far advanced; and it is a great doubt, whether there was at that time a single poem of the epic kind, for Homer to imitate or improve upon. Homer is undoubtedly a wonderful genius, perhaps the greatest that ever existed: his fire and the boldness of his conceptions, are inimitable.[33]

Adam Ferguson spoke of the language of the early ages as 'simple and confined' and 'varied and free', and preferred Homer to Virgil. The primitive poet

delivers the emotions of the heart, in words suggested by the heart: for he knows no other. And hence it is, that while we admire the judgment and invention of *Virgil*, and of other later poets, these terms appear misapplied to *Homer*. Though intelligent, as well as sublime, in his conceptions, we cannot anticipate the lights of his understanding, nor the movements of his heart: he appears to speak of his thoughts and expressions by a supernatural instinct, not by reflection.[34]

James Beattie, in his 'Essay on poetry and music, as they affect the mind' (1762), attempted to sketch a theory of poetry which was closely related to the classical *ut pictura poesis* idea where 'the end of poetical description' is 'not only to relate facts but to paint them'.[35] His view was that a primitive society was the one most likely to create poetry on this principle of visualization: 'Homer's simple manners may disgust a Terrasson, or a Chesterfield; but will always please the universal taste, because they are more picturesque in themselves, than any form of artificial manners can be, and more suitable to those ideas of human life which are most familiar to the human mind.'[36] He argued, moreover, that these products of primitive poetry appeal to those basic feelings and ideas of man which relate to universal taste.

Hugh Blair took a similar view. He was the most authoritative defender of Macpherson's versions of Ossian's poems, and in his lectures, delivered during many decades at the University of Edinburgh, he constantly put forward primitivist arguments. In *A critical dissertation on the poems of Ossian* Blair spoke highly of the poetry of uncultivated ages which abounds with 'that enthusiasm, that vehemence and fire, which are the soul of poetry'.[37] In his lectures, Blair's critical interest was in that freedom of poetic genius which civilized society, with its preoccupation with contemporary taste, is bound to restrict.

A masterly genius, it is true, will of himself, untaught, compose in such a manner as shall be agreeable to the most material rules of Criticism; for as these rules are founded in nature, nature will often suggest them in practice. Homer, it is more than probable, was acquainted with no systems of the art of poetry. Guided by genius alone, he composed in verse a regular story, which all posterity has admired.[38]

The primitivists' study of the Homeric epic was occasionally impaired by their unreasonable idealism and insufficient factual information, but their interest in primitive societies, those distant from their own in both time and place, made them lay emphasis on aspects of ancient poetry which earlier had received only passing notice. Their idea that each culture is unique, and that between antiquity and the modern age no such continuity exists as certain similarities of themes and notions had led men to believe, made them give proper recognition to the fact that originality and creative genius were in essential ways dependent on primitive society.

The first problem formulated by John Brown, James Beattie and Lord Monboddo concerned the interrelationship of poetry and dance, in other words, words and music, and this had led to speculations about the development of language. Early poetry represented a special instance of the close connection between words and music, and all existing evidence about it seemed to support the theory that the origins of human communication, which finally resulted in the highly sophisticated system of language, were to be found in situations that involved play rather than practically useful achievement. The primitivists, notably Thomas Reid and Lord Monboddo, looked at children and how they acquired 'habits of sensation' in play situations of their early infancy, and made the assumption that early peoples and savages were the children of mankind.[39] This compelling analogue made them study the poetry of ancient Greece, Judea, China, Peru, India and Scandinavia, as well as that of the ancient Celts. As early as 1737 Edward Manwaring had written that 'the first Poets were Masters of Music, and the efficient Cause of Poetry was Happiness of Genius, with a Facility of expressing the Conceptions of the Mind according to the natural Ideas of Things',[40] expressing the line of theoretical speculation that the primitivists followed. The primitivists realized that music had formed an important part of ancient Greek poetry, epic, lyric and dramatic; and they assumed that poetry produced without any influence from 'a supposed Civilization' would be even more closely connected with simple sound values and melodious utterances.[41]

The second problem debated by the Scottish philosophers falls more precisely in the field of poetic theory, and goes back to the 1740s or even earlier. Pope, in his preface to the *Iliad* (1715), had analysed the poetic quality which he termed 'fire' and had rated Homer highest among epic poets because he had the greatest measure of it. Since Pope a new conception of poetry had grown up which found poetic virtue in vigour, vehemence and fire, and its champions were poets who influenced contemporary taste in that direction: Young, Smart, Chatterton and Collins. This conception was not only accepted in the ranks of the primitivists, but was carried to the extreme conclusion that the essence of poetry is precisely 'fire', that is, vigour, spontaneous force and vehemence.

Finally, the philosophers added a third notion to this new view of poetry by emphasizing that the origins of artistic expression could not be understood in isolation from the social context that produced them; and the Ossianic poetry seemed to be direct evidence for this theory. William Duff, James Dunbar and Lord Kames were the first to raise the question whether primitive poetry was the product of its society in the sense that the existing social conditions entirely determined its character, vigour and simplicity. If this were the case, the primitivists argued, could such a state be discovered again in parts of the world that had remained out of the reach of western civilization? And they answered this socially deterministic problem in the affirmative. Duff argued:

In the earliest and least cultivated periods of society, Poetry is by one great effort of nature, in one age, and by one individual, brought to the highest perfection to which human Genius is capable of advancing it; not only when the other Arts and Sciences are in a languishing state, but when they do not so much as exist. Thus *Homer* wrote his *Iliad* and *Odyssey*, when there was not a single picture to be seen in Greece; and *Ossian* composed *Fingal* and *Temora*, when none of the Arts, whether liberal or mechanical, were known in his country.[42]

In their writings on originality and early society, the primitivists put forward two allied but distinct hypotheses. One hypothesis set an inherent value on originality, regarding it as creative under unfavourable circumstances and as related in fact to a certain deprivation of literary models or cultural stimuli, but, because of this cultural isolation, falling ultimately short of the idea of the perfectly formed genius. This view can be seen in the writings of Brown, Gerard and Lord Kames. The other hypothesis regarded the poetic genius of primitive peoples as all the greater because it had lacked contact with the models and materials that civilized society offers and was untutored, revealing its innate power and developing the meanings of its art in the act of creation. This notion is supported by the writings of Duff, Ferguson and Blair, and appears later in some of the Romantic views on originality.

In the primitivists' discussion of original genius the question whether the ancient or modern culture was to be regarded as superior, which had been so much debated in the early part of the eighteenth century and had been one of the central questions of the *querelle*, had largely become meaningless. The primitivists did not even consider the idea of the continuity of cultures, whereby one could see a direct line of development from antiquity to the contemporary age, and could therefore argue meaningfully whether modern conditions represented a decline or an advance. They used examples from the classical epic largely because they were thoroughly acquainted with the material and perceived its relevance to their arguments. But they regarded each culture as unique, and as the result of an infinite number of coincidental factors that had combined to make it what it was. Each culture was thought to have its men of genius who, as poets, artists and philosophers, could analyse its ingredients and influence its development through practical measures.

Moreover, the primitivists had an interest in the universal aspects of the human mind. Their 'original genius' was the epic poet who possessed rich powers of invention and was authorized by his society to make free use of them. He was a man who created from the experiences provided by his culture a work of literature that gave objective form to conceptions which were implicit in those experiences, but which had not been previously expressed. Genius was understood to be a universal human faculty, and as such was considered to be independent of cultural progress or decline, being in the last resort simply superior intelligence. It could be shaped by culture, but the quality that raised it to the status of genius remained independent of the cultural scene. Holding these views, the primitivists could look upon popular, orally transmitted epics as the products either of one, or of several poets of creative genius, and were not essentially interested in the question whether the *Iliad*, for example, was the work of one or several authors. They could hold that certain cultures and periods produced an unusually large number of men of genius and could at the same time maintain that an individual genius had the power to raise the general level of his culture.

Homer had been the model of originality for poetic theorists since ancient times, but in the period we are considering certain changes occurred which affected the view men took of past centuries and of contemporary works. This was largely due to the fact that eighteenth-century writers and critics were beginning to see themselves as detached from Graeco-Roman culture, and were learning to set greater emphasis on social issues in whatever phenomena they were studying. 'Society then is the theatre on which our genius expands with freedom', said James Dunbar.[43] The primitivists' discussion of genius associated genius with the environment. Homer's genius was seen as related to the fact that he belonged to a primitive society. There existed, they maintained, an organic relationship between genius and a society that is close to nature and does not hamper the development of genius by excessive economic or moral control. This utopian relationship between the artist and the environment was seen to exist at the time of Homer, when poetry was orally transmitted.

11

Poetry is original 'imitation':
Robert Wood's theory of the Homeric epic

Robert Wood wrote in 1767 that Homer was 'the most original of all poets, and the most constant and faithful copier after nature'.[1] This statement, which may be puzzling in its apparently paradoxical use of the word 'original', coupled as it is with the practice of copying nature, expresses in fact one of the most interesting eighteenth-century views about the Homeric epics. Wood's *Essay* finds room for the notions that had been attached to Homer during the century, for example omniscience, imaginative scope and narrative simplicity, and it adds one more: that what we call 'originality' derives from the sharpness of the poet's responses to his environment and from the precision with which he can record these responses.[2] Wood rejects inspiration as an explanation of genius and gives the key role to the poet's scientifically accurate powers of observation. He ascribes Homer's excellence to his 'amazing Powers of original imitation' – a theory which not only made a significant contribution to classical studies, but also came to influence contemporary taste in literature, and it is important to see how Wood came to formulate it.[3]

Robert Wood (1717?–1771) had visited the scenes described in the *Iliad* and the *Odyssey* during his tour of Greece, the Greek Islands and Asia Minor with his friends James ('Jamaica') Dawkins and John Bouverie and the Italian artist Borra in 1750–1. Journeys to the classical sites of the Mediterranean were becoming increasingly common in the eighteenth century. They were made traditionally by younger members of rich families for educational and recreational purposes, and as such had earned the title of 'the grand tour'; but as time passed the prospect of such a tour came also to attract a growing number of educated middle-class travellers who visited cities of cultural and historical interest in Italy and central Europe. The immense educational importance of the grand tour cannot be overestimated. Even if the 'grand-tourists' were often poorly informed, young and superficial, they brought back to their country impressions and objects which did much to stimulate cultural activity.

Wood, however, belonged to a third and more influential group of travellers to the classical sites. This group comprised literary men and women, scholars, architects and artists, whose travels were in many instances financed by cultural bodies such as the influential Society of the Dilettanti, and who went for the purpose of exploring and recording the details of the classical scene. They disapproved of the predatory, treasure-hunting approach which was so much in evidence, especially in the case of Herculaneum and Pompeii from the first discovery of these sites in 1708 to the late eighteenth century; they prepared for the journey far more carefully than the ordinary visitor, and usually published an account of their experiences on their return.[4]

Wood's journey was not an antiquarian mission organized by a public body. He went as a private person in the company of his friends and met his costs out of his private means. This left him free to observe what he pleased and enabled him to develop a consistent imaginative viewpoint of his own, while remaining careful about the archaeological and historical accuracy of his findings.

The days when such cheerful and sentimental travellers as Thomas Coryate, William Lithgow or Pierre Belon explored Greece for the first time were long past; but even eighteenth-century accounts such as we have from Lady Mary Wortley Montagu and Pierre Augustin Guys could express joy at the first discovery of the places which had become familiar through books.[5] Classical ground could not be approached in quite the same way as other places on earth; consequently the travellers were led into seeing much of what they expected to see there, and Wood was not completely free from the tendency to anticipate his observations. He wrote soon after his tour in 1753 (expressing the sentiments of the average educated traveller): 'It is impossible to consider with indifference those countries which gave birth to letters and arts, where soldiers, orators, philosophers, poets and artists have shown the boldest and happiest flights of genius, and done the greatest honour to human nature.'[6] Accurate and critical as he was, he could not avoid idealizing the classical scene. Even in his *Ruins of Palmyra*, which was primarily an architectural survey, he shows himself fascinated by the opportunity the visit gave him to investigate the background to classical literature. He emphasized the importance of such background information: 'classical ground not only makes us always relish the poet, or historian more, but sometimes helps us to understand them better'. It is not surprising to find him pointing out that visits to an original Homeric site, even one in ruins, make a more powerful psychological impact than the most careful reading of the Homeric text: 'the *Iliad* has new beauties on the banks of the Scamander, and the *Odyssey* is most pleasing in the countries where Ulysses travelled and Homer sung'.

Robert Wood's spirit of discovery was shared by the members of the Society of the Dilettanti. A product of the philhellenism which flourished at this time in Britain,[7] this highly active association was founded for the purpose of studying Greek antiquities on their original sites and began its formal meetings in the 1770s. Its members seem to have been inspired by a somewhat naive enthusiasm, but they set great store by accuracy and precision, so that the quality of their work was reasonably good. Wood's preface to the travels of Richard Chandler can serve as an example. Chandler toured the Greek mainland and islands with the architect Nicolas Revett and the botanist William Pars, and the words which describe his first impressions of Asia Minor are such as any tourist might have used: 'And here the Father of *Poetry* produced a standard for Composition, which no Age or Country have dared to depart from, or have been able to surpass.'[8] But when Wood seeks to recommend his work, it is on the grounds of its truthfulness and historical accuracy: 'consisting rather of Matters of *Fact* than of *Opinion*, [it] derives Merit more from the Writer's Veracity than from his Talents for Composition'.[9]

Wood also set great store by accuracy, and this must be seen as a new departure from the fictionalized and unreliable accounts of earlier travellers. He and his contemporaries wanted to see the actual remains of the ancient world and to report about them truthfully, now that this had become materially possible. They romanticized classical antiquity, as the Renaissance had romanticized the New World, but they realized that their dream would be rapidly lost in unreality if it were not subjected to the censorship of a critical and investigating intellect.

Any final estimate of the eighteenth-century travellers and their
accounts of the classical sites must emphasize their essentially
enlightened approach to the problems facing them. They refrained, in principle anyway, from removing the ancient remains
from their original location, whatever the rubble around them,
but aimed at an accurate and faithful description of what they
saw. They provided detailed illustrations by professional artists
of architectural remains, fragments of sculpture, topographical
features and the Mediterranean fauna and flora. The more
literary travellers, such as Wood, commented in detail on the
scenery, climate, people and customs of the countries they visited,
and compared their experience with the actual situation that had
existed two or three thousand years before, though such a comparison was admittedly an imaginative rather than a scholarly
feat.

The work of these travellers meant that men opened their
minds for the first time to the sensuous aspects of classical
antiquity – an element which had not been prominent in earlier
estimations of the classics. Moreover, the travellers were able to
report on the classical scene with a veracity which cleared away
much of the fog and mystification that had come to obscure
classical literature. To have seen the actual size of a Greek temple,
and to have felt the wind that blew through its columns, meant
that proportion and reality entered into men's idea of classical
antiquity.

Wood's purpose in his *Essay on the original genius of Homer*
was to give an account of Homer as a poet who had worked in
circumstances with which Wood had become familiar during his
travels and studies. He believed that the historical and cultural
gap between past and present could be bridged, because writing,
in the last analysis, is a description of reality. Homer was 'the
most original of all Poets', Wood thought, because he had
depicted the reality with which he was personally familiar, and
was the best narrator of the things and events he had seen and
experienced.

I was the more confirmed in this judgment, the more I referred myself
back to the state of society and manners of that early period. I therefore examined the materials of the *Iliad* and the *Odyssey*, not only

where they were collected, but, as nearly as possible, in the same order, in the same light, and under the same point of view, in which I imagine they presented themselves to the Poet's choice; making it the chief object of my inquiry to investigate the several circumstances, and various relations of this kind, which may be supposed to have influenced his occupation of things.[10]

Wood concurred with Blackwell in regarding Homer as an original genius. But where Blackwell had tried to find social and cultural causes for Homer's achievement, Wood opted for a simpler approach and one which as a traveller he was particularly well equipped to follow.

Blackwell's *Enquiry into the life and writings of Homer* (1735) had shown that Homeric society possessed the primitive values, the fresh sensitivity, coupled however with some sophistication, which made epic writing possible. The heroic history of the Homeric age had provided suitable material for the poems. But in Wood's opinion Blackwell had failed in his purpose because he did not pay sufficient attention to the particular qualities that singled out Homer from the mass of his contemporaries and made him a poet. The parts of the *Enquiry* did not form a coherent whole: Homer emerged as 'a mighty Genius' but not as a writer. Wood wanted to add the insight of a modern educated traveller to Homeric studies. He explained his purpose as follows:

The place of Homer's birth and education is not so much the object of this inquiry, as it is to learn, if possible, from the Poet himself, where his fancy began to open to the wide field of matter, which he so happily collected and arranged in that wonderful epic form, that still continues to hold the first rank among compositions of genius.[11]

As Wood visited the areas where Homer had lived and where the actions of his poems were located, his interest was caught by the idea of relating the descriptions he found in Homer's text to the physical scenes around him, and he soon arrived at a position where he was led to defend Homer's veracity concerning geographical details and descriptions of natural phenomena, and to refute the arguments of critics like Perrault who had belittled Homer's learning. He became convinced of the factual truth of the Homeric epics, and convinced above all that Homer's metaphors and similes, the most personal features of his poet's technique, could be used to build up a picture of the poet's experience that

would be more true to life than the one Blackwell had created by
assembling data from external sources.

Wood therefore discarded all the evidence that ancient tradition
had preserved about Homer, and set out to compare the poet's
expressions and descriptions with the maps of the Mediterranean
area and with his own observations. 'It is from these natural and
unguarded appeals of original genius to the obvious and familiar
occurrences of common life,' he wrote about Homer's metaphors
and similes, 'that we may not only frequently collect the custom,
manners, and arts, of remote antiquity; but sometimes discover
the condition, and. . .the country of the Poet.'[12]

Wood's method of dealing with the Homeric text is illustrated
by the following example. He argued that the metaphorical
language revealed a world of reality which could be seen in
logical, naturalistic terms:

When the formidable march of Ajax with his corps is compared to a
threatening storm coming from the sea, I must observe (as an illustration, not of the obvious beauties of the simile, but of the Poet's country)
that this can be no other than an Ionian, or, at least, an Asiatic storm;
for it is raised by a West wind, which, in those seas, can blow on that
coast alone.[13]

Wood's theory was that Homer had been either an Ionian or an
Aeolian Greek, and had come from either Smyrna or Chios. Both
places had the advantage of being near the sea, and conformed
with the descriptions of landscape and natural phenomena in the
Iliad and the *Odyssey*. Wood favoured the Ionian theory. He had
first-hand knowledge of the Ionian and Asiatic coast line, and by
resorting to his own experience he intended to recreate for his
readers the Homeric world.

many beautiful allusions to the times, for which he wrote, are irretriev-
ably lost, even to the most conversant in antiquities. However, as we
found the manners of the *Iliad* still preserved in some parts of the
East, nay retaining, in a remarkable degree, that genuine cast of
natural simplicity, which we admire in his works and the sacred books,
it may not be improper to inquire how such an invariability in the
modes of life should be peculiar to that part of the world.[14]

The fact that Homer had lived in the vicinity of Troy, provided
him in Wood's opinion with exceptional opportunities for understanding the war. This was not just a reasonable guess. Wood
knew the controversial question about the location of Troy, and

saw it necessary to draw a map which could be proved correct on the evidence of the poems.[15] Being near Troy, Homer had had the opportunity, 'not only of being thoroughly acquainted with that spot, but of collecting circumstantial accounts of the most re-nowned achievements of the war, perhaps from those who were eye-witnesses of the siege, and had signalized themselves upon the Scamandrian plain; or at least from their children'.[16] Wood had to study the facts of Homer's life before he could continue his argument on a more general level. But even here, the focus was not on the person of Homer. What emerges from Wood's specu-lations is the image of a writer: 'Homer was a faithful historian, because he was a correct painter.'[17]

The technical problem of epic composition remained unsolved. How exactly did Homer compose? Both the *Iliad* and the *Odyssey* incorporated elements that Wood recognized as part of the popu-lar tradition of Greece – stories, fragments of tales and motifs that must have been known to the Homeric audience. Wood also realized that the state of Greek language and society in Homeric times must have been favourable for the creation of a popular epic. But he did not suggest that the epics might have been a com-pilation.

He nourished an ideal of the poet as a gifted individual, and of the poet's role as the creator of his work. This ideal prevented him from coming to the conclusion that Homer had simply been a folk poet, relating the related. In his view, the narrator of the *Iliad* and the *Odyssey* had been an independent observer of the events about which he sang. He had been an isolated individual capable of rising above the tradition that his contemporaries could only repeat. Homer, Wood said, 'had only the great book of nature to peruse, and was original from necessity, as well as by genius'.[18] But the crucial problem of the Homeric epics was their oral character.

Wood was among the first to argue that Homer was illiterate. He also understood that the growth of literacy must have effected important changes in the nature of poetry and the part it played in society. Yet, was it possible that two epics of such length and wealth of detail had been composed without the aid of writing? Did the poet himself resort to some kind of *aide-mémoire*? Were any systems of writing in use at the time for recording facts men needed to remember? If so, how were the epics written down? Or if they were not written down, what features can we find in them that indicate their originally oral nature? Wood had to deal with these questions with caution, because he knew that the educated public of his day assumed that an oral literature was inferior to a written one.

Wood argued that the epics themselves suggest the illiteracy of their poet, for 'there is nothing, that conveys the idea of letters, or reading; none of the various terms, which belong to those arts, are to be found in Homer'.[19] Wood's theory that the alphabet was not a Greek invention and that writing came to Greece proper some time during the seventh and sixth centuries B.C., before the Persian wars, has been confirmed by modern scholarship.[20] Homer composed the epics in a pre-literate society that was familiar with other means of poetic expression than the written word. The fact that the Homeric epics belong to the pre-literate age indicates the fidelity of oral tradition and the highly developed mnemotechnics of its oral poets.

The relation of poetry to the written word is not a question that can be viewed in separation from a social context.[21] In a pre-literate society poetry is the preferred method of communication; it provides formulaic structures and a metaphorical conciseness that act as aids to the memory and facilitate the preservation of knowledge. The agricultural calendar included in Hesiod's *Works and days* is an example of how useful information of educational importance was preserved in poetic form. The poetic conventions of a literate society produce different results, as only in a literate society can poetry develop towards a greater intimacy of content and unpredictability of expression, and poetry is then relieved of its public and didactic functions. Consequently, the oral poet has a social role from which the literate poet is free. The oral poet is dependent on an immediate response from his audience, which alone makes his work meaningful, whereas the literate poet is free to create an individual language which can reach an anonymous audience in privacy. The transition from an oral to a literate culture in ancient Greece can be traced in the works of Homer, Hesiod and the early writers of the lyric, Hesiod being the first poet whose poems mostly bear the marks of having been thought out and composed in a literary form, and Sappho, Alcaeus and Archilochus indicating a clearly developed individuality addressing itself not to the community but to the individual reader of a literate culture.

The immediate background to Wood's notion of the original genius of Homer was his own travel experience, which made him familiar with the Homeric scenes, just as Homer had been. Wood analysed originality in writing in an extremely practical manner, comparing it frequently with painting; and it would not be altogether unfair to say that his *Essay* was a product of a rather simplistic mission to prove the rightness of Horace's dictum *ut pictura poesis*:

the more we consider the Poet's age, country, and travels, the more we discover that he took his scenery and landscape from nature, his manners and characters from life, his persons and facts (whether fabulous or historical) from tradition, and his passions and sentiments from experience of the operations of the human mind in others, compared with, and corrected by, his own feelings.[22]

It is easy to understand the enthusiasm of such diverse writers as Goethe and Wolf for Wood's *Essay*. The *Essay* is a panegyric in praise of originality that at times has a Romantic sound. This originality is indebted to nature only, and nature is the totality of the external world, places and people, natural phenomena and human emotions, as perceived by the mind of the poet. But Wood's emphasis on the reality of the outside world, which exists apart from the author, which cannot be falsified for the purposes of writing, but which it is the poet's task to describe, also anticipated the notion of realism that emerged in the nineteenth-century novel. Original genius was the total response of the artist, by the means of art, to the world that had moulded him. Epic writing involved isolation, detachment and observation on the part of a superior mind, though the resultant poem suggests exuberance and generosity. Wood's analysis of the Homeric epic proposes that recording trivial things, such as the making of a wedding-bed, or a young warrior's anger in the middle of the fiercest battle, or the details of a blind poet's harp, is also part of the epic poet's art. 'Original imitation' emerges as the key term which characterizes not only the Homeric epic but epic writing in general. It defines a kind of imitation that does not rely on preconceived notions as regards the rules of epic composition and the patterns through which the world is perceived, but is faithful to the subject matter which the individual poet has chosen.

The development from the neoclassical position had proceeded along several lines in the eighteenth century; and one of these lines of change culminated in Wood's *Essay*. What the neoclassical critics, such as Rapin, Dacier and Le Bossu, had regarded as vulgarity in Homer, was now seen as valuable realism. Wood emphasized this realism, as he could argue on the basis of his own observations that Homer had described the world he had seen and had expressed his experience in terms with which his own age had been familiar. It is easy to see how the material Wood provided could be used to reinforce primitivist arguments. Homer had imitated nature, in the widest possible sense, by describing it in detail. Wood's important conclusion was that poetic originality consists in the accurate description of reality, and this reality must needs comprise the totality of human experience and the external world.

12

The originality of Homer: some conclusions

Homeric criticism of the eighteenth century is characterized by a pedantic preoccupation with the originality of the Greek poet. This is evident not only in the major works dealing with Homer's personality and poetry – the writings of Perrault, Mme Dacier, Pope, Voltaire, Vico, Blackwell, Macpherson and Wood, which have merited close study here – but also in the large corpus of minor critical works which built up the general intellectual climate of the day, such as the philosophical and anthropological treatises of the Scottish primitivists and the numerous letters, essays and poems written for didactic or literary critical purposes by men interested in the theory of education or of fine arts. These are works which do not directly attempt to evaluate Homer but use him indirectly as an example. And it is in them that we find repeated again and again the claim that Homer and the ancient authors were the 'great Originals' who drank 'at the breast of Nature',[1] coupled with the demand that modern poets should learn to do likewise and should rediscover the 'fountains and streams' of nature and culture which supposedly nourished Homer.[2]

This type of originality for which the eighteenth century thirsted cannot be seen as peculiarly Homeric. Though it was left undefined, we find it usually set in opposition to imitation which was regarded as an inferior poetic technique. The German art critic J. G. Sulzer, writing about originality, says that 'der Originalgeist wird dem Nachahmer entgegen gestellt',[3] and John Pinkerton, some ten years later (1785), argues that no man 'of real genius can be an imitator...originality is coessential with genius'.[4] Homer was thought to have originality because he had not imitated anyone.

The story is, however, more complicated than these simple

examples suggest. The increasing amount of interest shown by eighteenth-century criticism and philosophy in the meaning of genius and originality manifested itself in various characteristic ways from the time of the *querelle*, when the first attempts were made – notably by Perrault, Fontenelle and La Motte – to clarify the contemporary position with regard to the heritage of Greek and Roman antiquity. The authority of Homer suffered seriously because of the *querelle*. Since the *modernes* argued that the originality and progress of modern culture depended on its scientific achievements and necessitated a firm departure from ancient thought, they naturally wanted to discard the literary and artistic productions of classical antiquity, on the ground that they reflected the elementary concepts of its science and natural philosophy. Similarly, as the *modernes* placed special emphasis on the development of contemporary vernacular literatures – this was an aspect of the *querelle* which had received vigorous support in England even independently of the educational claims of the *modernes* – the poems of Homer lost their place as models of a perfectly conceived epic but remained, either in translations or in their Greek form, examples of vernacular poetry produced by an alien culture. Consequently, when we look at the development of ideas about Homeric genius over a period of some sixty years, we can say that during the *querelle* the authority of Homer was questioned and decisively rejected by a large part of the educated public, which however enabled the originality of the poet to be revaluated in a genuinely historical and poetic context by critics and poets who often had only a tenuous involvement with the classical tradition.

The problem for those critics and writers who were interested in the rehabilitation of Homer was to prove that the poet was inimitable, not only by the modern age but also by his own contemporaries, and that originality was precisely the asset which Homer possessed, when his claim to be the perfect genius was in question.

The purpose of the present chapter is to summarize the most important eighteenth-century views of Homer's originality and to see how these were linked with current theories concerning originality. The ways in which the writers, critics and poets of the period discussed Homer's originality and genius were in part at least familiar to them from the classical tradition. But as they were faced with the task of having to assess ancient art on the basis of the new knowledge that was rapidly accumulating about it, they discovered, partly inadvertently, definitions of originality, which differ in many interesting ways from any previous views.

We can distinguish four different ideas about Homer. Two of these had been current in antiquity and had been much discussed during the Renaissance and the seventeenth century: the notion of Homer as *the first human poet* and the notion of him as *the omniscient author*. Two others were then contributed by the eighteenth century; the notion of Homer as *the primitive bard* and the idea of the Homeric epic as the collective mind of a culture, which can be named, borrowing from Vico, *the true Homer*. During the period we are considering these four ideas were presented as arguments for Homer's originality, as poets and scholars came to emphasize that Homer was a representative of the creative poets of the Greek peoples, and that the special value of his epics lay in the fact that they were the original expression of a creative nation.[5]

I. THE FIRST POET AND THE OMNISCIENT AUTHOR

The notion that Homer was the first human poet, and for this reason the original all later poets copied, was supported by classical, hellenistic and Byzantine writers, who distinguished Homer from his mythical predecessors Musaeus and Orpheus largely because the Homeric epics were the first complete texts available to them, and because his were the earliest writings that had a definitely secular character. The poems which were attributed (however mistakenly) to Orpheus were prophetic and mystical in tone. Homer was not only the first object of ancient poetic criticism, but also the first educator of the Greek peoples. The first-century rhetorician Heraclitus, a Stoic, testified to this: 'Right from the early infancy that tender minds of the children who engage in studies are nourished by Homer, and like sweet milk are his words to us, who from the babies in swaddling clothes thereby grow stronger in our understanding. . .and men know all but one end to Homer, that of their lives.'[6] When the notion of Homer's being the first poet reappeared in the seventeenth and eighteenth centuries, it was associated with a certain pseudo-classicist tendency, being one of the half-examined views that the later ages had inherited *en bloc* from antiquity. Gerard Croese, who wrote a study in 1704 comparing Homer and the Old Testament, a topic popular at the time, said of the primacy of Homer: 'Homerum, poetarum omnium, Graecorum, aliorumque, antiquissum, mirum quantum veteres non unis principibus viris in Graecia, sed etiam inter barbaras, etiam Eoäs atque extremas genteis, in amore et deliciis fuisse testentur.'[7] Ludolph Kuester, in his study of Homer's age, native country and textual tradition (1696), wrote of the antiquity of Homer: 'utut autem accurate definiri non possit, quo tempore Homerus vixerit: Illud saltem constat, omnibus, qui hodie extant Poëtis, eum vetustiorem esse'.[8] Homer, esteemed as the first poet to have emerged from the mythical age, was also valued for having provided a model for the later epic poets of antiquity. The analysis of how Virgil had copied from him became a critical commonplace during the eighteenth century, as this was an indebtedness that could be neatly and objectively established, and the primacy of Homer was regarded moreover as having some value, even when the Virgilian epic was preferred. Dryden's criticism of the epic provided the standard view in England.[9] Richard Hurd, in his *Letter to Mr Mason* (1757) which formed part of their argument on the nature of poetry and the classics, referred to an old painting in which 'the figure of Homer with a fountain streaming out of his mouth, and the other poets watering at it' had been, rather absurdly, depicted. Hurd argued that Homer and the Greeks were the originals of all later literature: 'even in this our age, when good letters, they say, are departing from us, the Greek and Roman stamp is still visible in every work of genius, that has taken with the public'.[10] Roger Kedington, a minor critic, who gleaned his ideas from Terrasson, eulogized Homer, 'this greatest and original genius':

It has been observed very justly of *Homer*, that he not only transcends all poets whatever, but that he has in this most ornamented *poem*, outgone in perspicuity and clearness of expression even all writers in *prose*: as this uncommonly easy and happy flow must needs recommend him universally, as the perfectest pattern, and the best model in good writing of all others whatever, to imitate and copy after.[11]

John Aikin, whose criticism of poetry had primitivistic tendencies, praised Homer for his 'rich and creative invention, which is the very soul of poetry'. Homer was 'an original':

it requires very little judgment to see, that no succeeding poet whatever can with any propriety be compared with *Homer*: that great father of the *Grecian* poetry and literature, had a genius too fruitful and comprehensive to let any of the striking parts of nature escape his observation; and the poets, who have followed him, have done little more than transcribing his images, and giving a new dress to his thoughts.[12]

The idea that Homer was the first poet and the original which could not be surpassed or even properly imitated (but only copied) gave eighteenth-century English criticism of the epic a characteristically pessimistic slant.[13] Dr Johnson gave expression to this in his 'Preface to Shakespeare' by stating that the poet of later times was not able to do much more than 'new name his characters'.

But the critics who praised Homer on the grounds of priority did not raise the kindred issue that the Homeric poetry had perhaps been perfected by generations of epic poets who had shared a common folklore and technique. The idea of the epic cycles, which is unanimously accepted by modern Homeric scholarship, was belittled by the defenders of Homer as an impoverished method of creation. It is a curious fact that the critics who did understand the value of existing literary traditions as an enrichment of poetic expression should have eulogized Homer for having been the first poet in the history of western civilization whose only debts were to the poetic lore of eastern nations. It may be suggested that the primacy of Homer became a virtue of some importance for the literary critics of the eighteenth century, because it presented a standard of excellence in the form of a myth and a metaphor to a predominantly rational school of criticism.

The notion of Homer's omniscience had its origins in Plato, who frequently lets Socrates characterize the reverend master as the source of all wisdom and all folly,[14] and also in the numerous lives of Homer which contain fifth-century elements and were collected little before the time of Augustus. The notion is a commonplace in hellenistic, Roman and Byzantine writings on the poet, which largely reflect the simple fact that Homer was the staple diet of every schoolboy in the Roman Empire. Pseudo-Plutarch's *Vita Homeri* (first century A.D.) speaks of Homer as the greatest poet as regards his 'eloquence, philosophy and experience and knowledge of all matters'. Quintilian mentions Homer's polymathy: 'Ceterum, ut de Homero taceam, in quo nullius non artis aut opera perfecta aut certe non dubia vestigia reperiuntur';[15] the Byzantine critic Tzetzes praises Homer as an omniscient author and 'the ocean of all poetry'.[16] This already highly suggestive notion then became an integral part of the poetic theory of the Renaissance platonists.[17] They added to it the important idea that Homeric poetry drew upon the sources of esoteric wisdom. Homer's knowledge was regarded by them not so much as factual and scientific but rather as the *arcana,* the hidden wisdom that opened its true meaning only to a select minority who possessed the right key for reading and understanding it. They similarly assumed that this wisdom had been deliberately hidden under the veil of esoteric language.[18] The difficulties posed by Homeric Greek were understood to be only half the problem; the fact that Homeric wisdom was concealed in riddles and ambiguity constituted the other half, which from the educational point of view was considered the more important. In the humanistic scheme of Politian's thought the omniscience of Homer came to represent the ideal towards which an educated man should strive with great labour and effort, but which in the last resort could be achieved only by an individual who had poetic sensibility and an understanding of the essentially esoteric nature of that encyclopedic knowledge.[19] A similar point was made later by Rabelais, who in his prologue to *Gargantua* (?1534) argued that Homer's omniscience was an ideal worth emulating because his perfect mastery of language concealed knowledge both of all the arts and sciences and of the basic human condition, which becomes obvious to those who trouble to enquire further.[20]

The eighteenth-century critics also discussed Homer as an omniscient author, but their arguments have a new context, for two reasons. First, as the Homeric poems became gradually more accessible through the increasing number of translations and a growing knowledge of Homeric Greek, the reading public was better placed to check the truth of the myth that Homer was omniscient. Second, the spread of scientific knowledge during the eighteenth century had the effect of revealing even to ordinary readers that there were serious gaps in Homer's ideas on astronomy, say, when judged by the knowledge available in modern times. Most men (though Wood was an exception here) were in any case sceptical about the value of early Greek science even apart from Homer.

Although it is debatable whether the more penetrating criticism of Homer was influenced by these general trends, we can see the esoteric interest in omniscience surviving to some extent in the eighteenth century. The inherent fascination in the idea that there had been a single poetic genius who had absorbed and expressed the totality of what can fall within the human ken is apparent in the eighteenth-century discussions of the epic as the most universal genre of literature as well as incidentally in the writings of Pope, Blackwell and Wood. Homer was valued for an omniscience that comprised the knowledge of all human virtues and vices, the goodness and depravity of human nature and all the scientific knowledge of his age. If the interpretation of Homer's poems was held to be difficult and to require 'esoteric' knowledge, this was because the notion of omniscience in eighteenth-century criticism implies not so much a knowledge of accumulated facts as a certain level of understanding in the poet, and emphasizes, in contrast to the neoplatonist idea of esoteric wisdom, the knowledge of moral and human realities.

The seventeenth-century Homeric critic James Duport made a detailed study of selected passages in the *Iliad* and *Odyssey*, referring to Greek, Latin and Hebrew authors for support of his theory of Homer's omniscience. It is of interest that he compared Homer with Christ: 'Est, inquam, *Homerus* immensus scientiarum Oceanus. . .Sed Christus multo magis abyssus veritatis, et fons vitae ac Salutatis aeternae. In *Homeri* scriptis (teste *Plutarcho*) omnium bonarum artium elementa atque semina, omnium virtutum et vitiorum exempla, omnium scientiarum documenta continentur: At in *Christo* multo magis (teste *Paulo*) sunt omnes thesauri sapientiae ac scientiae absconditi.'[21] The frequent comparisons between Christ and Homer during the seventeenth and early eighteenth centuries – Duport is one of the best examples of this tradition – were obviously motivated by the desire to place Homer in his proper secular and pagan context as regards education. The supporters of the Jesuits, even the most humanistically minded educators within the Roman Catholic Church who favoured the study of the Greek language, looked askance at things Greek on doctrinal grounds, insofar as the pagan values of classical antiquity were clearly opposed to the Christian life and the papacy.

But we can also see the fundamental opposition between

pagan and Christian *learning* being evoked in these comparisons, and this was undoubtedly an issue even at the time of the *querelle*. The opposition was between two kinds of erudition; one that leads to secular, scientific and humanistic wisdom and another that aims at religious, mystical and spiritual wisdom; and ultimately between two texts, Homer and the Bible, that open themselves to two totally different types of intelligence. The former has a firm grasp of reality, of the moral, social and educative universe; the latter offers a sense of the transcendental reality and hidden truths of man's future. Two basically different epistemological ideas were also presented in these comparisons: Homer, the secular text, being itself the totality of human achievement and omniscience acquired by man's intelligence; and the Bible, the sacred text, being only the means to a knowledge that man ultimately cannot obtain without divine dispensation.

During the eighteenth century the efforts of the humanists to establish an autonomous place for the study of Homer and of Greek language and culture gradually began to bear fruit. René Rapin gives the standard neoclassical view of Homer's omniscience. He emphasizes the educational value of the wisdom contained in the epics: Homer was the teacher of mankind.

Homer, who had a Genius accomplish'd for *Poetry*, had the vastest, sublimest, profoundest, and most universal Wit that ever was; 'twas by his Poems that all the Worthies of Antiquity were form'd: from hence the Law-makers, took the first Platform of the Laws they gave to Mankind; the Founders of Monarchies and Commonwealths, from hence took the Model for their Polities. Hence the Philosophers found the first Principles of Morality, which they have taught to the People. Hence Physicians have studied Diseases, and their Cures; Astronomers have learn'd the Knowledge of Heaven, and Geometricians of the Earth: Kings and Princes have learn'd the Art to govern, and Captains to form a Battle, to encamp an Army, to besiege Towns, to fight and to gain Victories...In fine, *Homer* has been...the first Founder of all Arts and Sciences, and the Pattern of the Wise-men in all Ages.[22]

Rapin's views on omniscience, like all his critical writings, were eagerly received in England. Anthony Collins, who was engaged in a controversy with Bentley on the issue of Homer's universality (Bentley did not accept it), thought that 'the Principles of all Arts and Sciences are contained' in Homer. Collins discussed Homer's knowledge in a more specific way than Rapin; some of the ideas he put forward foreshadowed Blackwell's and Wood's: 'Homer could never have describ'd as he ought, nor in the manner he has done, a *Chariot* or a *Chariot-Wheel*, without the particular Knowledge of a Coachmaker.'[23] Where Rapin had distinguished between Genius and Knowledge, Edward Manwaring, a critic who valued originality, emphasized Homer's omniscience and scope as the distinguishing mark of the genius that made the poet inimitable: 'To know the Poet [Homer] in all his Parts requires almost infinite Knowledge. Many have indeed endeavoured to imitate him, but no one as yet could ever equal him. He had all the Gifts Nature could give, and all the Art that could be derived from the greatest Experience and the deepest Judgment.'[24] Manwaring regarded th*e Iliad* as 'the most complete poem in the world' which contained the 'grounds of all Arts and Sciences'; it presented 'a compleat Picture of all natural Things, which nothing but Almighty Power could create'.[25] For all their intuitive understanding of Homer's originality and genius, which we see emerging in the middle of the eighteenth century in England, critics and poets continued to discuss these notions in the terms established in antiquity. But the important fact to be emphasized here is that they did regard omniscience as a valid critical concept which could perhaps be used in the assessment of contemporary works.

The explanation for Homer's outstanding creativity has been looked for either in the theory of divine inspiration, or in the idea of the optimum realization of a natural, human potentiality, and these two incompatible views have coexisted at every stage of history. The classical tradition contained both theories of inspiration and theories of rational creativity. The former view has been endorsed by poets who are, reasonably enough, opposed to the analysis of something of which they themselves know very little, so that a familiar metaphor often seems to them better able to convey what is essential in the creative act. T. S. Eliot's remark that Coleridge was a changed man after 'a visitation of the Muses'[26] is meaningful to those who know what is meant by the metaphor of the Muse. It does not rule out the possibility of an analysis of Coleridge's creativity; it only means that knowledge of Coleridge's literary influences, of his opium habits, of his frustrated relations with his family, of his love for two Saras, gives no answer to the problem of his extraordinary literary output. We gain an understanding of something else, no doubt, but in the final analysis we are faced with the fact that over the ultimate issue of creativity more mythical explanations might have done just as well or better. The inspirational and the rational hypotheses do not explain the same thing, but describe different aspects of the creative act. Insofar as we maintain that mystery is an essential element of poetry, and that without mystery poetry is merely words, we can say that all inspirational explanations of poetic creation are better and truer than the rational ones, even if one cannot understand the meaning of the inspirational explanation without having participated in the mystery of creating.

Consequently, there was a good deal of confusion when the modern critics tried to explain Homer's genius as if he had been a cross between a Hebrew prophet and an eighteenth-century critic. They were attempting to reconcile what they saw as the human and the divine aspects of the Homeric epic, and were misled by the ancient modes of discussing the problem. They were also influenced by the biblical tradition, which showed instances of a different type of poetic creativity. Some writers, such as Bogan, Grotius, Duport, Croese and Barnes, wrote treatises comparing the Bible and the classical epic. The differences were obvious; and yet the critics were intrigued by the fact that the tradition of antiquity, which was theirs as well, had seen Homer as a divinely inspired, omniscient poet. The ancient metaphor was read quite literally in Anglican England, even after Blackwell's work, and one suspects that Homer was sometimes regarded as the supreme model of epic literature for having supposedly been the first poet who had derived his poetry from the gods.

2. THE TRANSFORMATION OF HOMER

It is a feature of the Homeric tradition that it has included as its vital parts even those readings of the Greek epic which are clearly incorrect. If the purpose of scholarship is the seeking of truth, however, we can see that during the eighteenth century scholars and critics were gradually coming closer to what must be at least an approximation to the truth about Homer. This process involved a great many false starts and strange paths, but it was, all the same, a process which was characterized by the desire to understand the secret of Homer's appeal. The Homeric studies of the period included all those approaches which are now regarded as cornerstones of our conception of the Greek epic: textual criticism, classical scholarship which was preoccupied with the Homeric question, and actual criticism of the epics themselves. Though one type of Homeric interpretation was lacking, namely the literature of imagination based on Homeric themes and motifs (with the exception of Fénelon's *Télémaque*), which began to flourish only at the end of the nineteenth century, the eighteenth century provided examples of how the Homeric epics could be used as evidence for theories of individual and social creativity, which neither the preceding nor the following centuries have done.

At the very beginning of the eighteenth century (taking this to have started with the *querelle des anciens et des modernes*), the prevailing view of Homer was that offered by the neoclassical critics. They saw Homer as the traditionally eminent poet whose majesty and omniscience were praised but who was actually much inferior to Virgil when it came to the writing of the epic. At the end of the eighteenth century, the dominant criticism of the Homeric poems was already very much coloured by Romanticism. Homer then emerged as the collective voice of a tribal society, which was passingly noted to have been Greek, but the Greekness did not much matter. The fact that Homer was an epic poet of ancient Greece had been of prime importance to Mme Dacier and to Blackwell, who believed in the personal Homer but who emphasized the genius of the people that had produced him, as well as to Vico, who regarded Homer as the collective name for a class of ancient Greek singers. It had also been important to Macpherson, who tried to justify his Ossianic poems by their supposedly close similarity with the time-hallowed Homeric epics. But at about the same time the primitivists in Scotland and Herder on the Continent focused their interest on the creative power that manifested itself in a particular type of early society, and the Homeric poems provided valuable material for their theories. Their hopes were raised by the belief that a natural creative potentiality was concealed in the common people whose lives were organized similarly to Homeric society. It was characteristic of this pre-Romantic trend that folk poetry of European peoples was not only collected but also admired and intentionally composed, so the appearance of many new epic poets of the Homeric type was regarded not as too remote a possibility.

But men's expectations were betrayed: what they received was an Ossian, not a Homer. When the poets of the Romantic period emerged, their greatest achievements were not based on popular culture as the so-called pre-Romantic writers in England had advocated, but on the recognition of individuality and lyricism which can sometimes manifest itself in true folk poetry, and they could argue with considerable evidence that this, too, could be discovered in the Homeric epic. Those men in England and France who had preferred the elements of individual heroism, adventure and fairy-tale of the *Odyssey* to the wild cataracts, torrents and solemn gloominess of the *Iliad* were preparing the way for the restoration of the idea of the poet as the seer and the bard which the Romantics were to adopt.

The complex history of Homer in the eighteenth century is not, therefore, the history of Homeric scholarship and learning – although the discoveries by d'Aubignac, Bentley, Villoison and F. A. Wolf significantly reflected the general trends. It is, as I have shown in this book, the history of ideas about Homer's originality and genius. The problems presented by the figure and poetry of Homer were genuinely more intriguing and perplexing to the eighteenth century than they had been to the seventeenth, which saw in Homer the somewhat remote classical model and never came properly to terms with its 'father of poesie'.

Homer had been the model of originality for poetic theorists since antiquity, and when eighteenth-century criticism and philosophy became increasingly interested in the questions of genius and originality, he was used as an outstanding example. The nature of the questions eighteenth-century writers put was such as could find an answer in the study of his works. Consequently men's interest in Homer ranged from the biographical to the mythical and the critical. There were studies of the poet's life and attempts to solve the nature-nurture dilemma by collecting facts about the historical person called Homer (Parnell, Blackwell, Wood); there were treatises concerning the background of myth and religion of the Homeric epic (Gravina, Mme Dacier, Vico); and there were also a great number of discourses on the Homeric method of composition, poetic technique, inspiration and treatment of the subject matter (Rapin, Blackmore, Felton, Pope, Kedington, Pinkerton, Cowper and a host of translators as well as minor critics). The latter group provided a Homeric criticism which was a substantial eighteenth-century contribution to criticism of the methods and mechanisms of literary creation, applicable to genres other than the epic.

Although eighteenth-century Homeric criticism was largely based on the assumptions and speculations of earlier generations, a certain shift of emphasis took place during the period, a shift which reflects the versatility of the classical tradition. It would be an exaggeration to suggest that the tools of literary criticism applicable to a new type of poetic sensibility were developed by the critics of Homer, or that the subtle changes of literary taste were fully evident in the notions about Homer's original genius. But as the *Iliad* and the *Odyssey* came to be studied as products of specific cultural conditions, the nature of their poetry was revaluated on new grounds. What had earlier been regarded as vulgarity in Homer came to be seen as valuable realism and originality, and what had been condemned as primitive in the Homeric epic came to be considered, by the middle of the eighteenth century, as the main explanation for the originality and creative genius of the Greek poet; and this shift of emphasis largely corresponds with the general development in the theory and practice of poetry and the novel. The multitude of ways in which Homer was used in contemporary culture suggests that the eighteenth century was seeking in the epic poet a myth by which to explain its own complex myths of tradition and originality in a historical situation which was evolving towards new solutions.

It is instructive to observe how development in Homeric studies reflected precisely those preoccupations that were to be characteristic of the nineteenth century: the interest in the primitive which led to Herder's concern with national origins and in England to the rise of anthropology; the liking for realistic description which explains much of Dickens and Balzac; the concept of individual genius as an inner fire finding expression through the imagination, which we associate with the Romantic movement. It would be misleading to suggest that these preoccupations originated in the study of Homer. The interest in the primitive goes back to Montaigne, realism to Defoe, and the Romantic view of genius is more closely related to 'Longinus' than to Homer. But there is no doubt that the study of Homer forwarded these trends. It was one of the areas in the eighteenth century in which cultural growth was unmistakably vigorous; and the remote past proved the matrix of the future.

Notes

INTRODUCTION

1 V. Bérard, *La résurrection d'Homère* (Paris 1930), pp. 15ff;
F. Buffière, *Les mythes d'Homère et la pensée grecque* (Paris 1956),
pp. 22ff; G. S. Kirk, 'Dark age and oral poet', *PCPS*, n.s. 7 (1961),
34–48; A. Lesky, 'Homeros', *RE*, suppl. 11 (1967); M. P. Nilsson,
Homer and Mycenae (London 1933); A. Parry, 'Have we Homer's
Iliad?', *YCS*, 20 (1966), 177–216; W. J. Woodhouse, *The composition of Homer's Odyssey* (London 1930).

2 G. M. A. Richter, *The portraits of the Greeks* (London 1965), pp.
17ff, 46ff. She has distinguished four types of Homeric portrait: the
Epimenides type, the Modena type, the Apollonias of Tyana type
and the hellenistic blind type.

3 Lucian, *The panegyric of Demosthenes*, 9, in *Lucianus: works*,
trans. H. W. Fowler and F. G. Fowler (Oxford 1905).

4 Pseudo-Plutarch, *Homeri vita et de Homeri poesi*, in the Renaissance Latin translation by J. A. Ernesti, *Homeri opera*, vol. 5
(Leipzig 1764), pp. 141ff, 153–4, 229. H. I. Marrou, *Histoire de
l'éducation dans l'antiquité* (Paris 1948, 6th edn 1965), pp. 39ff,
81ff, 88, 97, 100 and passim.

5 G. A. Kennedy, *The art of persuasion in Greece* (Princeton 1963);
L. P. Wilkinson, *Golden Latin artistry* (Cambridge 1962).

6 W. K. C. Guthrie, *A history of Greek philosophy*, vol. 3 (Cambridge
1969), pp. 265ff, 271ff; see also P. Shorey, *What Plato said*
(Chicago 1933); E. A. Havelock, 'The evidence for the teaching of
Socrates', *TAPA*, 65 (1934), 282–95; P. Vicaire, *Platon: critique
littéraire* (Paris 1960).

7 *Homeri vita*, p. 153. See also Cicero, *Tusc. disp.* 1, 26.

8 G. A. Cary, *The medieval Alexander*, ed. J. A. Ross (Cambridge
1956); see also M. W. Howard, *The influence of Plutarch in the
major European literatures of the eighteenth century* (Chapel Hill
1970); Marrou, *Histoire de l'éducation*, pp. 40, 44 and passim;
J. M. Steadman, 'Achilles and Renaissance epic: moral criticism
and literary tradition', in *Lebende Antike*, ed. H. Meller and
H. J. Zimmermann (Berlin 1967), pp. 139ff.

9 P. Courcelle, *Les lettres grecques en Occident, de Macrobe à Cassiodore* (Paris 1948).

10 E. Sandvoss, *Sokrates und Nietzsche* (Leiden 1966).

11 L. Schucan, *Das Nachleben von Basilius Magnus' 'Ad adolescentes'* (Geneva 1973); see also St Jerome, *Epistolae*, 22; Dante, *Inferno*, IV, 88.

12 E. L. Curtius, *Europäische Literatur und lateinische Mittelalter* (Berne 1948, 2nd edn 1954), pp. 208ff; S. Weinstock, 'Die platonische Homerkritik und ihre Nachwirkung', *Philologus*, 82 (1926), 121–53.

13 Karl Langosch, 'Überlieferungsgeschichte der mittellateinischen Literatur', in *Geschichte der Textüberlieferung der antiken und mittelalterlichen Literatur*, ed. H. Erbse et al., vol. 2 (Zurich 1964), p. 14.

14 E. von Leutsch, 'Homer im Mittelalter', *Philologus*, 12 (1857), 366–8; P. Costil, 'La question homérique et l'évolution du goût littéraire en France', *Annales de l'Université de Grenoble*, n.s. 19 (1943), 95–168, esp. 96–9; E. Franceschini and A. Pertusi, 'Un'ignota Odissea latina dell'ultimo trecento', *Aevum*, 33 (1959), 323–55, esp. 323–4; J. Madden, *Classical learning in Ireland* (London 1908).

15 Remigio Sabbadini, *Le scoperte dei codici latini e greci ne' secoli XIV e XV* (1905), Biblioteca storica del Rinascimento, 4 (Florence 1967), pp. 43ff; A. Pertusi, *Storiografia umanistica e mondo bizantino* (Palermo 1967), pp. 11–12; see also Vincenzo di Giovanni; *Filologia e lettera Siciliana*, n.s. (Palermo 1879), p. 198; G. Voigt, *Il risorgimento dell'antichitá classica ovvero il primo secolo dell'umanesimo* (*Die Wiederbelebung des classichen Altertums*, Berlin, 1888), trans. O. Valbusa, Biblioteca storica del Rinascimento, 5 (Florence 1968), vol. 1, pp. 262–5; K. M. Setton, 'The Byzantine background to the Italian Renaissance', *Proceedings of the American Philosophical Society*, 100 (1956), 1–76. I am also indebted in this discussion to the MS of the paper 'The Greek poets in the Renaissance' by Carlotta Griffiths, given at the Warburg Institute, 4 February 1976.

16 A. Pertusi, *Leonzio Pilato fra Petrarca e Boccaccio. Le sue versioni omeriche negli autographi di Venezia e la cultura greca del primo umanesimo* (Venice and Rome 1964), pp. 265ff, 521ff; G. Cammelli, *I dotti bizantini e le origini dell'umanesimo* (Florence 1942), pp. 88–92.

17 J. R. Calonja, 'Alfonso el Magnánimo y la traducción de la "Ilíada" por Lorenzo Valla', *Boletín de la Real Academia de buenas letras de Barcelona*, 23 (1950), 109–15; V. Zaccaria, 'Sulle opere di Pier Candido Decembrio', *Rinascimento*, 7 (1956), 13–74.

18 I. Maier, *Ange Politien. La formation d'un poète humaniste (1469–1480)* (Geneva 1966), pp. 38, 100–3.

19 B. Botfield ed., *Prefaces to the first editions of the Greek and Roman classics and of the sacred scriptures* (London 1861). See also P. de Nolhac, *Pétrarque et l'humanisme* (Paris 1892), esp. vol. 1, pp. 318ff; J. E. Spingarn, *A history of literary criticism in the Renais-*

sance (New York 1899), pp. 107ff; B. Weinberg, *A history of literary criticism in the Italian Renaissance* (Chicago 1961), vol. 1, pp. 571–2, 600ff.

20 Scholia minora were also printed in Strasbourg in 1539. See C. G. Heyne, 'De editionibus Homeri', in *Homeri carmina*, vol. 2 (Leipzig 1802); H. Erbse, *Beiträge zur Überlieferung der Iliasscholien* (Munich 1960), and *Scholia Graeca in Homeri Iliadem* (Berlin 1969–71).

21 W. H. Woodward, *Vittorino de Feltre and other humanist educators* (Cambridge 1905), pp. 161ff.

22 E. J. Kenney, *The classical text* (London 1974); R. Pfeiffer, *History of classical scholarship from 1300 to 1850* (Oxford 1976).

23 V. Hall, 'The preface to Scaliger's Poetices libri septem', *MLN*, 60 (1945), 447–53; 'Scaliger's defense of poetry', *PMLA*, 63 (1948), 1125–30; and 'Life of J. C. Scaliger', *TAPS*, 40 (1950), 85–165.

24 Meric Casaubon, *De nupera Homeri editione* (London 1659), p. 8.

25 G. Castor, *Pléiade poetics* (Cambridge 1964); I. Silver, *Ronsard and the hellenic Renaissance in France* (Washington 1961); see also Costil, 'La question homérique', esp. pp. 106–9.

26 P. de Nolhac, *Ronsard et l'humanisme* (Paris 1921), pp. 69–70, 85–6; W. H. Storer, *Virgil and Ronsard* (Paris 1923); M. Dassonville, *Ronsard, Etude historique et littéraire* (Geneva 1968).

27 N. Hepp, *Homère en France au XVIIe siècle* (Paris 1968), p. 2; and *Deux amis d'Homère au XVIIe siècle. Textes inédits de Paul Pellisson et de Claude Fleury* (Paris 1970).

28 René Le Bossu's definition in his influential *Traité du poëme épique* (1675), translated into English in 1695. Since some of the issues raised by neoclassical criticism are discussed in chs. 1 and 6, the views are here given a summary account without detailed reference.

CHAPTER I

1 Hans Baron, in 'The *querelle* of the ancients and the moderns as a problem for Renaissance scholarship', *JHI*, 20 (1959), 3–22, discusses the reformatory character of the *querelle* against the sixteenth-century background. R. F. Jones, in his *Ancients and moderns. A study of the rise of the scientific movement in seventeenth-century England*, 2nd rev. edn (Washington 1961), looks at the *querelle* as a revolt largely from Aristotle and as a phase which finally established the Baconian view of scientific experimentation (p. x). G. W. Shaw, in his 'Homère, sujet de discussion pendant la querelle des anciens et des modernes' (unpubld MA thesis, Liverpool 1959), remarks of the *querelle*: 'c'est la fin de l'esprit de la Renaissance, de l'autre la querelle est à l'origine d'un renouvellement de la critique littéraire' (introduction).

2 The first historian of the *querelle*, Hippolyte Rigault, says in his *Histoire de la querelle des anciens et des modernes* (Paris 1856): 'Au fond du débat il y avait une idée philosophique, une des plus

grandes qui puissent être proposées à l'esprit humain, parce qu'elle intéresse la dignité de sa nature, l'idée du progrès intellectuel de l'humanité. Il y avait une idée littéraire corrélative, l'idée de l'indépendance du goût et de l'emancipation du génie moderne, affranchi de l'imitation des anciens' (p. 11). L. Wencelius, 'La querelle des anciens et des modernes et l'humanisme', *XVIIe siècle*, 9–10 (1951), 15–34, remarks that 'un souci humaniste manifeste' during the *querelle* (p. 16). G. S. Santangelo, in his bibliographical study of the querelle, *La 'querelle des anciens et des modernes' nella critica del '900* (Bari 1975), analyses the debate as follows: 'La querelle è dunque, innanzi tutto, punto essenziale dal quale la *critica nuova* dà avvio alla propria evoluzione' (p. 104). He speaks of the *querelle* as 'il problema dell'uomo' in which the following questions came into focus: 'quello della realtà umana', 'quello dei metodi che permettano di esprimerla al massimo livello di perfezione' and 'quello del significato profondamente umano del progresso delle idee' (p. 133).

3 La Bruyère, *Discours sur Théophraste* (Paris 1688); B. le B. Fontenelle, *Nouveaux dialogues des morts* (1683), ed. Jean Dagen (Paris 1971), p. 135. To the extent that man is a function of his feelings and emotions, human nature does not change: 'le génie sérieux ou badin, ce ne sont là que les dehors de l'Homme, et tout cela change; mais le coeur ne change point, et tout l'Homme est dans le coeur' (*Nouveaux dialogues*, p. 175); and in this Fontenelle endorses the static view of man in accordance with the 'ancient' view.

4 Fontenelle saw nature as a kind of sculptor, or one who weighs: 'La nature a entre les mains une certaine pâte qui est toujours la même, qu'elle tourne et retourne sans cesse en mille façons et dont elle forme les hommes, les animaux, les plantes; et certainement elle n'a point formé Platon, Démosthène ni Homère d'une argile plus fine ni mieux preparée que nos philosophes, nos orateurs et nos poètes d'aujourd'hui' (*Digression sur les anciens et les modernes* (1688), ed. R. Shackleton (Oxford 1955), p. 161), and 'Je peindrais volontiers la nature avec une balance à la main, comme la justice, pour marquer qu'elle s'en sert à peser, et à égaler à peu près tout ce qu'elle distribue aux hommes' (*ibid.* p. 173).

5 Saint-Evremond, *Oeuvres en prose*, ed. R. Ternois, vol. 3 (Paris 1966), p. 358.

6 Fontenelle, *Digression*, p. 175.

7 Fontenelle, *A plurality of worlds*, trans. G. Glanvill (London 1688), p. 140.

8 Montaigne speaks in several instances in his *Essais* (1580–95) about classical literature in terms of 'la science que j'y cherche', and his need to learn through his reading of the classics: 'j'apprends à ranger mes humeurs', 'moi qui ne demande qu'à dévenir plus sage'.

9 C. Perrault, *Parallèle des anciens et des modernes en ce qui regarde la poësie* (1692), p. 95.

10 François Fénelon, *The adventures of Telemachus, the son of Ulysses: done from the last edition printed at Paris...with a discourse upon epick poetry; shewing the excellency of this poem of Telemachus in particular*, Mr Ozell, 3rd edn (London 1720). Fénelon was appraised in England as Homer and Virgil combined: 'He joins Truth of Design to Beauty of Colouring; the Fire of *Homer* to the Majesty of *Virgil*' (*ibid.* p. xlix); 'The Fire of *Homer*, especially in the *Iliad*, is hot and impetuous, like Whirlwind of Flames that devour all around it. The Fire of *Virgil* has more Light than Heat, and always shines in an equal and uniform Manner. That of *Telemachus* warms and enlightens at the same Time' (*ibid.* p. 1); 'Thus our illustrious Author has brought into his Poem the greatest Beauties of the Antients. He has all the Enthusiasm and Abundance of *Homer*, all the Magnificence and Regularity of *Virgil*' (*ibid.* p. lxi).

11 A member of the French Academy, he wrote a reconciliatory pamphlet about the *querelle*, *Lettre sur les occupations de l'Académie française* (written in 1714, published posthumously in 1716). In ch. 10, called 'Sur les anciens et les modernes', he remarked 'Je commence par souhaiter que les modernes surpassent les anciens', but, 'Il resteroit toujours aux anciens la gloire d'avoir commencé, d'avoir montré le chemin aux autres, et de leur avoir donné de quoi encherir sur eux' (par. 1). And he concludes: 'Je ne vante point les anciens comme des modèles sans imperfections; je ne veux point ôter à personne l'espérance de les vaincre, je souhaite au contraire de voir les modernes victorieux par l'étude des anciens mêmes qu'ils auront vaincus' (par. 10). Fénelon's place in French literature and ideas has been studied by Albert Cherel, *Fénelon au XVIIIe siècle en France (1715–1820)* (Paris 1917).

12 In England the tradition was continued by Richard Blackmore, who wrote two unsuccessful epic poems, *Prince Arthur* (1695) and *King Arthur* (1697), and an analysis of his models, *Homer and Virgil not to be compared with the two Arthurs* (1700).

August Buck, in the introduction to Boileau's *L'art poëtique* (Munich 1970) discusses the growth and principles of the French epic in the latter half of the seventeenth century. The most important epics produced on classical principles were Saint-Amant, *Moïse sauvé* (1653, 6 edns by 1664), Le Moyne, *Saint Louis* (1653, 8 edns by 1685), Chapelain, *La Pucelle* (1656, 7 edns by 1664), Scudéry, *Alaric* (1654, 8 edns by 1685), Desmarets de Saint-Sorlin, *Clovis* (1657, 5 edns by 1674), Le Laboureur, *Charlemagne* (1664, 3 edns by 1687) and Carel de Sainte-Garde, *Childebrand* (1666), which became *Charles Martel* (1679, 5 edns by 1680). The Christian nationalistic epic in France is discussed by Hans Kortum, *Charles Perrault und Nicolas Boileau. Der Antike-Streit im Zeitalter der klassischen französichen Literatur* (Berlin 1966), pp. 136–45.

13 Pierre Daniel Huet, in his *Traité de l'origine des romans* (1670), ed. F. Gégou (Geneva 1971), trans. as *A treatise of romances* [sic]

and their original (1672), makes the distinction between the epic poem, the novel and the fable, based on seventeenth-century French material: 'Les romans sont plus simples, moins élevés et moins figurés dans l'invention et dans l'expression; les poèmes ont plus du merveilleux quoique toujours vraisemblables; les romans ont plus du vraisemblable quoiqu'ils aient quelquefois du merveilleux; les poèmes sont plus réglés et plus châtiés dans l'ordonnance et reçoivent moins de matière, d'événements et d'épisodes; les romans en reçoivent davantage parce qu'étant moins élevés et moins figurés, ils ne tendent pas tant l'esprit et le laissent en état de se charger d'un plus grand nombre de différentes idées; enfin les poèmes ont pour sujet une action militaire ou politique et ne traitent l'amour que par occasion; les romans au contraire ont l'amour pour sujet principal et ne traitent la politique et la guerre que par incident' (pp. 47–8). And he continues on the fable: 'les romans sont des fictions de choses qui ont pu être et qui n'ont point été, et les fables sont des fictions de choses qui n'ont point été, et et qui n'ont pu être' (p. 50).

14 Perrault published *Griselidis* in 1691, followed by *Souhaits ridicules* in 1693, *Peau d'ane* in 1694, *La belle au bois dormant* in 1696, and the whole collection of *Contes* in 1697. The most important contemporary collectors of fairy-tales were Mme D'Aulnoy, who brought *L'oiseau bleu* and *La belle aux cheveux d'or* to the public, Mlle Lhéritier and Mlle Bernard. The standard text is *Contes, textes établis, avec introduction sommaire biographique, bibliographie, notices, relevé de variantes, notes et glossaire*, ed. Gilbert Rouger (Paris 1967), and there are studies by Theodor Pletscher, *Die Märchen Charles Perraults* (Berlin 1906), Jacques Barchilon, *Perrault's tales of Mother Goose* (New York 1956), and Marc Soriano, *Les contes de Perrault. Culture savante et traditions populaires* (Paris 1968). Soriano makes some connections between Perrault's work as the collector of fairy-tales and the *querelle*; he sees Perrault's interest in folklore as a result of his criticism of the classical epic (p. 312).

15 See Paul Delarue, 'Les contes merveilleux de Perrault et la tradition populaire', *Bulletin Folklorique de l'Ile-de-France*, n.s. 13 (1951), 195–201, 221–7, 251–60, 283–91, and 'Les contes merveilleux de Perrault et les récits parallèles (Paris 1923); M. E. Storer, *Une Populaires*, 1–3 (1954), 1–22, 251–70; Pierre Saint-Yves, *Les contes de Perrault et les recits parallèles* (Paris 1923); M. E. Storer, *Une épisode littéraire de la fin de XVIIe siècle. La mode des contes de fées 1685–1700* (Paris 1928). For some parallel texts, see *Les contes de Perrault*, ed. Marcel Aymé (Paris 1964), which includes texts by Boccaccio, Straparole, Basile, Mlle Bernard and Mlle Lhéritier.

16 Perrault, *Histoires*, preface.

17 For a history of this story, see Elie Golenistcheff-Koutnezoff, *L'histoire de Griselidis au XIVe et XVe siècle* (Paris 1933). The recurrence of some of its elements can be traced through D. P.

Rotunda, *Motif-index of the Italian novella in prose* (Bloomington, Ind. 1942).

18 La Fontaine, 'Epitre à Monsieur l'évêque de Soissons' [i.e. Pierre Daniel Huet], pubd with a letter to de Bonrepous (Paris 1687), in *Oeuvres complètes*, ed. H. Regnier, vol. 9 (Paris 1892), pp. 200–5.

19 La Motte, 'Of the nature of the fable', *One hundred new court fables*, trans. Mr Samber (London 1721), p. 13.

20 Louis Sebastien Mercier, *L'an deux mille quatre cent quarante. Rêve s'il en fut jamais*, ed. Raymond Trousson (Paris 1971). His comment on Perrault and the *Iliad* is in the *Nouvel examen de la tragédie française* (1778), quoted in the introduction by Trousson.

21 On the terminology of the first translations of d'Aubignac, Boileau and Rapin see I. Simon, 'Critical terms in Restoration translations from the French', *Revue Belge de Philologie et d'Histoire*, 42, 2 (1964), 853–79 and 43, 2 (1965), 902–26; see also G. Saisselin, 'Ancients and moderns', in *The rule of reason and the ruses of the heart* (Cleveland 1970), pp. 5–15; N. Hepp, 'Esquisse du vocabulaire de la critique littéraire de la querelle du Cid à la querelle d'Homère', *Romanische Forschungen*, 69 (1957), 332–408; Barbara M. H. Strang, 'Dryden's innovations in critical vocabulary', *Durham University Journal*, 51 (1958–9), 114–23.

22 Le Clerc, *Parrhasiana: or, thoughts upon several subjects...*(London 1700), pp. 4–5.

23 *Ibid.* p. 5.

24 Temple praises Homer as 'the greatest universal Genius' and the ancients as 'those golden and inexhausted Mines of Invention'; see *Critical essays of the seventeenth century*, ed. J. E. Spingarn, vol. 3 (Oxford 1909), p. 80.

25 Temple argued for the values of ancient learning and for the esteem that the classics merit in his 'Essay upon the ancient and modern learning' (1690), in *Critical essays*, ed. Spingarn, vol. 3, pp. 32ff. In answer to this, William Wotton wrote in the *Reflections upon ancient and modern learning* (1694): 'It is evident therefore, that though in some sense the Moderns may be said to have learned their Politicks and Ethicks from the Ancients, yet there is no convincing argument that can be brought from those Sciences, singly considered, that the Ancients had a greater Force of Genius than the wise and prudent Men of those later generations' (p. 18). Of the humanities Wotton said: 'But there are other Parts of Learning, that may seem capable of farther Improvement; of which, the Advocates for the Ancients do not only pretend that they were the Inventors, but that their Performances have never since been equalled, much less out-done.' (*Ibid.*) He concluded: 'Poesie, Oratory, Architecture, Painting, and Statuary, are of the first Sort' (i.e. not evidently progressing), and 'Natural History, Physiology, and Mathematics, with all their Dependencies, are of the second' (i.e. dependent on the accumulation of knowledge) (*ibid.* p. 19).

26 C. Gildon, 'An essay on the art, rise, and progress of the stage in

Greece, Rome and England', prefixed to the *Works of Shakespeare*, vol. 7, ed. Dr Sewell (London 1725), p. 11.

27 *Spectator*, no. 417 (28 June 1712).

28 P. Whalley, *An enquiry into the learning of Shakespeare* (London 1748), p. 15. Dryden compared Jonson and Shakespeare in his *Essay of dramatic poesy* (1668): 'If I would compare him [Jonson] with Shakespeare, I must acknowledge him the more correct poet, but Shakespeare the greater wit. Shakespeare was the Homer, or father of our dramatic poets; Jonson was the Virgil, the pattern of elaborate writing; I admire him, but I love Shakespeare' (*Of dramatic poesy and other critical essays*, ed. G. G. Watson (London 1962), vol. 1, p. 70). John Dennis, in his 'Essay on the genius and writings of Shakespeare' (1712), made the comparison between Homer and Shakespeare: '*Shakespear* was one of the greatest Genius's that the World e'er saw for the Tragick Stage. Tho' he lay under greater Disadvantages than any of his Successors, yet he had greater and more genuine Beauties than the best and greatest of them. And what makes the brightest Glory of his Character, those Beauties were entirely his own, and owing to the Force of his Nature; whereas his Faults were owing to his Education, and to the Age that he liv'd in. One may say of him as they did of *Homer*, that he had none to imitate, and is himself inimitable' (*The critical works*, ed. E. N. Hooker, vol. 2 (Baltimore 1943), p. 4).

29 *Ibid.* vol. 1 (Baltimore 1939), p. 203.

30 L. Welsted, *Epistles, odes, etc.* (London 1724), preface, p. xviii.

31 Ambrose Philips, to whom *A collection of old ballads* (London 1723–4) is attributed, remarked: 'Had the Writers in Question ow'd all to Learning, and Nothing to Nature, we should frequently in our Ballads, instead of that remarkable Simplicity have met with stiff Pedantry' (vol. 2, p. x).

CHAPTER 2

1 The *Parallèle* was published in four volumes from 1688 to 1697 in Paris, as follows: *Parallèle des anciens et des modernes en ce qui regarde les arts et les sciences* (1688), *Parallèle...en ce qui regarde l'éloquence* (1690), *Parallèle...en ce qui regarde la poësie* (1692) and *Parallèle...où il est traité de l'astronomie, de la géographie, de la navigation, de la guerre, de la médecine, etc.* (1697). It is discussed in H. Baron, 'The *querelle* of the ancients and the moderns as a problem for Renaissance scholarship', *JHI*, 20 (1959), 3–22; H. Rigault, *Histoire de la querelle des anciens et des modernes* (Paris 1856), pt 1, chs. 10 and 12; Ruth Cherniss, 'The ancients as authority in seventeenth-century France', in *The Greek tradition*, ed. G. Boas (Baltimore 1939), pp. 139–70; H. Kortum, *Charles Perrault und Nicolas Boileau. Der Antike-Streit im Zeitalter der klassischen französischen Literatur* (Berlin 1966); G. S. Santangelo, *La 'querelle des anciens et des modernes' nella critica del '900*

(Bari 1975), pp. 19–20; and the introduction to the facsimile reprint of the first edition of the *Parallèle*, ed. H. R. Jauss and Max Imdahl (Munich 1964).

2 In his little-known autobiographical fragment, *Mémoires de ma vie, et voyage à Bordeaux* (1669), ed. P. Bonnefon (Paris 1909), Perrault writes: 'Ensuite je composai le petit poëme de *Siècle de Louis le Grand*, qui reçut beaucoup de louanges dans la lecture qui s'en fit à l'Académie françoise, le jour qu'elle s'assembla pour témoigner la joie qu'elle ressentoit de la convalescence de Sa Majesté après la grande opération qui lui fut faite. Ces louanges irritèrent tellement M. Despréaux qu'après avoir grondé longtemps tout bas, il s'éleva dans l'Académie, et dit que c'étoit une honte qu'on fît une telle lecture, qui blamoit les plus grands hommes de l'antiquité. M. Huet, alors évêque de Soissons, lui dit de se taire, et que, s'il étoit question de prendre le parti des anciens, cela lui conviendroit mieux qu'à lui, parce qu'il les connoissoit beaucoup mieux, mais qu'ils n'étoient là que pour écouter. Depuis, le chagrin de M. Despréaux lui fit faire plusieurs épigrammes qui n'alloient qu'à m'offenser, mais nullement à ruiner mon sentiment touchant les anciens. M. Racine me fit compliment sur cet ouvrage, qu'il loua beaucoup, dans la supposition que ce n'étoit qu'un pur jeu d'esprit qui ne contenoit point mes véritables sentimens, et que dans la vérité je pensois tout le contraire de ce que j'avois avancée dans mon poëme. Je fus fâché qu'on ne crût pas ou du moins qu'on fît semblant de ne pas croire que j'eusse parlé sérieusement, de sorte que je pris la résolution de dire sérieusement en prose ce que j'avois dit en vers, et de le dire d'une manière à ne pas faire douter de mon vrai sentiment là-dessus. Voilà quelle a été la cause et l'origine de mes quatre tomes de Parallèles' (pp. 136–7).

3 *Parallèle*, vol. 1, preface.

4 The standard biography of Perrault is by Paul Bonnefon, 'Charles Perrault. Essai sur sa vie et ses ouvrages', *Revue d'Histoire Littéraire de la France*, 11 (1904), 365–420; 'Charles Perrault, littérateur et académicien. L'opposition à Boileau', *ibid.* 12 (1905), 549–610; 'Les dernières années de Charles Perrault', *ibid.* 13 (1906), 606–57.

5 The poem was published by P. Bonnefon in *Revue d'Histoire Littéraire de la France*, 8 (1901), 110–42. See also Marc Soriano, *Le dossier Perrault* (Paris 1972), p. 47.

6 Boileau's subsequent *Réflexions critiques* (1694) was a criticism of Perrault's views. On the side of the ancients H. B. Longpierre published his *Défense des anciens* (1687), F. de Callières the *Histoire poëtique de la guerre nouvellement déclarée entre les anciens et les modernes* (1688), P. D. Huet his *Lettre à Monsieur Perrault* (1692, published 1712), and A. Arnauld his *Lettre à Monsieur Perrault* (1694).

7 Boileau, *L'art poëtique*, ed. August Buck (Munich 1970), I, 1–6.

8 Boileau's *Réflexions* was translated into English in 1712. Boileau wrote to Perrault: 'you always continue resolv'd not to admire *Homer* or *Virgil* too much, and I think I can never admire them enough' (*The works of M. Boileau*, vol. 2 (London 1711), p. 170); and he asked: 'And yet can you deny that 'tis to this Imitation alone all our greatest Poets have ow'd their Success?' (*ibid.* p. 172.) Boileau expressed a large part of his attack on Perrault in satirical verse. Epigrams 19–27, 'Sur ce qu'on avoit lu à l'Académie des vers contre Homère et contre Virgile', were written against Perrault.

9 L'Abbé and le Chevalier, *Parallèle*, vol. 3, p. 31.

10 L'Abbé, *ibid.* p. 35.

11 *Ibid.* p. 33.

12 Bentley argued: 'He [Homer] wrote a sequel of Songs and Rhapsodies, to be sung by himself for small earnings and good cheer, at Festivals and other days of Merriment; the *Ilias* he made for the Men, and the *Odysseis* for the other Sex. These loose Songs were not collected together in the form of an Epic Poem, till Pisistratus's time about 500 years later' (*Remarks upon a late Discourse of free-thinking* (London 1713), p. 18).

13 Introduction to his edition of *Conjectures académiques* by V. Magnien (Paris 1925), pp. v, xii–xiii. Adrien Baillet discusses d'Aubignac in *Jugements des Savants*, III, 1 (1685), pp. 277ff; his review is sceptical but favourable.

14 *Parallèle*, vol. 3, p. 23.

15 L'Abbé, *Parallèle*, vol. 3, p. 126.

16 *Ibid.* p. 93.

17 *Ibid.* p. 95.

18 L'Abbé, *Parallèle*, vol. 2, p. 29.

19 L'Abbé. *Parallèle*, vol. 3, pp. 7–8.

20 C. Perrault, *Characters historical and panegyrical of the greatest men that have appeared in France, during the last century*, trans. John Ozell, vol. 1 (London 1704), preface.

21 *Ibid.* p. 189; vol. 2 (London 1705), pp. 152, 158.

CHAPTER 3

1 Mme Anne Dacier, *L'Iliade d'Homère traduite en françois, avec des remarques* (Paris 1711), *L'Iliade d'Homère. Seconde édition, revue et augmentée avec quelques réflexions sur la préface angloise de M. Pope* (Paris 1719) and *l'Odyssée d'Homère, traduite en françois, avec des remarques* (Paris 1716); Antoine Houdar de La Motte, *L'Iliade, poëme, avec un discours sur Homère* (Paris 1701–14).

2 Mme Dacier's editions are *L. A. Flori rerum Romanarum epitome* (Paris 1674); *Callimachi hymni, epigrammata et fragmenta, graece et latine* (Paris 1674); *Sex. Aurelii Victoris historiae Romanae* (Paris 1681); *Eutropii historiae Romanae breviarum* (Paris 1683); *Dictys Cretensis et Dares Phrygius de bello et excidio Trojae*

(completed 1680, Paris 1684). Her translations, apart from Homer, are *Les poësies d'Anacréon et de Sapho* (Paris 1681); *L'Amphitryon, comédie de Plaute* (Paris 1683); *L'Epidicus, comédie de Plaute* (Paris 1683); *Le Rudens, comédie de Plaute* (Paris 1683); *Le Plutus et les Nuées d'Aristophane* (Paris 1684); *Les comédies de Térence* (Paris 1688); *Réflexions morales de l'empéreur Marc-Antonius* (Paris 1691). N. Hepp, in *Homère en France au XVIIe siècle* (Paris 1968), comments: 'Enorme entreprise, sur laquelle nous croirons plutôt le *Journal des Savants* qui parle de quinze à seize années de travail que les *Nouvelles de la République des lettres*, qui affirmaient dès 1700 que l'ouvrage était achevé' (p. 634). There are two brief monographs on Mme Dacier: Paul Mazon, *Madame Dacier et les traductions d'Homère en France* (Oxford 1936), and E. Malcovati, *Madame Dacier, una gentildonna filologa del gran secolo* (Florence 1952).

3 The *Lettres sur Homère et les anciens*, his correspondence with Fénelon, was not published until the nineteenth century. Fontenelle thought highly of La Motte, according to the 'Portrait de M. de La Motte', by Mme la marquise de Lambert, in *Oeuvres de La Motte* (Paris 1754), vol. I, pt I, pp. iff.

4 'Les belles infidèles' was the term used to describe French translators before Mme Dacier and La Motte. See Roger Zuber, *Perrot d'Ablancourt et 'les belles infidèles': traduction et critique de Balzac à Boileau* (Paris 1968). Before Mme Dacier translation of classical literature was held in low esteem in France (*ibid.* p. 26). See also E. Cary, 'Mme Dacier, Houdar de La Motte et "les belles infidèles"', *Les grands traducteurs français* (Geneva 1963), pp. 29ff.

5 Voltaire's note, BM Add. MS 35122, fol. 27, quoted in T. Bestermann, *Voltaire* (London 1969), p. 501.

6 There is some discussion of the war in H. Rigault's *Histoire de la querelle des anciens et des modernes* (Paris 1856), pt III, chs. 1–7; in Hepp, *Homère en France*, pp. 629ff, which is perhaps the most adequate account; and in G. S. Santangelo, *La 'querelle des anciens et des modernes' nella critica del '900* (Bari 1975), pp. 137ff. There is an eighteenth-century account of the war by the abbé A. S. Irailh, *Querelles littéraires, ou mémoires pour servir à l'histoire des révolutions de la république des lettres, depuis Homère jusqu'à nos jours* (Paris 1761).

7 The abbé de Pons took the side of La Motte in his *Lettre sur l'Iliade de La Motte* (Paris 1714). Père Jean Boivin wrote in defence of La Motte in his *Apologie d'Homère* (Paris 1715), and he had earlier published similar views in his *La querelle entre les partisans d'Homère et ceux de Virgile* (Paris 1707). François Gacon gave his support to Mme Dacier in his collection of twenty letters, *Homère vengé, ou réponse à M. de La Motte sur l'Iliade* (Paris 1715). Père Claude Buffier, in his *Homère en arbitrage* (Paris 1715), took the intermediate position, trying to see the good in both views. Later, the abbé de Pons wrote against Mme Dacier's views in his

Dissertation sur le poëme épique, contre la doctrine de Mme Dacier (Paris 1717), published in *Oeuvres* (Paris 1738), pp. 95–145.

8 *L'Homère travesti, ou l'Iliade en vers burlesques* is now conclusively attributed to Marivaux, by F. Deloffre, in the introduction to his edition of Marivaux's *Le Télémaque travesti* (1736) (Geneva and Lille 1956), p. 23.

9 *L'Iliade*, preface, vol. I, p. i.

10 *Ibid.* p. xxiv.

11 *Ibid.* pp. v–vi.

12 Paul Dupont, in his monograph *Houdar de La Motte* (Paris 1898), gives a final estimate of La Motte's translation: 'la prodigieuse ignorance de l'histoire, la confusion des époques et surtout la méconnaissance de tout ce qui est spontané, génial et primitif... Il ne conçoit pas ce qu'a été Homère; il ne soupçonne rien de l'art ni des moeurs antiques' (p. 33). In his preface to the first book of the *Iliad* (1701) La Motte remarks: 'je le traduis moins que je ne l'imite'.

13 In the preface to *L'Iliade* Mme Dacier said: 'La plûpart des gens sont gâtés aujourd'hui par la lecture de quantité de livres vains et frivoles, et ne peuvent souffrir ce qui n'est pas dans le même goût. L'amour, après avoir corrompu les moeurs, a corrompu les ouvrages. C'est l'âme de tous nos écrits (p. v). In *Corruption du goût* (1714) she analysed this more closely. There were two reasons for the corruption: 'L'une, ce sont ces spectacles licentieux qui combattent directement la Réligion et les Moeurs, et dont la Poësie et la Musique également molles et effeminées communiquent tout leur poison à l'âme, et relachent tous les nerfs de l'esprit, de sorte que presque toute nostre Poësie d'aujourd'hui porte ce caractère' (pp. 27–8). And 'l'autre, ce sont ces ouvrages fades et frivoles, dont j'ai parlé dans la Préface sur l'Iliade, ces faux Poëmes Épiques, ces Romans insensés que l'ignorance et l'amour ont produits, et qui métamorphosent les plus grands Héros de l'Antiquité en Bourgeois Damoiseaux' (p. 28).

14 La Motte, preface to the 'Discours', in *Oeuvres*, vol. 2, unnumbered pp.

15 *Ibid.* p. 135.

16 In his preface to the first book of the *Iliad* he discusses his translation, the principles of which can be grouped under four headings: 1. 'Je n'ai presque rien retranché qu'une repetition qui m'a paru ennuieuse et n'avoir aucun fondement'; 2. 'Pour la clarté, j'ai évité autant que j'ai pû les transpositions et les longues périodes'; 3. 'J'ai pris la liberté d'ajoûter de certaines choses pour en éclaircir d'autres, et de changer l'arrangement dans quelques endroits'; 4. 'cette différence du siècle Homère et du nôtre m'a obligé à beaucoup de ménagements pour ne point altérer mon original, et ne point choquer aussi les lecteurs imbus de moeurs toutes différentes'.

17 *Ibid.* p. xliii.

18 *Ibid.* p. xxxviii.

19 La Motte's shorter poems 'L'ombre d'Homère' and 'Homère' make it clear that he had some respect for Homer. In his *Réflexions* he said: 'J'évoque l'ombre d'Homère, avec tout le respect que lui doit un Poëte, pour apprendre de lui même comment je dois l'imiter pour plaire à mon siècle' (*Oeuvres*, vol. 3, p. 7). In the 'Discours' he said 'Homère...est dévenu, de siècle en siècle, un objet important de la vanité et de la curiosité humaine' (*Oeuvres*, vol. 2, p. 2). La Motte's fable of Homer and the deaf man tells a story of the old ballad-maker Homer who was flattered by the attention of a man whom he did not know to be deaf.

20 See N. Hepp, *Homère en France*. It was only after the victory of the 'demi-habiles' that the 'habiles' could again restore their position, and this did not happen until nearly the middle of the eighteenth century (p. 759).

21 *Corruption du goût*, pp. 2–3.

22 Mme Dacier, *Homère défendu*, p. 4.

23 'Si l'on souffre que de faux principes leur gâtent l'esprit et le jugement, il n'y a plus de ressource; le mauvais Goût et l'ignorance achèveront de prendre le dessus, et voilà les Lettres entièrement perdues; les Lettres qui sont la source ce du bon Goût, de la Politesse et de tout bon Gouvernement' (*Corruption du goût*, p. 7).

24 See H. Klein, *There is no disputing about taste: Untersuchungen zum englischen Geschmacksbegriff im achtzehnten Jahrhundert* (Münster 1967), pp. 146ff; F. Schümmer, *Die Entwicklung des Geschmackbegriffs in der Philosophie des 17. und 18. Jahrhunderts* (Bonn 1955). In her study of Shaftesbury's influence on eighteenth-century ideas of taste, *L'estetica del gusto nel settecento inglese* (Florence 1962), Lia Formigari argues that the eighteenth century, following Shaftesbury, saw the classics and nature as equal norms and objects of imitation when it came to form its views of good taste (pp. 155ff).

25 *Corruption du goût*, p. 10.

26 *Ibid.* pp. 10–12.

27 *Ibid.* p. 11.

CHAPTER 4

1 Letter to William Broome (16 June 1715) in *The correspondence of Alexander Pope*, ed. G. Sherburn (Oxford 1956), vol. 1, p. 297. The project was conceived about 1707; the volumes of the translation appeared at yearly intervals from 1715 to 1720. See Norman Callan, 'Pope and the classics', in *Alexander Pope*, ed. P. Dixon (London 1972), pp. 230–49. Pope's early translations of Homer include 'The episode of Sarpedon', in *Poetical miscellanies*, vol. 6 (1709), 'The gardens of Alcinous', in the *Guardian*, no. 173 (1713), and 'The arrival of Ulysses in Ithaca', in *Poetical miscellanies consisting of original poems and translations*, ed. R. Steele (1713).

The translations are edited by M. Mack, *The poems of Alexander Pope* (London 1967), vols. 7–10.

2　Pope wrote to the Duke of Buckingham (1 September 1718): 'I cannot think quite so highly of the Lady's learning, tho' I respect it very much' (*Correspondence*, vol. 1, p. 492). Meanwhile Mme Dacier, in her 'Quelques reflexions sur la préface angloise de M. Pope', in the third volume of *L'Iliade*, 3rd edn (1719), expressed a complete misunderstanding of Pope's *Iliad*. For a discussion of Pope's relations with French criticism see E. Audra, *L'influence française dans l'oeuvre de Pope* (Paris 1931), esp. pp. 58ff.

3　John Jortin translated Eustathius's notes on Homer for Pope; see *J. Nichols's anecdotes of W. Bowyer* (London 1782), pp. 258–9; William Broome assisted with the Greek, as did Parnell, who also wrote 'An essay on the life, writings and learning of Homer' in the first volume of the *Iliad* (1715). The progress of Pope's work is covered, apart from his letters, in Joseph Spence, *Anecdotes, observations and characters of books and men*, ed. B. Dobrée (London 1964), pp. 102–81, and O. Ruffhead, *The life of A. Pope* (London 1769). See also D. Knight, 'Pope as a student of Homer' *CL*, 4 (1952), 75–82; Callan, 'Pope and the classics'; George Sherburn, *The early career of Alexander Pope* (Oxford 1934).

4　See D. Knight, 'The augustan mode', in *On translation*, ed. R. A. Brower (New York 1966), p. 199. See also H. A. Mason, *To Homer through Pope. An introduction to Homer's Iliad and Pope's translation* (London 1972). The eighteenth-century translations of the Homeric epic have a special place in the literary history of the period. Since Chapman (1614) the translation of Homer had been attempted in full only twice, by John Ogilby (*Iliad*, 1660, *Odyssey*, 1669) and Thomas Hobbes (*Odyssey*, 1674, *Iliad*, 1676). In the eighteenth century Homer was translated, in part or in full, fifteen times. The four full renderings of the *Iliad* were by John Ozell, in prose (1712); by Pope, in heroic couplets (1715–20); by Macpherson, in prose (1773); and by William Cowper, in blank verse (1791). The first book of the *Iliad* was translated by Dryden in 1700; by Thomas Tickell in 1715; by Samuel Langley in 1767; by Alexander Geddes in 1792; and by William Tremenheere in 1792. The *Odyssey* was translated only twice, by Pope (1725–6) and Cowper (1791). There was a gap of 53 years after the publication of Pope's *Iliad*, and a gap of 65 years after Pope's *Odyssey*, before each work was again translated.

5　On the history and composition of the preface and its changes see D. Knight, 'The development of Pope's Iliad preface: a study of the manuscript', *MLQ*, 16 (1955), 237–46. See also H. J. Zimmermann, *Alexander Popes Noten zu Homer. Eine Manuskript- und Quellenstudie* (Heidelberg 1966).

6　'To the reader', *Chapman's Homer*, ed. Allardyce Nicoll (New York 1956), vol. 1, l. 142.

7　Chapman's method of translation and his indebtedness to the Latin of Spondanus have been studied by Phyllis Bartlett, 'Chapman's revisions in his Iliads', *ELH*, 2 (1935), 92–119. See also A. Warren, 'Pope on the translators of Homer', *MP*, 29 (1931), 229–32.

8 Preface to the *Iliad* (1715), p. 21.

9 *Ion* 534 A–B, *Phdr.* 238 D, 278 B. The notion of *furor poeticus* has been discussed notably by E. N. Tigerstedt, 'The poet as creator: origins of a metaphor', *CLS*, 5 (1968), 455–88; from antiquity to Romanticism, by V. Rüfner, 'Homo secundus deus: eine geistesge-schichtliche Studie zum menschlichen Schöpfertum', *Philosophisches Jahrbuch der Görresgellschaft*, 63 (1955), 248–91; H. Thüme, *Beiträge zur Geschichte des Geniebegriffs in England*, Studien zur englischen Philologie, 71 (Halle 1927); M. W. Bundy, *The theory of imagination in classical and medieval thought* (Urbana 1927), and ' "Invention" and "imagination" in the Renaissance', *Journal of English and German Philology*, 29 (1930), 535–45, which makes the useful distinction of four kinds of sources for poetic theories: (1) a psychological view of imagination, with its roots in Aristotle, (2) an ethical and pathological view with roots in the pre-Socratics of Pythagoreans, (3) a great mystical theory of Plato, and (4) the rhetorical teachings of the *trivium* with its notions of *inventio dispositio* and *elocutio* (p. 538). Only the first three are thus related to the concept of 'fire'.

10 See Grahame Castor, *Pléiade poetics* (Cambridge 1964).

11 See George G. Watson, 'Contributions to a dictionary of critical terms: *imagination* and *fancy*', *Essays in Criticism*, 3 (1953), 201–14.

12 Preface, p. 3.

13 *Ibid.* p. 12.

14 *Ibid.* p. 4; see also letter (5 April 1708) in *Correspondence*, vol. 1, p. 44.

15 In his earliest ode, *P.* X, 53ff and *P.* IV, 60, for instance. The bee metaphor appears also in the early Greek poets Simonides and Bacchylides.

16 Preface, p. 4.

17 *Ibid.* pp. 17–18.

18 *Ibid.* pp. 4–5.

CHAPTER 5

1 F. D. White, in her introduction to *Voltaire's Essay on epic poetry. A study and an edition* (New York 1915), discovered 'a marked change in tone and opinion' in the chapters dealing with Homer (p. 48). Her conclusion that the French chapter differed from the English 'radically in plan, detail and spirit' (p. 89) seems, however, something of an exaggeration.

2 On the background to Voltaire's view of the war about Homer and the epic see the introduction to *La Henriade*, ed. O. R. Taylor, Studies on Voltaire and the eighteenth century, 38–40 (Geneva

1965): 'La conception voltairienne de l'épopée', vol. 1, pp. 89–148; Voltaire on Homer, pp. 120ff.

3 'Lettres sur Oedipe' no. 3, in *Oedipe, tragédie* (Paris 1719): 'Je vous rendrai seulement compte avec simplicité des endroits qui m'ont revolté, et sur lesquels j'ai besoin des lumières de ceux qui connoissant mieux que moi les anciens, peuvent mieux excuser tous leurs défauts' (p. 93). The plot betrays 'absurdité' and is 'éloigné du sens commun' (p. 95). Oedipus's murder of Laius is 'sans aucune raison, sans aucun fondement, sans que le moindre jour puisse autoriser ses soupçons et...avec une extravagance dont il n'y a guère d'exemples parmi les modernes, ni même parmi les anciens' (p. 98).

4 'Essay on epick poetry' (1727), p. 38.

5 *Treatise of the epick poem*, trans. W. J. (London 1695): 'Man being the chief and the most noble of all the Effects which God produc'd, and nothing being so proper, nor more useful to *Poets* than this Subject, they have added it to the former, and treated of the Doctrine of *Morality* after the same Manner as they did that of *Divinity* and *Philosophy*: And from Morality thus discours'd of, has Art form'd that kind of *Poem* and *Fable*, which we call the *Epick*' (p. 6). And: 'The Epopea is a Discourse invented by Art, to form the Manners by such instructions as are disguis'd under the Allegories of some one important Action, which is related in Verse, after a probable, diverting, and surprising Manner.' (*Ibid.*)

6 'Essay on epick poetry', p. 38.

7 'An *Epick* poem is a Discourse in Verse. Use alone has prefix'd the Name of *Epick*, particularly to those Poems which relate some great action' (*ibid.* p. 39).

8 *Ibid.* p. 46.

9 He wrote on Shakespeare in *Letters concerning the English nation* (1733): 'Shakespeare boasted a strong, fruitful genius: He was natural and sublime, but had not so much as a single Spark of good taste, or knew one Rule of the Drama' (p. 166), and 'the great Merit of this Dramatic Poet has been the Ruin of the English Stage' (p. 167). See D. Flower, *Voltaire's England* (London 1950).

10 'Essay on epick poetry', p. 56.

11 *Essai sur les moeurs et l'esprit des nations* (1756), written between 1745 and 1756, ed. René Pomeau (Paris 1963). In the chapters 'De la religion des premiers hommes' and 'Des usages et des sentiments communs à presque toutes les nations anciennes' and in various chapters on ancient Greek beliefs and customs as compared with the Chinese, Jewish, Indian and North American, Voltaire discusses the Homeric epic as if it were a true record of the Greek peoples. On the concept of soul he says: 'Remarquons, en passant, que dans l'âge moyen de la Grèce, du temps d'Homère, l'âme n'était autre chose qu'une image aérienne du corps. Ulysse voit dans les enfers des ombres, des mânes: pouvait-il voir des esprits purs?' (I, p. 12.) On human sacrifices: 'Il fallait bien que cet usage fût reçu du

temps de la guerre de Troie, puisque Homère fait immoler par Achille douze Troyens à l'ombre de Patrocle. Homère eût-il osé dire une chose si horrible, n'aurait-il pas craint de révolter tous ses lecteurs, si de tels holocaustes n'avaient pas été en usage?' And he concludes: 'Tout poète peint les moeurs de son pays' (I, p. 127).

12 'Essay on epick poetry', p. 49.

13 *Ibid.* pp. 48–9.

14 *Ibid.* p. 49.

CHAPTER 6

1 Letter to John Murray (Ravenna, 7 February 1821), in *Works, letters and journals*, ed. R. E. Prothero (London 1904), vol. 5, p. 554.

2 See H. T. Swedenberg, 'Rules and English critics of the epic 1650–1800', *SP*, 35 (1938), 566–87; E. N. Hooker, 'The discussion of taste, from 1750 to 1770, and the new trends in literary criticism', *PMLA*, 49 (1934), 577–92; L. I. Bredvold, 'The rise of English classicism: a study in methodology', *CL*, 2 (1950), 253–68; R. S. Crane, 'A neglected mid-eighteenth century plea for originality and its author', *PQ*, 13 (1934), 21–9, and 'An early eighteenth century enthusiast for primitive poetry: John Husbands', *MLN*, 37 (1922), 27–36; F. Gallaway, *Reason, rule and revolt in English classicism* (New York 1940, 2nd edn 1966), esp. p. vii.

3 R. Le Bossu, *Treatise of the epick poem*, trans. W. J. (London 1695), p. 6. Pope's definition of the epic followed Le Bossu's word for word, although his concept of poetry owes nothing of importance to Le Bossu.

4 C. Gildon, 'An essay on the art, rise and progress of the stage in Greece, Rome and England', prefixed to the *Works of Shakespeare*, vol. 7, ed. Dr Sewell (London 1725), p. v.

5 C. Gildon, *The compleat art of poetry* (London 1718), vol. I, p. 129.

6 R. Rapin, 'A comparison of Homer and Virgil', in *The whole critical works*, trans. by several hands (London 1706), vol. I, p. 156.

7 *Ibid.* pp. 198–9.

8 *Ibid.* p. 210.

9 R. Blackmore, preface to *King Arthur, an heroic poem, in 12 books* (London 1697), p. xv.

10 A. Blackwall, *An introduction to the classics* (London 1718), pp. 7–8.

11 D. Hume, 'Of the rise and progress of arts and sciences' (1741), in *Essays, moral, political and literary* (Edinburgh 1748), World's Classics edn (Oxford 1963), p. 115.

12 The preface was written for Johnson's edition of Shakespeare's works (1765). 'Milton' was printed first in his *Prefaces, biographical and critical, to the works of the English poets*, vol. 2 (London 1779). For these texts I have used *Johnson's prose and poetry*, ed. Mona Wilson (London 1950, repr. 1970).

13 Johnson's *Dictionary* (1755) gives the following definitions: *Enthusiasm*: 1. A vain belief of private revelation; a vain confidence

of divine favour or communication. 2. Heat of imagination; violence of passion; confidence of opinion. 3. Elevation of fancy; exaltation of ideas.

Fire (Johnson lists 11 meanings): 8. Ardour of temper; violence of passion. 9. Liveliness of imagination; vigour of fancy; intellectual activity; force of expression; spirit of sentiment. 10. The passion of love.

Genius: 1. The protecting or ruling power of men, places, things. 2. A man endowed with superior faculties. 3. Mental power or faculties. 4. Disposition of nature by which any one is qualified for some peculiar employment. 5. Nature; disposition.

Invention: 1. Fiction. 2. Discovery. 3. Excogitation; act of producing something new. 4. Forgery. 5. The thing invented.

Judgment (Johnson lists 12 meanings): 1. The power of discerning the relations between one term or one proposition and another. 5. The quality of distinguishing propriety and impropriety; criticism. 6. Opinion, notion.

Nature (Johnson lists 10 meanings): 1. An imaginary being supposed to preside over the material and animal world. 2. The native state or properties of any thing, by which it is discriminated from others. 5. The regular course of things. 6. The compass of natural existence. 10. Sentiments or images adapted to nature, or conformable to truth and reality. Note that Johnson does not recognize the sense of 'nature' the Romantics knew, i.e. rivers, forests, rocks etc.

Original: adj.: Primitive; pristine; first. *sb*: 1. Beginning. 2. Fountain, source; that which gives beginning or existence. 3. First copy; archetype; that from which any thing is transcribed or translated. 4. Derivation; descent.

14 Johnson, 'Preface to Shakespeare', *Prose and poetry*, p. 490.
15 Johnson, 'John Milton', *ibid.* p. 834.
16 Thomas Parnell, 'An essay on the life, writings and learning of Homer', in *The Iliad of Homer*, trans. A. Pope, vol. 1 (London 1715), p. 51.
17 G. V. Gravina, *Della ragion poetica libri due* (Rome 1708), ed. with introduction by G. Natali (Lanciano 1921). The best modern edition is in *Gian Vincenzo Gravina; scritti critici e teorici*, ed. A. Quondam, Scrittori d'Italia, 255 (Rome and Bari 1973), pp. 195–327. Gravina's work, known in England, was criticized there for its platonism, according to John Pinkerton, *Letters of literature* (London 1785), p. 206, who reveals, however, a profound misunderstanding of Gravina's views.
18 Gravina's major work in jurisprudence was *Originum juris civilis libri tres* (Leipzig 1708). See V. Julia, *Saggio sulla vita e sulla opere di G. V. Gravina* (Cosenza 1879); F. Balsano, *Delle dottrine filosofiche e civili di G. V. Gravina* (Cosenza 1880); E. Reich, *G. V. Gravina als Aesthetiker. Ein Beitrag zur Geschichte der Kunstphilosophie*, Sitzungsberichte der Philosophisch-historischen Classe der Kaiserlichen Akademie der Wissenschaften, 120 (Vienna 1890);

F. Moffa, 'Gian Vincenzo Gravina', in *Studi di letteratura italiana,*
val. 7 (Naples 1907), pp. 165–349.

19 T. Blackwell, *An enquiry into the life and writings of Homer*
(London 1735), p. 142. On Gravina and Vico, see B. Barillari,
G. V. Gravina come precursore del Vico (Naples 1942); E. Vidal,
*Saggio sul Montesquieu con particolare riguardo alla sua concezione
dell'uomo* (Milan 1950), pp. 21–2, 88–9; C. Ghisalberti, *Gian
Vincenzo Gravina. Giurista e storico* (Rome 1962), pp. 7–19.

20 Gravina, *Della ragion poetica*, ed. Quondam, p 199.

21 *Ibid.* p. 203.

22 *Ibid.* p. 210.

23 *Ibid.* p. 273.

CHAPTER 7

1 *La scienza nuova seconda* (Naples 1730, rev. 1744), ed. F. Nicolini
(Bari 1942). About his method Vico says: 'We must therefore go
back with the philologians and fetch it from the stones of Deucalion
and Pyrrha...Our treatment...must take its start from the time
these creatures began to think humanly...to discover the way in
which this first human thinking arose in the gentile world, we
encountered exasperating difficulties which have cost us the research
of a good twenty years' (par. 338). Vico makes it even more pointed
by saying 'Thus it is that with the help of the preceding philosophical proofs, the philological proofs both confirm their authority
by reason and at the same time confirm reason by their authority'
(par. 359). References are to Vico's own paragraph numbers and to
the English text, *The new science of Vico*, trans. T. G. Bergin and
M. H. Fisch (New York 1948), which has preserved many of Vico's
Italian idioms in an attempt to be literal.

2 *La scienza nuova prima* (Naples 1725), ed. F. Nicolini (Bari 1968),
contained only the rudiments of the later version, and can be regarded as an independent work, although its main argument is
similar: 'Condotta delle materie, con la quale le nazioni, in diversi
luoghi, in diversi tempi, sopra gli stessi principi delle religioni e
lingue hanno gli stessi nascimenti, progressi, stati, decadenze e fini,
e si propagano di mano in mano nel mondo dell'umana generazione'
(bk 5). The Homeric chapters are in bk 3, pars. 288–305. Homer is,
as in the later version, 'il primo istorico che abbiamo della greca
nazione' (par. 288).

3 The best discussion of the meaning of Homer in Vico's work is still
Benedetto Croce's 'Homer and primitive poetry', *The philosophy
of Giambattista Vico*, trans. R. G. Collingwood (London 1913),
pp. 183–96. Croce remarks: 'The errors which intellectualism and
neoclassical criticism discovered in Homer led the critics to repeat
freely the saying of Horace that "good Homer nods at times":
whereas Vico on the contrary exclaims, "if he had not nodded so
often he would never have been good!" (*nisi ita saepe dormitasset,*

numquam bonus fuisset Homerus). Homer was the greatest poet precisely because he was not a philosopher' (p. 191). See also F. Nicolini, 'Sugli studi omerici di Giambattista Vico', *Atti della Academia nazionale dei Lincei*, ser. 7, vol. 5, 10 (1954), 469–519; A. Pagliaro, 'Omero e la poesia popolare in Vico', in *Altri saggi di critica semantica* (Messina, d'Anna 1961).

4 Bacon argues that men have been kept back, as by a kind of enchantment, from progress in the sciences by reverence for antiquity, by the authority of men accounted great in philosophy, and then by general consent (*History of the reign of King Henry the Seventh* (1622), ed. R. Lockyer (London 1971), pp. 190–1). See an account of Bacon's methods in L. A. Jardine, *Francis Bacon: discovery and the art of discourse* (Cambridge 1974); also F. H. Anderson, *The philosophy of Francis Bacon* (Chicago 1948); R. Metz, 'Bacon's part in the intellectual movement of his time', in *Seventeenth century studies presented to Sir Herbert Grierson*, ed. J. Dover Wilson (Oxford 1938), pp. 21–32; R. C. Cochrane, 'Francis Bacon in early eighteenth century literature', *PQ*, 37 (1958), 57–79.

5 *The autobiography of Giambattista Vico*, trans. T. G. Bergin and M. H. Fisch (Cornell 1944), p. 187, and introduction, p. 34. The attitudes of the Catholic Church in Italy to the classics have been discussed in this light by G. Voigt. *Il risorgimento dell'antichità classica ovvero il primo secolo dell'umanesimo* (*Die Wiederbelebung des classischen Altertums* (Berlin 1888), trans. O. Valbusa, Biblioteca storica del Rinascimento, 5 (Florence 1968), vol. 1, pp. 11–12.

6 *The new science*, par. 780.

7 *Ibid.* par. 779.

8 *Ibid.*

9 E. R. Dodds in his *The Greeks and the irrational* (Berkeley 1951) has studied the conglomerate personality type of the poet, priest, explorer and philosopher which was well known in archaic and classical Greece, the most notable examples being the semi-mythical Orpheus, Musaeus and Linus and some possibly real persons such as Aristeas, Epimenides and Salmoxis. They had in common with Homer, who was regarded entirely as a historical person, the fact that they were also writers of epic or originators of poetic genres. See also W. K. C. Guthrie, *A history of Greek philosophy*, vol. 3 (Cambridge 1969), chs. 3–9.

10 B. Weinberg, *A history of literary criticism in the Italian Renaissance* (Chicago 1961), and the collection of relevant documents by de Conti, Trissino, Salviati, Lionardi et al., in *Trattati di poetica e retorica del cinquecento*, ed. B. Weinberg (Bari 1970). See also studies by E. N. Tigerstedt, 'The poet as creator: origins of a metaphor', *CLS*, 5 (1968), 455–88, and V. Rüfner, 'Homo secundus deus: eine geistesgeschichtliche Studie zum menschlichen 'Schöpfertum', *Philosophisches Jahrbuch der Görresgesellschaft*, 63 (1955), 248–91, esp. pp. 264ff. See also Edgar Wind, *Pagan mysteries in the Renaissance* (London 1958).

11 Plato's references to Homer in the *Ion*, *Apology* and *Republic* can be interpreted in a number of ways. In the *Republic* he said that Homer was the first teacher and guide of all the tragic poets, *R.* 595 B: 'ἔοικε μὲν γὰρ τῶν καλῶν ἁπάντων τούτων τῶν τραγικῶν πρῶτος διδάσκαλός τε καὶ ἡγεμὼν γενέσθαι'. In the later dialogues, *Phaedrus* and the *Laws*, he himself renounced Homer. Vico realized that Plato had been misinterpreted, but he nevertheless regarded Plato as the source of error: 'Plato left firmly fixed the opinion that Homer was endowed with sublime esoteric wisdom (and all the other philosophers have followed in his train, with [pseudo-]Plutarch foremost, writing an entire book on the matter)' (*The new science*, par. 780).

12 *The new science*, par. 41.

13 *Ibid.* par. 787.

14 *Ibid.* par. 782.

15 *Ibid.* par. 787.

16 *Ibid.* par. 806.

17 *Ibid.* par. 808.

18 'One that poetic sublimity is inseparable from popularity, and the other that peoples who have first created heroic characters for themselves will afterwards apprehend human (or civilized) customs only in terms of characters made famous by luminous examples' (*ibid.* par. 809). See also I. Berlin, *Vico and Herder* (London 1976).

19 *The new science*, par. 201.

20 *Ibid.* par. 202.

21 *Ibid.* par. 34. Here the Italian original makes Vico's thought clearer than the translation: 'Principio di tal'origini e di lingue e di lettere si truova essere stato di natura, furon poeti, i quali parlarono per caratteri poetici.' The confusion arises from the use of 'character' in the English version. In Italian, *carattere* has the meanings character, disposition, type, nature, property, peculiarity, character part, style, literary portrait, sketch, letter, print, type, handwriting. In the Neapolitan dialect, which was Vico's, *carattere* means *indole, natura, carattere, forma e maniera di scrivere*. Vico's statement that early peoples spoke 'per caratteri poetici' suggests that he had in mind the poetic mode of expression in general, not the specialized language of poetry. The poetic mode was thus contrasted with the discursive mode of philosophy.

22 *Ibid.* par. 816.

23 *Ibid.* pars. 899–903.

24 *Ibid.* par. 873.

CHAPTER 8

1 However, many of the period's greatest natural scientists, like Newton, saw their philosophy as perfectly compatible with religion (*Opticks*, 1704). See A. O. Lovejoy, *The great chain of being* (Cambridge, Mass., 1936), pp. 227ff; C. L. Becker, *The heavenly city of the eighteenth-century philosophers* (New Haven 1932);

M. H. Nicolson, *Newton demands the muse* (Princeton 1946, London 1963); N. Hampson, *The Enlightenment* (Harmondsworth 1968), introduction; P. Gay, *The Enlightenment: an interpretation*, vol. 2, *The science of freedom* (London 1970); *The forerunners of Darwin 1745–1859*, ed. H. Glass et al. (Baltimore 1959), pp. 114–49.

2 Ernst Cassirer, *The philosophy of the Enlightenment* (1932), trans. F. C. A. Koelln and J. P. Pettegrove (New York 1951). In the *Tractatus theologico-politicus* (1670) Spinoza directed all the vehemence of his attack on the ignorance of theologians who did not understand the true nature of the scriptures, saying 'Praejudicia theologorum; scio enim, ea maxime impedire, quo minus homines animum ad philosophiam applicare possint', in his letter to Henry Oldenburg (1665), and maintaining that his ultimate purpose was 'libertas philosophandi dicendique quae sentimus'; Ep. 30, *The correspondence of Spinoza*, ed. A. Wolf (London 1928). See also *The political works of Spinoza*, ed. and trans. A. G. Wernham (Oxford 1958), pp. 109–11. On the tradition of the critique of religion and on Spinoza's work see Leo Strauss, *Spinoza's critique of religion* (New York 1965), pp. 111ff.

3 T. Blackwell, *An enquiry into the life and writings of Homer* (London 1735), pp. 3–4.

4 Some reviews give an idea of the current indignation against Blackwell: 'As to the *Life of Homer*, it must certainly be commended by every Man who has Taste of learned and ingenious Compositions; by every Man, who, according to the old Rule, is not offended with a few Faults, and is ready without Envy, to give Merit its due Praise. And this I can assure you, if it is *Anti-Christian* to commend it, infidelity has made a strange Progress in this University; the Performance is here universally applauded, without any Exceptions to those obnoxious Places which I am told Dr R. [Thomas Rundle] pointed out when he spoke most in its Favour'; *The old whig: or, The consistent protestant*, no. 10 (15 May 1735). G. Costa, *La critica omerica di Thomas Blackwell (1701–1757)*, Publicazione dell'Istituto di Filosofia dell'Università di Roma, 6 (Florence 1959), traces some of this controversy, pp. 21ff.

5 Blackwell had begun his study on Homer as early as May 1732, after his stay with Dr Richard Mead in Great Ormond Street, London. Dr Mead's house, an international meeting place for artists and scholars, was the starting point for the European reputation of the *Enquiry*. Mead counted among his intimate friends Pope, Bentley, Roger Gale and Sir John Clerk (see *DNB*). His library and collections of antiquities were renowned. The British Museum has a list of 6491 volumes of the *Bibliotheca Meadiana, sive catalogus librorum R. M.*, auctioned on 18 November 1754 and 7 April 1755 for £5499 4s. 5d. (note on front leaf). The library contained the works of Vico. Mead's life was written by M. Maty, *Authentic memoirs of the life of Dr Mead* (London 1755).

6 The first edition (March 1735) of 1500 copies sold rapidly.

7 The *Enquiry* was reviewed in most positive terms in the *Bibliothèque britannique*, vol. 5, pp. 388–404, vol. 6, pp. 320–49: 'un ouvrage intéressant et utile' and 'une grande connoissance des livres anciens et jugement solide', though 'y souhaiterait peutêtre un peu plus d'ordre' (vol. 6, p. 349). The reviewer in the *Literary magazine* said: 'The author has bestow'd a great deal of pains and learning in discoursing on a subject which will ever be thought worthy of attention', and spoke of it as an 'elegant performance' (vol. 1, p. 169). *The present state of the republick of letters* was not so favourable: 'I praise where I can, but it is always my Duty to be impartial' (reviews in vol. 15, pp. 113–18, 179–202, 291–309), and the reviewer considered it in general obscure (p. 294). Mrs Cockburn, in a letter of 28 August 1735, bears witness to the reception of the *Enquiry* among the general public: it 'has had a great vogue in London' (*The works of Mrs Cockburn* (London 1751), vol. 2, p. 278).

8 In *Sammlung critischer, poetischer, und anderer geistvollen Schriften*. It was fully translated by Johann Heinrich Voss in 1776. Dorothy Knight, 'Thomas Blackwell and J. J. Bodmer: the establishment of a literary link between Homeric Greece and medieval Germany', *German Life and Letters*, n.s. 6 (1953), 249–58, argues that Bodmer's work, *Critische Betrachtungen über die poetischen Gemählde der Dichter* (Zürich 1741), had considerable similarities with Blackwell's *Enquiry* (p. 252).

9 Herder was among the first to call serious attention to the *Enquiry* on the Continent. He speaks of it as a 'precious book': 'Thomas Blackwells *Untersuchung über das Leben und die Schriften Homers* (und leider ist dies schätzbare Buch, das in England so hoch aufgenommen ward, kaum halb ins Deutsche übersetzt), eine Untersuchung, die sich den hohen Satz aufgibt: "Welch ein Zusammenschluss von natürlichen Ursachen konnte den einzigen Homer hervorbringen?" die diesen Satz aus den Geheimnissen der griechischen Literatur und Geschichte mit wahrem kritischen Geist erklärt und zum Homer ein Schlüssel ist – diese Abhandlung sollte statt Einleitung sein, eine Einleitung, die fast nie so notwendig ist als wenn wir uns dem ältesten, dem göttlichsten, dem unübersetzbaren Homer nähern' (*Über die neuere deutsche Literatur* (1767), ed. A. Gillies (Oxford 1969), pp. 64–5). See also R. Nünlist, *Homer, Aristoteles und Pindar in der Sicht Herders* (Bonn 1971), pp. 35ff.

10 Thomas Blackwell, snr (1660?–1728) was a Presbyterian minister who took a prominent part in the affairs of the Scottish Church both through his writings and through his work to improve the constitution of the Church of Scotland. Thomas Blackwell, jnr (1701–57) was professor of Greek at the Marischal College, Aberdeen, in 1728–57, and principal from 1748 until his death.

11 The *Biographia britannica*, which gives credit to the information provided by Alexander Gerard, says of Blackwell: 'He had a dignity of address which commanded the attention of the students. . .To his

zeal and diligence in discharging the duties of his station, it is probable that the world is, in part, indebted for such men as Campbell, Gerard, Reid, Beattie, Duncan, and the Fordyces' (vol. 2 (London 1780), p. 335). Other contemporary accounts of Blackwell are contained in John Nichols's *Literary anecdotes of the eighteenth century*, enlarged from his *Anecdotes biographical and literary* (1778), vol. 5 (London 1812), p. 641, and his *Illustrations of the literary history of the eighteenth century*, vol. 2 (London 1817), pp. 35, 69, 814, 820, 851, vol. 4 (London 1822), p. 84; in Lord Kames's *Sketches of the history of man* (Edinburgh 1774); and in James Beattie's 'On the utility of classical learning' (1769), in *Essays* (London 1776).

12 The *Enquiry* was closely connected with his other works on ancient literature and mythology. *The memoirs of the court of Augustus* (London, vols. 1–2 1753–5, vol. 3 (posthumous) 1763) defines a problem that is essentially the environmental one of the *Enquiry*: why 'there never was an Age more productive of Poets, Historians, Memoir-writers, and indeed writers of all kinds, than from the end of the Civil Wars, to the middle of the reign of Tiberius' (vol. 1, p. 2). The hero of this work was Horace. Blackwell produced substantial evidence for the conclusions of the *Enquiry* in his *Proofs of the Enquiry into Homer's life and writings, translated into English; being a key to the Enquiry* (London 1747). This was published because there had been a 'general Complaint among the Readers of the Enquiry' that 'though the chief Facts in it seem to be supported by Proof and Authority, yet they were obliged to take the *Proofs themselves* upon Trust; because the greatest part of them were adduced from Authors in the ancient Languages, *Hebrew, Greek*, and *Latin*, which it does not fall to every one's share to understand: And the others were taken from modern Authors in *Spanish, Italian* and *French*, which Languages were as rarely possessed by the Proficients in the Ancient' (p. 3).

13 *Enquiry*, p. 2.

14 Thomas Parnell's 'An essay on the life, writings and learning of Homer', in *The Iliad of Homer*, trans. A. Pope, vol 1 (London 1715), pp. 1–70, proved helpful for his contemporaries, but had no analytic approach to its subject.

15 The genesis of the *Enquiry* is described in the correspondence between Blackwell and the famous Scots antiquarian Sir John Clerk: see Costa, *Blackwell*, p. 18. In May 1732 he was engaged on a work whose general principle was similar to that of the *Enquiry* – *The memoirs of the court of Augustus*. On 7 February 1734 the MS of the *Enquiry* was more or less ready.

16 For Blackwell and the Aberdeen circle see *Fasti academiae Mariscallanae Aberdoensis: selections from the records*, ed. P. J. Anderson (Aberdeen 1889); J. MacCosh, *The Scottish philosophy, biographical, expository, critical, from Hutcheson to Hamilton* (London 1875), pp. 467ff; J. Valentine, 'A Society of Aberdeen

philosophers a hundred years ago', *Macmillan's Magazine*, 8 (1863), 436–44; J. Ramsay, *Scotland and Scotsmen in the eighteenth century* (Edinburgh 1888), vol. 1, p. 469; W. Smellie, *Literary and characteristical lives* (Edinburgh 1800), p. 5; D. D. McElroy, *Scotland's age of improvement* (Washington 1969), pp. 10, 44, and 'The literary clubs and societies of eighteenth century Scotland, and their influence on the literary productions of the period from 1700 to 1800' (unpubd PhD thesis, Edinburgh 1952), in which McElroy studies the problem of how ideas may have spread through personal contacts, listing some 200 clubs, societies, and associations in Scotland (vol. 2). H. Graham, *Scottish men of letters in the eighteenth century* (London 1901), is anecdotal but informative.

17 In *Letters concerning mythology*, which is in many ways a key to the *Enquiry*, Blackwell comments: 'In order to resolve it [i.e. the central question of the *Enquiry*] you must either ascribe his Superiority to Supernatural divine Assistance, which many of the Ancients firmly believed, tho' *We* do not; or, allowing him to have been an ordinary Man, you must enquire into every *Cause*, natural or accidental, that can possibly have Influence upon the human Mind, towards forming it to Poetry and Verse' (p. 37).

18 *Enquiry*, p. 3. Blackwell here seems to have misinterpreted for his own purposes the implicit meaning of the cynical and godless Tacitus in the *Germania*.

19 See MacCosh, *Scottish philosophy*, pp. 467ff, and Valentine, 'Aberdeen philosophers'.

20 Lois Whitney, 'Thomas Blackwell, a disciple of Shaftesbury', *PQ*, 5 (1926), 196–211. D. M. Foerster, 'Scottish primitivism and the historical approach', *PQ*, 29 (1950), 307–23, regards Blackwell as the pioneer of the historical criticism of literature. Lois Whitney, 'Eighteenth century primitivistic theories of the epic', *MP*, 21 (1924), 337–78, and *Primitivism and the idea of progress in English literature of the eighteenth century* (Baltimore 1934), puts Blackwell in the context of Scottish primitivism. E. L. Tuveson, *Millenium and utopia: a study in the background of the idea of progress* (Berkeley 1949), suggests the influence of Burnet's *Sacred theory of the earth* on Blackwell's view of Homer as an early religious poet (pp. 210ff). On Shaftesbury's influence on the Romantics and on this eighteenth-century link see R. L. Brett, *The third Earl of Shaftesbury. A study in eighteenth century literary theory* (London 1951); A. O. Aldridge, 'Lord Shaftesbury's literary theories', *PQ*, 24 (1945), 46–64; Robert Marsh, 'Shaftesbury's theory of poetry: the importance of the "inward colloquy"', *ELH*, 28 (1961), 54–69.

21 *Enquiry*, p. 4.

22 Third Earl of Shaftesbury, *Characteristics of men, manners, opinions, times*, 3rd edn (1723), ed. J. M. Robertson (London 1900), vol. 1, p. 129.

23 *Ibid.* p. 155.

24 *Enquiry*, pp. 10–11.
25 *Ibid.* p. 70.
26 *Ibid.* p. 81.
27 *Ibid.* pp. 22–3, 315.
28 *Ibid.* p. 46.

CHAPTER 9

1 The origins of this interest can be seen in the *querelle* and in the publication of Perrault's *Contes* and La Motte's *Fables* in France. C. A. Sainte-Beuve, 'Homère', *Journal des Débats* 27 (January 1843), in *Aperçus de l'oeuvre critique de C.-A. Sainte-Beuve*, ed. G. Corbière-Gille (Paris 1973), wrote about the development which culminated in the mid-eighteenth-century belief in the popular genius: 'On a beaucoup et très-éloquemment parlé à ce propos de poësie populaire, de génie instinctif, d'épopée toute spontanée, et l'on a cru par là, retrouvant la grandeur, suppléer à l'unité. Chaque époque a ses préjugés; il en est de plus d'une sorte. Il me semble qu'à un certain moment, et par réaction contre les quatres siècles classiques de Périclès, d'Auguste, de Léon X et de Louis XIV, dont on se sentait rebattu, on est devenu soudainement crédule aux poësies dites populaires: on y a été crédule comme certains athées le sont aux molécules organiques et aux générations spontanées' (p. 204). In England it was the periodicals that initially showed interest in popular literature. 'Chevy chase' was among the first published specimens of folk literature in England, in the *Spectator* (1711), with essays on the ballad by Addison. See G. S. Marr, *Periodical essayists of the eighteenth century* (New York 1924); R. D. Havens, 'Simplicity, a changing concept', *JHI*, 14 (1953), 3–32; René Wellek, *The rise of English literary history* (Chapel Hill 1941). The interest continued after Addison's writings on 'Chevy chase'. Allan Ramsay drew attention to Scottish songs in his *The ever-Green, being a collection of Scots poems* (Edinburgh 1724), Ambrose Philips published *A collection of old ballads* (London 1723–4), and Thomas Percy produced his *Reliques of ancient English poetry* (London 1765). The literary value of the Psalms had of course long been recognized. Also in England, two theoretical treatises on ancient poetry appeared: Robert Lowth's *De sacra poesi Hebraeorum* (Oxford 1753) and Richard Hurd's *Letters on chivalry and romance* (London 1762).

2 W. J. Watson, in his introduction to *Scottish verse from the book of the Dean of Lismore* (Edinburgh 1937), writes about the MS known as the book of the Dean of Lismore, which has the earliest entry in 1512 and was known to Macpherson: 'at some time in the eighteenth century...[it] became the property of the Highland Society of London' (p. xii); 'four poems relate to the earlier Cúchulaina or Ulster cycle, twenty-four to the later Ossianic or Fionn cycle' (p. xvii). According to D. S. Thomson, *Introduction to Gaelic*

poetry (London 1974), surviving MSS contain poems which date back to the fifteenth century: 'the surviving corpus of bardic poetry in Scotland consists of approximately 160 items, ranging in size from fragmentary quatrains to poems of over two hundred lines in length...the bulk of it belongs to the period 1450 to 1650, and more than half of it – a rough total of eighty-six items – belongs to the century between 1450 and 1550. Approximately forty poems can be assigned to the period 1600 to 1700, and a mere handful, hardly exceeding ten poems, to the post-1700 period' (p. 20). Thomson has also identified 'the medieval professional bard in Gaelic Scotland' (p. 19) – a figure which Macpherson tried to recreate. Macpherson may have also known the so-called MacDiarmid MS collection (1770), which is as yet unpublished. Some specimens available to Macpherson were included in John Toland's *A critical history of the Celtic religion and learning, containing an account of the Druids* (London 1740). John Smith, inspired by Macpherson, published a number of Gaelic poems which were authentic, in his *Sean Dana: le Oisian, Orran, Ulann, etc. Ancient poems of Ossian, Orran, Ullin, etc. collected in the Western Highlands and Isles; being the originals of the translations some time ago published in the Gaelic antiquities* (Edinburgh 1787). His poems were written down 'from oral recitation' (advertisement).

Various reasons have been suggested for the rise and fall of Gaelic oral literature. According to A. Carmichael, *Carmina Gadelica* (Edinburgh 1900; 2nd edn by E. Watson, Edinburgh 1928), 'Gaelic oral literature was widely diffused, greatly abundant and excellent in quality – in the opinion of scholars, unsurpassed by anything similar in the ancient classics of Greece or Rome' (p. xxii), reasons for this achievement being 'the crofting system, the social customs, and the evening "ceilidh"' (p. xxii). But Gaelic poetry was rapidly disappearing even in the eighteenth century. Carmichael writes: 'Several causes have contributed towards this decadence – principally the Reformation, the Risings, the evictions, the Disruption, the schools, and the spirit of the age...The Reformation movement condemned the beliefs and cults tolerated and assimilated by the Celtic Church and the Latin Church' (p. xxv). See also D. S. Thomson, 'Bogus Gaelic literature c1750–c1820', *Transactions of the Gaelic Society of Glasgow*, 5 (1958), 172–88.

3 Notably such well-known works as Olaus Magnus's *Historia de gentibus septentrionalibus* (Rome 1555), trans. (in epitome) as *A compendious history of the Goths, Swedes and Vandals* (1568); Sebastian Muenster's *De regnis septentrionalibus* (bk 4 of his *Cosmographia*, Basle 1544), adapted by George North as *The description of Swedland, Gotland and Finland* (1561); and Albertus Krantzius's *Chronica regnorum aquilonarium Daniae, Sueciae et Norvegiae* (Strasbourg 1546).

Scottish and English travellers went in increasing numbers to the arctic wastes during the following two centuries. Literary accounts include Fynes Moryson's *An itinerary containing his ten yeares travell* (London 1617); Robert Monro's *His expedition with the worthy Scots regiment levied in 1626 for his Majesties service in Denmark* (London 1637); and Bulstrode Whitelocke's *Journal of the Swedish embassy 1653–54*, ed. G. Morton (London 1772). Eighteenth-century travellers brought valuable scientific and anthropological evidence from northern parts. The Académie française des sciences sent Maupertuis to study the phenomenon of the aurora borealis in 1736–7, and he published his diary in *Le voyage en Laponie*; see Pierre Brunet, *Maupertuis* (Paris 1929). Regnauld Outhier's *Journal d'un voyage au nord en 1736 et 1737* was published in 1744, and was translated into English. P. H. Mallet's *Northern antiquities*, trans. by Thomas Percy from *L'histoire de Dannemarch*, 1755 (London 1770), proved a valuable source of northern mythology, poetry and languages. J. F. Lafitau's popular *Moeurs des sauvages Ameriquains, comparées aux moeurs des premiers temps* (Paris 1724) introduced the societies of the American Indians to the reading public.

4 The impact of Ossian in Europe is discussed in Theodor Drechster, *Der Stil des Macphersonschen Ossian* (Berlin 1904); Theodor Hasselquist, '*Ossian*' *i den svenska dikten och litteraturen* (Malmö 1895); L. M. Price, *English literature in Germany* (Berkeley 1953), pp. 122ff; P. van Tieghem, *Ossian en France* (Paris 1917), and *Ossian et l'ossianisme dans la littérature européenne au XVIIIe siècle* (The Hague 1920); R. Tombo, *Ossian in Germany: bibliography, general survey, Ossian's influence upon Klopstock and the Bards* (New York 1901); Karl Weitnauer, *Ossian in der italienischen Literatur bis etwa 1832* (Munich 1905).

5 The standard biography of Macpherson is T. B. Saunders, *The life and letters of James Macpherson* (London 1894). See also J. S. Smart, *James Macpherson. An episode in literature* (London 1905); and *Folk and hero tales*, ed. and trans. D. MacInnes, with a study of the development of the Ossianic saga by Alfred Nutt (London 1890).

6 Macpherson's publications of Ossian (1760–73) are: 'Two fragments of ancient poetry collected in the Highlands of Scotland, and translated from the Gaelic or Erse language', *Gentleman's Magazine* (June 1760), 287–8; *Fragments of ancient poetry, collected in the Highlands of Scotland, and translated from the Gaelic or Erse language* (Edinburgh 1760); *Fragments of ancient poetry*, 2nd edn (Edinburgh 1760) (poem no. 13 of this edition is a new addition); *Fingal, an ancient epic poem, in six books: together with several other poems, composed by Ossian the son of Fingal* (London 1762); *Temora, an ancient epic poem, in eight books: together with several other poems, composed by Ossian the son of Fingal. Translated from the Gaelic language, by James Macpherson* (London 1763); *The works of Ossian, the son of Fingal. In two volumes. Translated from the Gaelic language by James Macpherson*, 3rd edn (London

1765); *The poems of Ossian, translated by James Macpherson, esq.,
2 vols. A new edition, carefully corrected and greatly improved,
with dissertations on the era and poems of Ossian; and Dr Blair's
critical dissertation* (London 1773).

7 David Hume, 'Of the authenticity of Ossian's poems', in *Philosophical works*, ed. T. H. Green and T. H. Grose, vol. 4 (London 1882), pp. 415–24. Hume regarded Blair's position as 'the only real wonder in the whole affair' (p. 424).

8 Boswell's *Life of Johnson* (London 1791) gives Johnson's opinions on the subject: vol. 1, pp. 245, 513–14, 517–18; vol. 2, p. 443. Johnson published his views on Ossian after a visit to the birthplaces of the poems, in *A journey to the Western Islands of Scotland* (London 1775).

9 W. Wordsworth, *The Excursion* (London 1814), 'Essay supplementary to the preface'.

10 *Report of the committee of the Highland Society of Scotland, appointed to inquire into the nature and authenticity of the poems of Ossian, drawn up, according to the direction of the committee by Henry MacKenzie* (Edinburgh and London 1805). Malcolm Laing in his *History of Scotland with a dissertation of the poems of Ossian* (London 1804) and in *The poetical works of Macpherson* (Edinburgh 1805) put forward views similar to the report. Macpherson's Gaelic MSS were published by the Highland Society, but eleven original texts were found to be missing: *The Poems of Ossian, in the original Gaelic, with a literal translation into Latin, by the late Robert MacFarlan. Together with a dissertation on the authenticity of the poems, by Sir John Sinclair* (London 1807).

11 Herder expressed his views on Ossian on several occasions. In 'Homer und Ossian', *Beiträge zu den Horen* (1795–6), he engages in comparative analysis: 'Schon das unterscheidet Homer von Ossian ganz und gar, dass Jener, wenn ich so sagen darf, *rein-objektiv*, dieser *rein-subjektiv* dichtet' (*Herders Werke*, ed. B. Suphan, vol. 18 (Berlin 1883), p. 453). And he specifies the difference: 'Er [Homer] ist *rein epischer*, Ossian ist, wenn man so will, ein *lyrisch-epischer* Dichter' (p. 454). Ossian is important to Herder as a contrast to Homer, whose poetry he also utilizes for his theory of the folk epic: 'seine [Ossian's] Gestalten sind Nebelgestalten, und sollten es sein; aus dem leisen Hauch der Empfindung sind sie geschaffen und schlupfen wie Lufte vorüber' (p. 455). He sums up: 'Die intensive Kraft des Gesanges, wiewohl in einem engern Kreise ist Ossians; die extensive, wieweitesten Felde der Mittheilung bleibt Homers grosser Vorzug' (p. 456). Herder's pair of opposites can be stated as follows: *Homer* – east, morning, spring; *Ossian* – west, evening, autumn. 'Ossians Gedichte bezeichnen den Herbst seines Volkes' (p. 458).

12 In the *Journal Etranger* (September 1760). Between January and September 1762 the *Journal Etranger* published 95 pages of Ossianic poetry.

13 Mme de Staël, *De la littérature* (Paris 1800), ch. 11.

14 There are pictorial presentations of this theme, by Anne-Louis Girodet, 'Ossian receiving the Napoleonic officers' (1802), with the full title of 'The shades of the French warriors led by victory to the palace of Odin, and received by the Homer of the north and the phantoms of Fingal and his kin', at the Château Rueil-Malmaison, and by F. Gerard, 'Ossian evoking the phantoms on the edge of the Lora' (1801), originally a contribution to Malmaison, now at the Kunsthalle, Hamburg.

15 Hasselquist, '*Ossian*'; Weitnauer, *Ossian*; Werner Söderhjelm, *Åboromantiken och dess samband med utländska idéströmningar* (Porvoo 1915), pp. 13, 22ff.

16 Doubts about the genuineness of the Orphic poems came to a head with Thomas Tyrwhitt's publication of *De lapidibus* (1781), which he assigned to the fourth century A.D.

17 'He [Homer] seems to have trusted to the immediate resources of his genius, for the means of carrying him, through his journey. He advances, with apparent ease: Nor seems he ever to exert all his strength. He never deviates from his course, in search of ornament. In sublimity of expression and language he may be equalled: In simplicity and ease, it is difficult to ascend to his sphere' (*The Iliad of Homer* (London 1773), preface, vol. 1, pp. x–xi).

18 Macpherson justified his own translation in the following terms: 'His [Macpherson's] thoughts, concerning his [Homer's] person and the age, in which he lived, are so singular in themselves, that, without a more minute examination of the subject, he shall not venture to lay them before the Public. The extent of his design has been, to give Homer as he really is: And to endeavour, as much as possible, to make him speak English, with his own dignified simplicity and energy' (*ibid.* p. xx). Hume commented on Macpherson's Homeric translation in his essay on Ossian, where he also rejected the poet's Ossianic fragments, seeing in them only 'insipid correctness' and 'uniformity which betrays a man without genius': 'Finding the style of his [Macpherson's] Ossian admired by some, he attempts a translation of Homer in the very same style. He begins and finishes, in six weeks, a work that was for ever to eclipse the translation of Pope, whom he does not even deign to mention in his preface' (*Philosophical works*, vol. 4, p. 423).

19 J. Macpherson, *An introduction to the history of Great Britain and Ireland: or, an inquiry into the origin, religion, future state, characters, manners, morality, amusements, persons, manner of life, houses, navigation, commerce, language, government, kings, general assemblies, courts of justice, and juries, of the Britons, Scots, Irish and Anglo-Saxons* (London 1771, 3rd edn rev. and greatly enlarged, 1773), pp. 258–9.

20 J. Gordon, *Occasional thoughts on the study and character of classical authors* (London 1762), pp. 109–11.

21 Ossian's poems were seen to have Hebraic sublimity by Suard

(*Journal Etranger*, December 1761) and Chateaubriand (*Essai sur la littérature anglaise*); they were regarded as Pindaric odes by Marmontel ('Lyrique', *L'encyclopédie*), as ancient epic by Denis (*Die Lieder Sineds des Barden*), as lyrical songs by Melchior Grimm (*Correspondance*), as Scots folk poetry by Herder (*Über die neuere deutsche Literatur*) and as folk songs by Diderot (*Discours sur la poësie dramatique*). See discussion in van Tieghem, *Ossian et l'ossianisme*, p. 53.

22 John Aikin, a collector of English folk songs and poems, presented his work to his readers as an alternative to 'the modish insipidity of the age; and to gratify such real lovers of genius as yet remain amongst us' (*Essays on song-writing* (London 1772), p. iv). Aikin comments on Homer and Ossian, pp. viii, 4.

23 *An essay on original genius* (London 1767), p. 286.

24 J. Macpherson, 'A dissertation concerning the poems of Ossian', prefixed to the 1773 edn of *The poems of Ossian*.

25 H. Blair, 'A critical dissertation on the poems of Ossian', prefixed to the 1765 edn of *The works of Ossian*.

26 Voltaire had considerable fun at the expense of Ossian. See his 'Anciens et modernes', in *Questions sur l'encyclopédie* (Geneva 1770), I, 277–305. See also van Tiegham, *Ossian en France*, vol. I, p. 273.

27 *Temora, poëme épique en VIII chants, composé en langue Erse ou Gallique, par Ossian fils de Fingal. Traduit d'après l'édition anglaise de Macpherson, par M Le Marquis de St Simon* (Amsterdam 1774): 'Discours préliminaire', pp. 1–54. Maximilien Henri, Marquis de Saint Simon (1720–99), was a man of letters who worked for most of his life in Holland. His publications include various historical, political and botanical works, and an *Essai de traduction littérale et énergique* (1771) which shows his familiarity with English literature (translations from Pope, Milton, Shakespeare, Addison, Prior, Gay).

28 Saint-Simon, 'Discours préliminaire', p. 15.

29 *Ibid.*

30 *Ibid.*

CHAPTER 10

1 T. Blackwell, *An enquiry into the life and writings of Homer* (London 1735), pp. 54–5.

2 E. Manwaring, *An historical and critical account of the most eminent classic authors in poetry and history* (London 1737), p. 2.

3 R. Lowth, *De sacra poesi Hebraeorum, praelectiones academicae Oxonii habitae* (Oxford 1753), trans. G. Gregory, *Lectures on the sacred poetry of the Hebrews* (London 1787).

4 *Ibid.* vol. I, p. 37.

5 *Ibid.* vol. I, p. 38.

6 *Ibid.* vol. I, pp. 11–12.

7 R. Hurd, *Letters on chivalry and romance* (London 1762), p. 5.

8 *Ibid.* p. 59.

9 J. Beattie, 'An essay on poetry and music, as they affect the mind' (1762), in *Essays* (London 1776), p. 4.

10 J. Warton, in his *An essay on the genius and writings of Pope* (London 1756) writes: 'So *didactic* a genius would have been deficient in that *sublime* and *pathetic*, which are the main nerves of the epopea' (p. 280). In his edition of *The works of Virgil* (London 1763) Warton writes about Homer: 'He that peruses Homer, is like the traveller that surveys mount Atlas; the vastness and roughness of its rocks, the solemn gloominess of its pines and cedars, the everlasting snows that cover its head, the torrents that rush down its sides, and the wild beasts that roar in its caverns, all contribute to strike the imagination with inexpressible astonishment and awe' ('Prefatory dedication' (1753), vol. 1, p. vi). See the study of the Wartons by J. Pittock, *The ascendancy of taste* (London 1973), esp. pp. 141ff.

11 See J. McCosh, *The Scottish philosophy, biographical, expository, critical, from Hutcheson to Hamilton* (London 1875), p. 228.

12 Blackwell, *Enquiry*, p. 125.

13 J. Brown, *Essays on the Characteristics of the Earl of Shaftesbury*, 3rd edn (London 1752), p. 386.

14 W. Duff, *Critical observations on the writings of the most celebrated original geniuses in poetry* (London 1770), p. 4.

15 J. Brown, *A Dissertation on the rise, union, and power of poetry and music* (London 1763), p. 63.

16 *Ibid.* p. 66.

17 A. Gerard, *An essay on genius* (Edinburgh 1774), p. 11.

18 *Ibid.* p. 7.

19 *Ibid.* pp. 41–57; this is a summary of his analysis.

20 *Ibid.* p. 68.

21 A. Gerard, 'Appendix: whether poetry be properly an imitative art?' in *An essay on taste* (1759), 3rd edn (Edinburgh 1780), p. 283.

22 Gerard, *Essay on genius*, p. 12.

23 *Ibid.* pp. 128–9.

24 W. Duff, *An essay on original genius* (London 1767), pp. 131–2.

25 *Ibid.* p. 159.

26 *Ibid.* pp. 176–7.

27 *Ibid.* pp. 96–7.

28 On English seventeenth- and eighteenth-century ideas of enthusiasm see Susie Tucker, *Enthusiasm: a study in semantic change* (Cambridge 1972).

29 Duff, *Essay*, pp. 169–70.

30 *Ibid.* p. 286.

31 *Ibid.* p. 264.

32 *Ibid.* pp. 271–2.

33 Lord Kames, *Sketches of the history of man* (1774), 3rd edn (Edinburgh 1779), vol. 1, p. 159.

34 A. Ferguson, 'Of the history of literature', in *An essay on the history of civil society* (Edinburgh 1767), p. 266.

35 J. Beattie, *Essays*, p. 97.

36 *Ibid.* pp. 67–8.

37 H. Blair, *A critical dissertation on the poems of Ossian* (1765), 1809 edn, p. 41.

38 H. Blair, *Lectures on rhetoric and belles lettres* (London 1787), p. 21.

39 Lord Monboddo, in *Of the origin and progress of language*, vol. 1 (Edinburgh 1773), stated that 'every Faculty is the result of a previous habit or disposition' (p. 13), and that 'a great part of our infancy is spent in acquiring habits of sensation' (p. 35). He then made a study of wild peoples found in remote parts of the world, of wild children discovered in the woods (*l'enfant sauvage*) and of orang-outangs, and compared their capacity to acquire speech (pp. 180–8). The wild people could, the apes could not learn to speak (p. 188). See also his preface to the *Account of a savage girl, caught wild in the woods of Champagne* (Edinburgh 1768): 'For it is impossible to suppose, that language, the most wonderful art among men, should have been born with us, and practised by us from mere instinct, unless we could at the same time suppose, that other arts came into the world with us in the same manner' (p. xvii). See E. L. Cloyd, *James Burnett, Lord Monboddo* (Oxford 1972). Thomas Reid, *Essays on the intellectual powers of man* (Edinburgh 1785), agreed with Lord Monboddo in emphasizing the importance of early childhood in the acquisition of habits of sensation (ch. 1).

40 Manwaring, *Historical account*, p. 2. See also D. M. Foerster, 'Scottish primitivism and the historical approach', *PQ*, 29 (1950), 307–23.

41 Brown, *Dissertation*, chs. 3–7, esp. ch. 3, 'Of music, dance, and poem, in the savage state', and ch. 4, 'Of the natural consequences of a supposed civilization'. He regarded Aeschylus as a better example of the primitive poet than Homer: 'Aeschylus epitomizes the rude Genius of early periods. His imagery and sentiments are great; his style rugged and abrupt; and of a cast so totally different from that of Homer...His writings present to us all the characters of a sublime, original, and uncultivated genius, which scorned any other tutoress than Nature' (p. 66).

42 Duff, *Essay*, p. 264.

43 James Dunbar [?], *Essays on the history of mankind in rude and cultivated ages* (London 1780), p. 5.

CHAPTER 11

1 Robert Wood, *An essay on the original genius and writings of Homer* (rev. edn, London 1775), p. 5. The first version was published in folio under the title *A comparative view of the ancient and present state of the Troade to which is prefixed an essay on the*

original genius of Homer (1767). This publication had the *Essay* but omitted the *Comparative view*. The latter was printed with *An Essay on the original genius of Homer* (1769), and an expanded and improved version with illustrations and maps was published posthumously (1775). For a study of Wood's travels and diaries, see C. A. Hutton, 'The travels of "Palmyra" Wood in 1750–51), *Journal of Hellenic Studies*, 47 (1927), 102–28. Wood's travels to the ancient sites of Troy have also been studied by T. J. B. Spencer, 'Robert Wood and the problem of Troy in the eighteenth century', *JWCI*, 20 (1957), 75–105.

2 The eighteenth-century meanings and usages of such words as 'original', 'originality', 'genius', 'nature', 'imitation', which occur frequently in this chapter, present a *crise de conscience* in any study of eighteenth-century literary history, as the discussion of these concepts is impossible without using the same words, which shifted in meaning even during the period we have been considering. See A. O. Lovejoy, 'Nature as esthetic norm', *MLN*, 42 (1927), 444–50; J. W. Draper, 'Aristotelian mimesis in eighteenth-century England', *PMLA*, 36 (1921), 372–400; E. L. Mann, 'The problem of originality in English literary criticism 1750–1800', *PQ*, 18 (1939), 97–118; M. L. Wiley, 'Genius: a problem in definition', *Studies in English*, 16 (1936), 77–83; G. Matoré and A. J. Greimas, 'La naissance de "génie" au XVIIIe siècle. Étude lexicologique', *Français moderne*, 25 (1957), 256–72. The word 'environment' on the other hand does not belong to the eighteenth century. It covers the meaning of 'nature' as the external world, but stands in opposition to 'nature' as man's inherited characteristics.

3 Rudolf Pfeiffer, *History of classical scholarship from 1300 to 1850* (Oxford 1976), assesses Wood as contributor to classical studies (p. 161). Goethe writes about Wood's *Essay* in *Dichtung und Wahrheit*, III, 12: 'Auch das Homerische Licht ging uns neu wieder auf, und zwar recht im Sinne der Zeit, die ein solches Erscheinen höchst begünstigte: denn das beständige Hinweisen auf Natur bewirkte zuletzt, dass man auch die Werke der Alten von dieser Seite betrachten lernte. Was mehrere Reisende zu Aufklärung der Heiligen Schriften getan, leisteten andere für den Homer. Durch Guys war man eingeleitet, Wood gab der Sache den Schwung' (*Goethes Werke*, ed. Erich Trunz, vol. 9 (Hamburg 1955), p. 538). The whole passage (pp. 537–8) is of great interest. F. A. Wolf, who in his day was to convince the scholarly world of the multiple authorship of the Homeric epics, described Wood's *Essay* as 'celebratissimus liber' (*Prolegomena ad Homerum* (Halle 1795), vol. 1, p. 40).

4 See F. Haskell, *The age of the grand tour* (London 1967); L. Cust and S. Colvin, *History of the Society of the Dilettanti* (London 1914). Robert Wood was elected a member of the society on 1 May 1763.

5 Lady Mary Wortley Montagu wrote in her *Letters...written during*

her travels in Europe, Asia and Africa to persons of distinction (London 1771): 'North of the promontory of Sigaeum we saw that of Rhaeteum famed for the sepulchre of Ajax. While I viewed these celebrated fields and rivers, I admired the exact geography of Homer, whom I had in my hand. Almost every epithet he gives to a mountain or a plain, is still just for it; and I spent several hours here in as agreeable cogitations, as ever Don Quixote had on mount Montesinos' (letter to abbé Conti, 31 July 1718, p. 189). P. A. Guys was an enthusiastic though rather ill-informed traveller whose *Voyage littéraire de la Grèce* (Paris 1771) was immediately translated into English as *A sentimental* [sic] *journey through Greece* (London 1772). He wrote: 'the poets, like the artists, consulted nature, and nature alone. Homer is an undeniable proof of it. What truth! What energy! what judgment in the choice of his images! It is in Greece only that the *Iliad* and *Odyssey* can be read with all their advantages' (vol. 3, p. 66). The travellers of the late eighteenth century had a serious topographical and archaeological interest in the classical sites: see M. G. Choiseul-Gouffier, *Voyage pittoresque de la Grèce* (Paris 1782), and Jean Baptiste Le Chevalier, *Description of the plain of Troy*, trans. A. Dalzel, *Transactions of the Royal Society of Edinburgh*, 3 (1794), 1–92. Le Chevalier criticizes, rather surprisingly, Wood's meagre results in finding correspondences between Homer's *Iliad* and the actual sites (pp. vi–vii). See also J. M. Osborn, 'Travel literature and the rise of neohellenism in England', *Bulletin of the New York Public Library*, 67 (1963), 279–300; W. C. Cable, 'The popularity of English travel books about the Near East 1775–1825', *PQ*, 15 (1936), 70–8.

6 R. Wood, *The ruins of Palmyra* (London 1753), 'To the reader', unnumbered pp.

7 Admittedly its roots go back to the Renaissance. See Roberto Weiss, *The Renaissance discovery of classical antiquity* (Oxford 1969); T. J. B. Spencer, *Fair Greece, sad relic: literary philhellenism from Shakespeare to Byron* (London 1954); S. A. Larrabee, *English bards and Grecian marbles* (New York 1943); Harry Levin, *The broken column: a study in romantic hellenism* (Cambridge, Mass., 1931); B. H. Stern, *The rise of romantic hellenism in English literature, 1732–1786* (Menasha 1940).

8 R. Wood, 'Address to the reader', in R. Chandler, N. Revett and W. Pars, *Ionian antiquities* (Society of the Dilettanti, London 1769), p. iii.

9 *Ibid.* p. i.

10 *Essay* (1775), p. 5.

11 *Ibid.* p. 7.

12 *Ibid.* p. 18.

13 *Ibid.* pp. 23–4.

14 *Ibid.* pp. 145–6.

15 The map was appended to the *Essay*. Others who had interested

themselves in drawing maps of Troy included Pope (*The Iliad of Homer*, vol. 2 (London 1716)); Choiseul-Gouffier, *Voyage*, vol. 2, pp. 177, 208, 347, a work which seems to be derivative from Wood; Le Chevalier, *Description*, who criticized Wood. The final statement was attempted in the nineteenth century by H. N. Ulrichs, 'An excursus on the topography of the Homeric Ilium', *Transactions of the Royal Society of Literature*, 2nd ser., 2 (1847), 103–78. He again raised Homer, Strabo and Demetrius of Scepsis as authorities on the matter. See also Spencer, 'Wood and the problem of Troy'.

16 *Essay*, p. 182.

17 *Ibid.* p. 181.

18 *Ibid.* p. 35.

19 *Ibid.* p. 249. The only passage in Homer that suggests knowledge of the art of writing is *Iliad*, vi, 165–75. All references to poetic techniques are to the oral ones.

20 The current theory being that the Greek mainland was illiterate before Linear B was imported from Crete (*c.*1460 B.C.), and that the Greeks were analphabets before contact with the Phoenicians. Illiteracy may have survived longer in certain parts and dialects, e.g. in the Aeolic round the coast of Asia Minor. See A. J. B. Wace and F. H. Stubbings, *A companion to Homer* (London 1962); S. Dow, 'The Greeks in the Bronze Age', *Le 10e congrès international des sciences historiques* (Stockholm 1960), pp. 1–34. On the question of literacy in the Homeric period, see R. Sealey, 'From Phemios to Ion', *Revue des Etudes grecques*, 70 (1957), 312–55; J. Russo and B. Simon, 'Homeric psychology and the oral epic tradition', *JHI*, 29 (1968), 483–98; G. S. Kirk, 'Dark age and oral poet', *PCPS*, n.s. 7 (1961), 34–48; H. L. Lorimer, 'Homer and the art of writing: a sketch of opinion between 1713 and 1939', *AJA*, 52 (1948), 11–23; E. R. Dodds, 'Homer', in *Fifty years of classical scholarship*, ed. M. Platnauer (Oxford 1954), pp. 1–17, 31–5.

21 Rousseau, who was interested in Homeric poetry, writes in his 'Essai sur l'origine des langues' (1749–55?): 'Il m'est venu bien souvent dans l'esprit de douter non seulement qu'Homère sût écrire, mais même qu'on écrivait de son temps' (ch. 6). He supports the view that Homer did not know the art of writing, and argues his point from the lack of internal evidence in the epics, and from the fact that Homer has preserved a diversity of dialects, a characteristic of oral culture. He concludes: 'For a long time these poems were written only in men's memories. Somewhat later they were laboriously collected in writing. That was when Greece began to abound in books and written poetry, whereby all the charm of Homer could be experienced by comparison. Other poets had written; Homer alone had sung' (*On the origin of language*, trans. J. H. Moran and A. Gode (New York 1966), p. 24).

22 *Essay*, p. 294.

CHAPTER 12

1 Edward Young, *Conjectures on original composition; in a letter to Sir Charles Grandison* (London 1759), pp. 9–13.

2 A. Bayly, *The alliance of musick, poetry and oratory* (London 1789), p. 268.

3 J. G. Sulzer, *Allgemeine Theorie der schönen Künste* (Leipzig 1771), p. 861.

4 John Pinkerton, *Letters of literature* (London 1785), p. 359.

5 This aspect has been hardly discussed by the main historians of Homer in eighteenth-century England, D. M. Foerster, *Homer in English criticism* (New Haven 1947), and J. L. Myres, *Homer and his critics* (London 1958); see, however, the essay by H. W. Eppelsheimer, *Homer – ein Originalgenie* (Fulda 1948); G. Finsler, *Homer in der Neuzeit, von Dante bis Goethe* (Leipzig und Berlin 1912); and the anthology by E. Stemplinger, *Griechisch-lateinischer Literaturführer von Homer bis auf unsere Zeit* (Munich 1934), pp. 38–9.

6 Heraclitus, *Quaestiones Homericae*, ed. F. Oelmann (Leipzig 1910), ch. 1, p. 2. The unique position of the *Iliad* and the *Odyssey* in Greek education has been discussed in Myres, *Homer and his critics*; W. Jaeger, *Paideia: the ideals of Greek culture*, trans. G. Highet, vol. 1 (Oxford 1939); F. Buffière, *Les mythes d'Homère et la pensée Grecque* (Paris 1956), pp. 10–22.

7 G. Croese, ΟΜΗΡΟΣ ΕΒΡΑΙΟΣ (Dordrecht 1704), p. 2r. See also anon., *Homerus S. Scripturae interpres sive observatio philologica qua Salomo Prov.IV.v.3. et Lucas V.3 ex Homero inter se conciliantur* (Coburg; in the Bibliothèque Nationale, Paris, 4° A.5110), and J. Barnes, *Praelectiones ecclesiasticae et in Homerum* (Emmanuel College Library, Cambridge, MS 11.3.10). Other critics of Homer with biblical tendencies include Bogan, Grotius, Bochart, Kluwer and Picinelli. See P. Costil, 'La question homérique et l'évolution du goût littéraire en France', *Annales de l'Université de Grenoble*, n.s. 19 (1943), 95–148, esp. 116–17; E. Shaffer, '*Kubla Khan*' and the fall of Jerusalem; the mythological school of biblical criticism and secular literature 1770–1880 (Cambridge 1975).

8 L. Kuester, *Historia critica Homeri* (Frankfurt 1696).

9 J. Dryden, Preface to *Albion and Albanus* (1685), in *Essays*, ed. W. P. Ker (Oxford 1900), vol. 2, pp. 271–2.

10 R. Hurd, *A letter to Mr Mason; on the marks of imitation* (London 1757), p. 9.

11 R. Kedington, *Critical dissertations on the Iliad of Homer* (London 1759), p. 23.

12 J. Aikin, 'Essay on the poetry of eastern nations', in *Poems, consisting chiefly of translations from the Asiatic languages* (Oxford 1772), p. 195.

13 Edward Young, though apparently writing in praise of originality,

epitomizes this view: 'copies surpass not their *Originals*, as streams rise not higher than their spring, rarely so high...' (*Conjectures*, p. 41). But he extols Homer's originality with reservations: 'After all, the first Ancients had no Merit in being Originals: They could *not* be *Imitators* (pp. 18–19).

14 Plato, *R.* 595 B and *R.* 600 E – 601 A, leading to similar arguments in *Ion* 533 D – 534 E and *Phdr.* 245 A.

15 Quintilian, *Inst. Or.* XII, ii, 21.

16 J. Tzetzes, *Chiliades*, XIII, 626ff.

17 The Renaissance platonist Partenio, in *Dell'imitazione poetica* (1560), speaks of Homeric poetry as 'pelaghi di scienzie', and says, 'Onde veramente detto fu che sì come dall'Oceano tutti i fiumi e i mari derivano, così vediano da questo poeta tutte le cose dette aver l'origine et il principio'; B. Weinberg, *Trattati di poetica e retorica del cinquecento* (Bari 1970), vol. 2, pp. 521, 523. On these notions see B. Weinberg, *A history of literary criticism in the Italian Renaissance* (Chicago 1961), vol. 1, pp. 41ff.

18 D. P. Walker, 'Esoteric symbolism', in *Poetry and poetics from ancient Greece to the Renaissance*, ed. G. M. Kirkwood (Ithaca, N.Y., 1975), pp. 218–32.

19 I. Maier, *Ange Politien. La formation d'un poète humaniste (1469–1480)* (Geneva 1966), pp. 93–4. See also P. Kristeller, 'The modern system of the arts: a study in the history of aesthetics, I', *JHI*, 12 (1951), 496–527, esp. 510.

20 F. Rabelais, 'Prologue', *Gargantua*, ed. Pierre Jourda (Paris 1965), pp. 59/61. In *Pantagruel* Rabelais claims that no man without Greek should be called erudite (ed. Jourda (Paris 1964), ch. 8, p. 131).

21 J. Duport, 'Epistola dedicatoria', *Homeri, poetarum omnium seculorum facile principis, gnomologia* (Cambridge 1660).

22 R. Rapin, 'Reflections on Aristotle's poesie', in *The whole critical works*, trans. by several hands (London 1706), vol. 2, p. 138.

23 A. Collins, *A discourse of free-thinking* (London 1713), p. 9.

24 E. Manwaring, *An historical and critical account of the most eminent classic authors in poetry and history* (London 1737), p. iii.

25 *Ibid.* p. 70.

26 T. S. Eliot, *The use of poetry and the use of criticism* (London 1933).

Bibliography

1 PRIMARY SOURCES

1.1 ESSAYS AND TREATISES ON HOMER

d'Aubignac, Abbé (François Hédelin), *Conjectures académiques ou dissertation sur l'Iliade* (1715), ed. V. Magnien, Paris 1925.

Blackwell, Thomas, *An enquiry into the life and writings of Homer*, London 1735.
  Proofs of the enquiry into Homer's life and writings, translated into English; being a key to the enquiry, London 1747.

Bogan, Zacharus, *Homerus* Ἑβραΐζων *sive, comparatio Homeri cum scriptoribus sacris quoad norman loquendi*, Oxford 1658.

Boivin, Jean, *Apologie d'Homère et le bouclier d'Achille*, Paris 1715.
  La querelle entre les partisans d'Homère et ceux de Virgile, Paris 1707.

Bryant, Jacob, *A dissertation concerning the war of Troy and the expedition of the Grecians as described by Homer*, London 1796.
  Some observations upon the vindication of Homer, and of the

ancient poets and historians, who have recorded the siege and fall of *Troy*, Eton 1799.

Buffier, P. Claude, *Homère en arbitrage*, Paris 1715.

Cordonnier, Hyacinthe, *Dissertation sur Homère et sur Chapelain*, La Haye 1714.

Croese, Gerard, ΟΜΗΡΟΣ ΕΒΡΑΙΟΣ *sive Historia Hebraeorum ab Homero Hebraicis nominibus ac sententiis conscripta in Odyssea et Iliade*, Dordrecht 1704.

Cuperus, Gilbert, *Apotheosis vel consecratio Homeri*, Amsterdam 1683.

Dacier, Mme (Anne Lefèvre), 'Preface', in *L'Iliade d'Homère*, Paris 1711.

Duport, James, *Homeri, poetarum omnium seculorum facile principis, gnomologia, duplici parallelismo illustrata*, Cambridge 1660.

Faydit, P. V., *Remarques sur Virgile et sur Homère, et sur le style poetique de l'écriture*, Paris 1705.

Fiddes, Richard, *A prefatory epistle concerning some remarks to be published on Homer's Iliad*, London 1714.

Fleury, Claude, *Remarques sur Homère*, (MS, 1665) ed. N. Hepp, in *Deux amis d'Homère*, Paris 1970.

Fourmont, E., *Examen pacifique de la querelle de Madame Dacier et de Monsieur de la Motte sur Homère; avec un traité sur le poëme épique et la critique des deux Iliades, et de plusieurs autres poëmes*, Paris 1716.

Fraguier, Abbé Claude F., 'Discours sur la manière dont Virgile a imité Homère', in *Histoire de l'Academie royale des Inscriptions et Belles-Lettres*, vol. 2, Paris 1718, pp. 141–60.

Gacon, François, *Homère vengé, ou réponse à M. de la Motte sur l'Iliade*, Paris 1715.

Gueret, Gabriel, *La guerre des auteurs anciens et modernes*, Paris 1671.

Hardouin, P. Jean, *L'apologie d'Homère*, Paris 1716.

An apology for Homer; wherein the true nature and design of the Iliad is explained, and a new system of his theomythology proposed, London 1717.

Kedington, R., *Critical dissertations on the Iliad of Homer*, London 1759.

Klotz, C. A., *Epistolae Homericae*, Altenburg 1764.

Kuester, Ludolph, *Historia critica Homeri*, Frankfurt 1696.

La Motte, Antoine Houdar de, *L'Iliade, poëme, avec un discours sur Homère* (Paris 1714), in *Oeuvres*, vol. 2, Paris 1754.

Réflexions sur la critique (Paris 1715), in *Oeuvres*, vol. 3, Paris 1754.

Le Chevalier, Jean-Baptiste, *Description of the plain of Troy*, trans. with notes and illustrations by Andrew Dalzel, *Transactions of the Royal Society of Edinburgh*, 3 (1794), 1–92.

Morritt, J. B. S., *A vindication of Homer, and of the ancient poets and historians, who have recorded the siege and fall of Troy*, in answer to two late publications of Mr Bryant, London 1798.

Additional remarks on the topography of Troy etc., as given by

Homer, Strabo, and the ancient geographers; in answer to Mr Bryant's last publications, London 1800.

Parnell, Thomas, 'An essay on the life, writings and learning of Homer', in *The Iliad of Homer*, trans. A. Pope, vol. 1, London 1715.

Pellisson, Paul, *Relation à Chyrotée des chants VI–IX de l'Odyssée. Avec la traduction des chants I–IX de l'Odyssée* (MS, 1650), ed. N. Hepp, in *Deux amis d'Homère*, Paris 1970.

Pope, Alexander, Preface to the *Iliad* (1715), in *The Poems of Alexander Pope*, vol. 7, ed. M. Mack, London 1967.

Prescot, Kenrick, *Letters concerning Homer the sleeper in Horace: with additional classic amusement*, Cambridge 1773.

Prior, Matthew, *Observations on Homer. A letter*, London 1715.

Ramus, J., *Ulysses et Outinus unus et idem, sive disquisitio historica et geographica, qua, ex collatis inter se Odyssea Homeri et Edda Island Homerizante, Outini fraudes deteguntur, ac, detracta larva in lucem protrahitur Ulysses*, Copenhagen 1713.

Rapin, René, *Discours académique sur la comparaison entre Virgile et Homère*, Paris 1668.

  Observations sur les poèmes d'Homère et de Virgile, Paris 1669.

Terrasson, J., *Dissertation critique sur l'Iliade d'Homère*, Paris 1715.

  Addition à la dissertation critique, Paris 1716.

  A critical dissertation upon Homer's Iliad. Where, upon occasion of this poem, a new system of the art of poetry is attempted, founded upon the principles of reason, and the examples of the most illustrious poets, both ancient and modern, trans. Francis Brerewood, London 1722.

Verdicts of the learned concerning Virgil's and Homer's heroic poems, London 1697.

Vico, Giambattista, 'Della discoverta del vero Omero' (1730), in *La scienza nuova seconda*, ed. F. Nicolini, Bari 1942.

Wood, Robert, *An essay on the original genius of Homer*, London 1769, repr. with additions as *An essay on the original genius and writings of Homer* (London 1775).

1.2 WORKS RELATED TO THE STUDY OF HOMER

Adams, John, *Curious thoughts on the history of man: chiefly abridged or selected from the celebrated works of Lord Kaimes, Lord Monboddo, Dr Dunbar, and the immortal Montesquieu*, London 1789.

Addison, Joseph, 'On genius', *Spectator* (1711), no. 160.

  'An essay on the pleasures of the imagination', *Spectator* (1712), nos. 411–21.

  A discourse on ancient and modern learning, 2nd edn, London 1739.

Aikin, John, *Poems, consisting chiefly of translations from the Asiatic languages. To which are added two essays; On the poetry of the*

25

eastern nations, and, On the arts, commonly called imitative, Oxford 1772.

Essays on song-writing: with a collection of such English songs as are most eminent for poetical merit. To which are added, some original pieces, London 1772.

Akenside, Mark, *The pleasures of imagination. A poem,* London 1744.

Armstrong, John, *Taste: an epistle to a young critic,* London 1753.

Bayly, Anselm, *An introduction to languages, literary and philosophical; especially to the English, Latin, Greek and Hebrew,* London 1758.

Beattie, James, 'An essay on poetry and music, as they affect the mind' (1762), in *Essays,* London 1776.

'On the Utility of Classical Learning' (1769), in *Essays,* London 1776.

Benson, William, *Letters concerning poetical translations, and Virgil's and Milton's arts of verse,* London 1739.

Bentley, Richard, *A dissertation upon the epistles of Phalaris,* London 1699.

Remarks upon a late discourse of free-thinking, London 1713.

Bibliothèque britannique, ou histoire des ouvrages des savans de la Grande-Bretagne, The Hague 1733–47.

Biographia Britannica, or, the lives of the most eminent persons who have flourished in Great Britain and Ireland, from the earliest ages to the present times, London 1747–66; 2nd edn, London 1778–93.

Biographia classica, or, the lives and characters of all the classic authors, the Grecian and Roman poets, historians, orators, and biographers, London 1740.

Blackmore, Richard, *Homer and Virgil not to be compared with the two Arthurs,* London 1700.

Essays upon several subjects, London 1716.

Blackwall, Antony, *An introduction to the classics,* London 1718.

The sacred classics defended and illustrated, pt I, London 1725, pt II, London 1731.

Blackwell, Thomas, *Letters concerning mythology,* London 1748.

Memoirs of the court of Augustus, pts I–II, London 1753–5, pt III, London 1763.

Blair, Hugh, *Lectures on rhetoric and belles lettres,* London 1787.

Blankenburg, Friedrich von, *Litterarische Zusätze zu J. G. Sulzers allgemeiner Theorie der schönen Künste,* Leipzig 1796.

Blount, Thomas, *De re poetica: or, remarks upon poetry with characters and censures of the most considerable poets, whether ancient or modern, extracted out of best and choicest criticks,* London 1694.

Boccalini, Trajano, *Advertisements from Parnassus (Ragguagli di Parnasso,* 1612), trans. N. N. esq., London 1704.

Boileau-Despréaux, Nicolas, *The works of M. Boileau,* trans. by several hands, London 1711–12.

Bouhours, Dominique, *Pensées ingénieuses des anciens et des modernes,* Paris 1693.

The art of criticism: or, the method of making a right judgment upon subjects of wit and learning, trans. by a person of quality, London 1705.

Bowden, Samuel, *Poems on various subjects, with some essays in prose,* London 1754.

Bowle, John, *Reflections on originality in authors,* London 1766.

Boyer, Abel, *The English Theophrastus: or, the manners of the age,* London 1702.

Broome, William, *Poems on several occasions, with the preface: being an essay on criticism,* London 1727.

Brown, John, *Essays on the Characteristics of the Earl of Shaftesbury,* 3rd edn, London 1752.

An estimate of the manners and principles of the times, London 1757–58.

A dissertation on the rise, union and power of poetry and music, London 1763.

Burke, Edmund, *A philosophical inquiry into the origin of our ideas of the sublime and beautiful,* London 1756.

Bysshe, Edward, *The art of English poetry,* London 1702.

Callières, F. de, *Histoire poétique de la guerre nouvellement declarée entre les anciens et les modernes,* Paris 1688.

Cameron, Ewen, *The Fingal of Ossian,* Warrington 1776.

Campbell, John, *Prolusions; or, select pieces of antient poetry,* London 1760.

Capell, E., *Reflections on originality in authors,* London 1766.

Clarke, John, *An essay upon study,* London 1731.

Clarke, Samuel, *Letters on literary subjects,* London 1785.

A collection of old ballads, London 1723–5.

Collins, Anthony, *A discourse of free-thinking,* London 1713.

A complete catalogue of modern books, London 1766.

Cooper, J. G. *Letters concerning taste,* London 1755.

Critical observations on books, antient and modern, London 1776.

Dacier, André, *Poétique d'Aristote traduite en françois avec des remarques,* Paris 1681.

Dacier, Mme (Anne Lefèvre), *Des causes de la corruption du goût,* Paris 1714.

Dennis, John, *The advancement and reformation of modern poetry,* London 1701.

The grounds of criticism in poetry, London 1704.

Remarks upon Mr Pope's translation of Homer, London 1717.

Dryden, John, *Fables, ancient and modern, translated into verse, from Homer, Ovid, Boccace and Chaucer, with original poems; with a preface,* London 1700.

Dubos, Abbé René, *Réflexions critiques sur la poësie et sur la peinture,* Paris 1719.

Duff, William, *An essay on original genius,* London 1767.

Critical observations on the writings of the most celebrated original geniuses in poetry, London 1770.

Dunbar, James, *Essays on the history of mankind in rude and cultivated ages*, 2nd edn, London 1781.

Evans, Theophilus, *The history of modern enthusiasm from the reformation to the present times*, London 1752.

Felton, Henry, *A dissertation on reading the classics, and forming a just style*, London 1713.

Fénelon, François de Salignac de la Mothe, *Les aventures de Télémaque* (Paris 1699), ed. J. L. Goré, Paris 1968.

Ferguson, Adam, *An essay on the history of civil society*, Edinburgh 1767.

Fontenelle, Bernard le Bovier de, *Nouveaux dialogues des morts*, Paris 1683.

    Digression sur les anciens et les modernes, in *Poésies pastorales* (Paris 1688); ed. R. Shackleton (Oxford 1955).

    Conversations with a lady on the plurality of worlds, trans. Mr Glanvill, 4th edn, *to which is also added, a discourse concerning the antients and moderns*, trans. by Mr Hughes, London 1719.

Geddes, James, *An essay on the composition and manner of writing of the ancients, particularly Plato*, Glasgow 1748.

Gerard, Alexander, *An essay on taste*, Edinburgh 1759.

    Dissertations on subjects relating to the genius and evidences of Christianity, Edinburgh 1766.

    An essay on genius, Edinburgh 1774.

Gildon, Charles, *The compleat art of poetry*, London 1718.

    'An essay on the art, rise and progress of the stage in Greece, Rome and England', in the *Works of Shakespeare*, vol. 7, ed. Dr Sewell, London 1725.

Glanville, Joseph, *Plus ultra: or, the progress and advancement of knowledge, since the days of Aristotle*, London 1668.

Gordon, John, *A new estimate of manners and principles: being a comparison between ancient and modern times, in three great articles of knowledge, happiness, and virtue*, Cambridge 1760–1.

    Occasional thoughts on the study and character of classical authors, London 1762.

Goujet, Abbé C., ed., *Bibliothèque française ou histoire de la littérature française*, Paris 1740–56.

Gravina, Gian Vincenzo, *Della ragion poetica libri due*, Roma 1708.

Gregory, John, *A comparative view of the state and faculties of men with those of the animal world*, London 1765.

Guys, Pierre Augustin, *Voyage littéraire de la Grèce, ou lettres sur les Grecs, anciens et modernes, avec une parallèle de leurs moeurs*, Paris 1771.

Harris, James, *Three treatises; the first concerning art; the second concerning music, painting, and poetry; the third concerning happiness*, London 1744.

    Hermes: or, a philosophical inquiry concerning language and universal grammar, London 1751.

Hartley, David, *Observations on man*, London 1749.

Helvétius, Claude Adrien, *De l'esprit: or, essays on the mind, and its several faculties*, trans. from the edition printed under the author's inspection, London 1759.

Herder, J. G. von, *Über die neuere deutsche Literatur* (1767), ed. A. Gillies, Oxford 1969.

Hiffernan, Paul, *Dramatic genius*, London 1770.

Huet, Pierre Daniel, *Traité de l'origine des Romans*, Paris 1670.

Hughes, John, *Poems on several occasions, with some select essays in prose*, London 1735.

Hume, David, 'Of the Authenticity of Ossian's Poems', in *Philosophical works*, ed. T. H. Green and T. H. Grose, vol. 4, London 1882, pp. 415–24.

'Of the Rise and Progress of the Arts and Sciences' (1741) in *Essays, moral, political and literary*, Edinburgh 1748.

'Of the standard of taste' (1742) in *Essays, moral, political and literary*, Edinburgh 1748.

Hurd, Richard, *A discourse concerning poetical imitation*, London 1751.

Letters on chivalry and romance, London 1762.

Husbands, John, *A miscellany of poems by several hands*, Oxford 1731.

Hutcheson, Francis, *An inquiry into the original of our ideas of beauty and virtue*, London 1725.

Irailh, Abbé A. S., *Querelles littéraires, ou mémoires pour servir à l'histoire des revolutions de la république des lettres, depuis Homère jusqu'à nos jours*, Paris 1761.

Johnson, Samuel, 'Preface to Shakespeare', in *The Plays of Shakespeare*, vol. 1, London 1765.

Jortin, John, *Miscellaneous observations upon authors, ancient and modern*, London 1731–2.

Kames, Lord (Henry Home), *The elements of criticism*, Edinburgh 1761.

Sketches of the history of man, Edinburgh 1774.

Knox, Vicesimus, *Essays moral and literary*, London 1778.

La Bizardière, M. D. de, *Caractères des auteurs anciens et modernes et les jugements de leurs ouvrages*, Paris 1704.

Lafitau, J. F., *Moeurs des Sauvages Ameriquains, comparées aux moeurs des premiers temps*, Paris 1724.

La Motte, Antoine Houdar de, *One hundred new court fables, written for the instruction of princes, and a true knowledge of the world, with a discourse on fable*, trans. Mr Samber, London 1721.

Lansdowne, Lord (George Granville), *The laws of poetry*, London 1721.

Le Bossu, P. René, *Traité du poëme épique*, Paris 1675.

A treatise of the epick poem: containing many curious reflexions, very useful and necessary for the right understanding and judging of the excellencies of Homer and Virgil, trans. with a preface by W. J., London 1695.

Le Clerc, Jean, *Ars critica, in qua ad studia linguarum Latinae, Graecae, et Hebraicae via munitur*, Amsterdam 1696.

Parrhasiana: or, thoughts upon several subjects: as, criticism, history, morality and politics, London 1700.

The literary magazine: or, select British Library, London 1735.

Lowth, Robert, *De Sacra poesi Hebraeorum, praelectiones academicae Oxonii habitae,* Oxford 1753, trans. G. Gregory, *Lectures on the sacred poetry of the Hebrews,* London 1787.

Macpherson, James, *Fragments of ancient poetry, collected in the Highlands of Scotland, and translated from the Gaelic or Erse language,* Edinburgh 1760.

   The poems of Ossian, translated by James Macpherson, with dissertations on the era and poems of Ossian; and Dr Blair's critical dissertation, London 1773.

Maidwell, Lewis, *An essay upon the necessity and excellency of education,* London 1705.

Manwaring, Edward, *An historical and critical account of the most eminent classic authors in poetry and history,* London 1737.

Mémoires de littérature, tirés des régistres de l'Academie Royale des Inscriptions et Belles Lettres, La Haye, 1719.

Monboddo, Lord (James Burnet), *Of the origin and progress of language,* Edinburgh 1773–92.

Montague, Elizabeth, *An essay on the writings and genius of Shakespear,* London 1769.

Montfaucon, Bernard de, *Antiquity explained, and represented in sculptures,* trans. D. Humphreys, London 1721–2.

Morris, Corbyn, *An essay towards fixing the true standards of wit, humour, raillery, satire, and ridicule...,* London 1744.

The occasional papers: 'Of genius', in *A collection of occasional papers,* no. 10, vol. 3, London 1719, pp. 1–32.

Ogilvie, John, *An essay on the lyric poetry of the ancients,* London 1762.

Pemberton, Henry, *Observations on poetry; especially the epic: occasioned by the late poem upon Leonidas,* London 1738.

Percy, Thomas, ed., *Reliques of ancient English poetry: consisting of old heroic ballads, songs, and other pieces of our earlier poets, (chiefly of the Lyric kind), together with some few of later date,* London 1765.

   Five pieces of runic poetry, translated from the Islandic language. London 1763.

Perrault, Charles, *Parallèle des anciens et des modernes en ce qui regarde les arts et les sciences* (Paris 1688); *Parallèle...en ce qui regarde l'éloquence* (Paris 1690); *Parallèle...en ce qui regarde la poësie* (Paris 1692); *Parallèle...où il est traité de l'astronomie, de la géographie, de la navigation, de la guerre, de la médecine, etc.* (Paris 1697), ed. H. R. Jauss and M. Imdahl, Munich 1964.

   Characters historical and panegyrical of the greatest men that have appeared in France, during the last Century, trans. J. Ozell, London 1704–5.

Pinkerton, John, *Letters of literature, by Robert Heron,* London 1785.

Pope, Alexander, *An essay on criticism*, London 1711.

The present state of the republic of letters, London 1728–36.

Prior, Matthew, *Miscellaneous works*, London 1740.

Pufendorf, Samuel, *The whole duty of man, according to the law of nature, now made English*, London 1691.

Purshouse, A., *An essay on genius*, London 1782.

Rapin, René, *The whole critical works of M. Rapin*, trans. by several hands, London 1706.

Reid, Thomas, *An inquiry into the human mind on the principles of common sense*, London 1764.

Reynolds, Joshua, *The discourses of Sir Joshua Reynolds, 1–15* (1778), Glasgow 1797.

Robertson, William, *The history of America*, London 1777.

Rollin, Charles, *De la manière d'enseigner et d'étudier les belles lettres*, Paris 1726.

Saint-Evremond, Charles de Marguetel de Saint-Denis, 'Sur les anciens' (1685?), in *Oeuvres en prose*, ed. R. Ternois, vol. 3, Paris 1966.

Shaftesbury, 3rd Earl of (Anthony Ashley Cooper), *Characteristics of men, manners, opinions, times* (3rd edn, London 1723), ed. J. M. Robertson, London 1900.

Sharpe, William, *A dissertation upon genius, or, an attempt to shew, that the several instances of distinction, and degrees of superiority in the human genius are not, fundamentally, the result of nature, but the effect of acquisition*, London 1755.

Spence, Joseph, *Anecdotes, observations and characters of books and men*, ed. B. Dobrée, London 1964.

An essay on Pope's Odyssey: in which some particular beauties and blemishes of that work are considered, London 1726.

Sulzer, Johann Georg, *Allgemeine Theorie der schönen Künste*, Leipzig 1771.

Swift, Jonathan, *A tale of a tub* and *The battle of books*, London 1704.

Temple, Sir William, *Essay upon the ancient and modern learning*, London 1690, in *Critical essays of the seventeenth century*, ed. J. E. Spingarn, vol. 3, Oxford 1909.

Of poetry, London 1690, in *Critical essays*, ed. Spingarn, vol. 3.

Trapp, Joseph, *Praelectiones poeticae*, 2nd edn, London 1722.

The universal magazine: 'An Essay on Genius', May 1771, pp. 227–30.

Usher, James, *Clio: or, a discourse on taste, addressed to a young lady*, London 1767.

Vauvenargues, L. de Clapiers, *Introduction à la connoissance de l'esprit humain, suivie de réflexions et de maximes*, Paris 1747.

Vico, Giambattista, *La scienza nuova seconda* (Naples 1744), ed. F. Nicolini, Bari 1942.

Voltaire, Marie Arouet de, *An essay upon the civil wars of France extracted from curious manuscripts, and also upon the epick poetry of the European nations from Homer down to Milton*, London 1727.

Warton, Joseph, *Odes on various subjects, with a preface*, London 1746.

An essay on the genius and writings of Pope, London 1756.

Warton, Thomas, *The history of English poetry*, London 1774–89.

Observations on the Faerie Queen of Spenser, London 1754, 2nd edn, London 1762.

Webb, Samuel, *Remarks on the beauties of poetry*, London 1762.

Welsted, Leonard, *Epistles, odes, etc., written on several subjects, with a translation of Longinus' treatise on the sublime, to which is prefix'd, a dissertation concerning the English language, the state of poetry, etc.*, London 1724.

Whalley, Peter, *An enquiry into the learning of Shakespeare, with remarks on several passages of his plays*, London 1748.

Wood, Robert, *The ruins of Palmyra*, London 1753.

The ruins of Baalbec, London 1757.

Wotton, William, *Reflections upon ancient and modern learning*, London 1694.

2 SECONDARY LITERATURE

2.1 THE HOMERIC QUESTION

Allen, T. W., *Homer, the origins and transmission*, Oxford 1924.

Bérard, Victor, *La résurrection d'Homère*, Paris 1930.

Bickel, Ernst, *Homer, die Lösung der homerischen Frage*, Bonn 1949.

Buffière, Felix, *Les mythes d'Homère et la pensée grecque*, Paris 1956.

Combellack, F. M., 'Contemporary unitarians and Homeric originality', *AJP*, 71 (1950) 337–64.

Havelock, E. A., 'The preliteracy of the Greeks', *New Literary History*, 8 (1977), 369–91.

Kirk, G. S., 'Dark age and oral poet', *PCPS*, n.s. 7 (1961), 34–48.

Lesky, Albin, 'Homeros', *RE*, suppl. 11 (1967).

Lord, Albert, *The singer of tales*, Cambridge, Mass., 1960; New York 1973.

Lorimer, H. L., 'Homer and the art of writing: a sketch of opinion between 1713 and 1939', *AJA*, 52 (1948), 11–23.

Margoliouth, D. S., *The Homer of Aristotle*, Oxford 1923.

Nilsson, M. P., *Homer and Mycenae*, London 1933.

Parry, Adam, 'Have we Homer's Iliad?' *YCS*, 20 (1966), 177–216.

Parry, Milman, 'Studies in the epic technique of oral verse-making, 1: Homer and Homeric style', *HSCP*, 41 (1930), 73–147.

Schadewaldt, W., ed., *Legende von Homer dem fahrenden Sänger*, Leipzig 1942.

Wade-Gery, H. T., *The poet of the Iliad*, Cambridge 1952.

Wilamowitz-Moellendorff, Ulrich von, *Homerische Untersuchungen*, Berlin 1884.

Woodhouse, W. J., *The composition of Homer's Odyssey*, London 1930.

2.2 THE HOMERIC 'NACHLEBEN'

Arnold, Matthew, 'On translating Homer', in *The complete prose works of Matthew Arnold*, vol. 1: *On the classical tradition*, ed. R. H. Super, Ann Arbor 1960.

Auerbach, Erich, 'Odysseus' scar', in *Mimesis, the representation of reality in western literature*, trans. W. R. Trask, Princeton 1953.

Bleicher, Thomas, *Homer in der deutschen Literatur (1450–1740): zur Rezeption der Antike und zur Poetologie der Neuzeit*, Stuttgart 1972.

Bush, Douglas, 'Checklist of English translations of Homer', *PMLA*, 41 (1926), 335–41.

Butler, Samuel, *The authoress of the Odyssey*, London 1897.

Chateaubriand, François-René de, 'La Bible et Homère', in *Génie du Christianisme* (1802), vol. 1, 2, bk 5, ed. T. Delarouzée, Paris 1955.

Costa, Gustavo, *La critica omerica di Thomas Blackwell (1701–1757), Publicazioni dell'Istituto di filosofia dell'Università di Roma*, 6, Florence 1959.

Costil, P., 'La question homérique et l'évolution du goût littéraire en France', *Annales de l'Université de Grenoble*, n.s. 19 (1943), 95–168.

Eppelsheimer, H. W. *Homer – ein originalgenie*, Fulda 1948.

Finsler, Georg, *Homer in der Neuzeit, von Dante bis Goethe: Italien, Frankreich, England, Deutschland*, Leipzig und Berlin 1912.

Foerster, D. M., *Homer in English criticism: the historical approach in the eighteenth century*, Yale Studies in English, 105, New Haven 1947.

Fumaroli, M., 'Sur Homère en France au xviie siècle', *Revue d'histoire littéraire de la France* 73 (1973), 643–56.

Gladstone, W. E., *Landmarks of Homeric study*, London 1890.

Goethe, J. W. von, 'Homer noch einmal' (1827), in *Schriften zur Literatur*, ed. E. Nahler, Berlin 1970.

Hepp, Noémi, 'Homère en France au xvie siècle', *Atti della Accademia delle scienze di Torino*, 96 (1961–2), 1–120.

Homère en France au XVIIe siècle, Paris 1968.

Herder, J. G. von, 'Homer, ein Günstling der Zeit' (1795–6), in *Herders Werke*, ed. B. Suphan, vol. 18, Berlin 1883, pp. 420ff.

Kenner, Hugh, 'Joyce's Ulysses: Homer and Hamlet', *Essays in Criticism*, 2 (1952), 85–104.

Kerényi, C., 'Homer and his Odyssey', in *The voyages of Ulysses*, ed. Erich Lessing, London 1966, pp. 233–74.

Kraus, Konrad, *Winckelmann und Homer*, Berlin 1935.

Leutsch, E. von, 'Homer im Mittelalter' *Philologus*, 12 (1857), 366–8.

Lloyd-Jones, Hugh, 'Gladstone on Homer', *TLS* (3 January 1975), 15–17.

Lord, George, *Homeric Renaissance: the Odyssey of George Chapman*, London 1956.

'The Odyssey and the western world', *Sewanee Review*, 62 (1954), 406–27.

Mason, H. A., *To Homer through Pope. An introduction to Homer's Iliad and Pope's translation*, London 1972.

Myres, J. L., *Homer and his critics*, London 1958.

Nicolini, Fausto, 'Sugli studi omerici di Giambattista Vico', *Atti della Academia nazionale dei Lincei*, ser. 7, vol. 5 (1954), 469–519.

Pertusi, Agostino, *Leonzio Pilato fra Petrarca e Boccaccio. Le sue versioni omeriche negli autografi di Venezia e la cultura greca del primo umanesimo*, Civiltà Veneziana Studi 16, Venice and Rome 1964.

Ramsey, W., 'Voltaire and Homer', *PMLA*, 66 (1951), 182–96.

Rank, Otto, 'Homer. Psychologische Beiträge zur Entstehungsgeschichte des Volksepos', *Imago*, 3 (1917), 133–69.

Sainte-Beuve, C. A., 'Homère', *Journal des Débats*, 27 (January 1843), in *Aperçus de l'oeuvre critique de C. A. Sainte-Beuve*, ed. G. Corbière-Gille, Paris 1973.

Scott, J. A., *Homer and his influence*, Norwood, Mass., 1924.

Shaw, G. W., 'Homère, sujet de discussion pendant la querelle des anciens et des modernes', unpubd MA thesis, University of Liverpool 1959.

Stanford, W. B., *The Ulysses theme*, Oxford 1963.

Steiner, George, ed., *Homer. A collection of critical essays*, New Jersey 1962.

Sühnel, Rudolf, *Homer und die englische Humanität; Chapmans und Popes Übersetzungskunst im Rahmen der humanistischen Tradition*, Tübingen 1958.

Wagner, Fritz, 'Herders Homerbild, seine Wurzeln und Wirkungen', Inaugural dissertation, University of Cologne, 1960.

Weil, Simone, 'L'Iliade ou le poème de la force', *Les Cahiers du Sud*, 19 (1940), 561–74, 20 (1941), 21–34; repr. in *La source grecque*, Paris 1953.

Weinstock, S., 'Die platonische Homerkritik und ihre Nachwirkung', *Philologus*, 82 (1926), 121–53.

Weiss, R., 'Notes on Petrarch and Homer', *Rinascimento*, 4 (1953), 263–75.

Zimmermann, H. J., *Alexander Popes Noten zu Homer. Eine Manuskript- und Quellenstudie*, Heidelberg 1966.

2.3   THE CLASSICAL TRADITION

Bolgar, R. R., *The classical heritage and its beneficiaries*, Cambridge 1954.

  ed., *Classical influences on European culture, AD 500–1500*, Cambridge 1971.

  ed., *Classical influences on European culture, AD 1500–1700*, Cambridge 1976.

Brower, R. A., *Hero and saint. Shakespeare and the Graeco-Roman tradition*, Oxford 1972.

Bush, Douglas, *Mythology and the Renaissance tradition in English poetry*, Minneapolis 1932.

Castor, Grahame, *Pléiade poetics*, Cambridge 1964.

Cioranescu, A., 'La Pléiade et le poème epique', *Lumières de la Pléiade*, Neuvième Stage International d'Etudes Humanistes, Tours 1965, pp. 75–86.

Clarke, M. L., *Greek studies in England 1700–1830*, Cambridge 1945. *The classical line*, YFS 38 (1968).

Croce, Benedetto, *Poesia antica e moderna*, 2nd edn., Bari 1943.

Curtius, E. R., *Europäische Literatur und lateinische Mittelalter*, 2nd edn, Berne 1954.

Durling, Robert M., *The figure of the poet in Renaissance epic*, Cambridge, Mass., 1965.

Ephraim, C. *Wandel des Griechenbildes im achtzehnten Jahrhundert*, Bern 1936.

Garin, Eugenio, *L'éducation de l'homme moderne* (1957), trans. Jacqueline Humbert, Paris 1968.

Gombrich, E. H., *Art and illusion*, London 1960, 4th edn 1972. *In search of cultural history*, Oxford 1969.

Hall, V., *Renaissance literary criticism. A study of its social content*, New York 1945.

Hepp, Noémi, 'De l'épopée au roman: l'Odyssée et Télémaque', in *La litterature narrative d'imagination*, Centre de philologie romane de Strasbourg, Paris 1961, pp. 97–113.

Highet, Gilbert, *The classical tradition. Greek and Roman influences on western literature*, Oxford 1949.

Kermode, Frank, *The classic*, London 1975.

Knight, Douglas, *Pope and the heroic tradition. A critical study of his Iliad*, New Haven 1951.

Larrabee, S. A., *English bards and Grecian marbles; the relationship between sculpture and poetry, especially in the romantic period*, New York 1943.

Lebende Antike. Symposium für Rudolf Sühnel, ed. H. Meller and H. J. Zimmermann, Berlin 1967.

Maskell, David, *The historical epic in France 1500–1700*, Oxford 1973.

Panofsky, Erwin, *Studies in iconology*, Oxford 1939.

Panofsky, Erwin and Dora, *Pandora's box. The changing aspects of a mythical symbol*, New York 1956.

Pfeiffer, Rudolf, *History of classical scholarship from 1300 to 1850*, Oxford 1976.

Spencer, T. J. B., *Fair Greece, sad relic: literary philhellenism from Shakespeare to Byron*, London 1954.

Stern, Bernard, *The rise of romantic hellenism in English literature 1732–1786*, Menasha 1940.

Trousson, Raymond, *Le thème de Promethée dans la littérature européenne*, Geneva 1967.

Voigt, Georg, *Il risorgimento dell'antichitá classica ovvero il primo secolo dell'umanesimo* (*Die Wiederbelebung des classischen*

Altertums, Berlin 1888), trans. O. Valbusa, Biblioteca storica del Rinascimento, 5, Florence 1968.

Warburg, Aby, *Die Erneuerung der heidnischen Antike; kulturwissenschaftliche Beiträge zur Geschichte der europäischen Renaissance*, Leipzig und Berlin 1932.

The Warburg Institute, ed., *England and the Mediterranean tradition*, Oxford 1945.

Weinberg, Bernhard, *A history of literary criticism in the Italian Renaissance*, Chicago 1961.

Weiss, Roberto, *The Renaissance discovery of classical antiquity*, Oxford 1969.

2.4 ANCIENTS AND MODERNS

Baron, Hans, 'The *querelle* of the ancients and the moderns as a problem for Renaissance scholarship', *JHI*, 20 (1959), 3–22.

Buck, August, 'Aus der Vorgeschichte der querelle des anciens et des modernes in Mittelalter und Renaissance', *Bibliothèque d'humanisme et Renaissance*, 20 (1958), 527–41.

Burlingame, Anne E., *The battle of books in its historical setting*, New York 1920.

Cherniss, Ruth, 'The ancients as authority in seventeenth-century France', in *The Greek tradition*, ed. George Boas, Baltimore 1939, pp. 139–70.

Crane, R. S., 'The quarrel of the ancients and moderns and its consequences', *The idea of the humanities*, Chicago 1967, vol. 1, pp. 72–89.

Dupont, Paul, *Houdar de la Motte (1672–1731), un poète-philosophe au commencement du dix-huitième siècle*, Paris 1898.

Gillot, H., *La querelle des anciens et des modernes*, Paris 1914.

Hope, Q. M., *Saint-Evremond. The honnête homme as critic*, Bloomington 1962.

Jones, Richard F., *Ancients and moderns: a study of the background of the Battle of books*, St Louis 1936, 2nd edn 1961.

Kortum, Hans, *Charles Perrault und Nicolas Boileau. Der Antike-Streit im Zeitalter der klassischen französischen Literatur*, Berlin 1966.

Little, K. D., *Fénelon, a personal portrait*, New York 1951.

Lombard, A., *Fénelon et le retour à l'antique au XVIIIe siècle*, Neuchatel 1954.

Malcovati, E., *Madame Dacier, una gentildonna filologa del gran secolo*, Florence 1952.

Mazon, Paul, *Madame Dacier et les traductions d'Homère en France*, Oxford 1936.

Rigault, Hippolyte, *Histoire de la querelle des anciens et des modernes*, Paris 1856.

Santangelo, G. S., *La 'querelle des anciens et des modernes' nella critica del '900*, Bari 1975.

Soriano, Marc, *Le dossier Perrault*, Paris 1972.
Wencelius, L., 'La querelle des anciens et des modernes et l'humanisme',
XVIIe Siècle, 9–10 (1951), 15–34.

2.5 THE ENLIGHTENMENT

Bestermann, Theodore, *Voltaire*, London 1969.
Bryson, Gladys, *Man and society. The Scottish inquiry of the eighteenth century*, Princeton 1945.
Cassirer, Ernst, *The philosophy of the Enlightenment* (1932), trans. F. C. A. Koelln and J. P. Pettegrove, New York 1951.
Croce, Benedetto, *The philosophy of Giambattista Vico*, trans. R. G. Collingwood, London 1913.
De Mas, Enrico, 'Vico's new method of a new science', *JHI*, 32 (1971), 85–94.
Dieckmann, Herbert, 'An interpretation of the eighteenth century' *MLQ*, 15 (1954), 295–311.
Flower, Desmond, *Voltaire's England*, London 1950.
Gay, Peter, *The Enlightenment: an interpretation*, London 1970.
Glass, H. B., et al., ed., *The forerunners of Darwin 1745–1859*, Baltimore 1959.
Hampson, Norman, *The Enlightenment*, Harmondsworth 1968.
Hazard, Paul, *The European mind 1680–1715 (La crise de la conscience européenne*, Paris 1935), trans. J. L. May, London 1953.
Huizinga, F., 'Naturbild und Geschichtsbild im 18. Jahrhundert', *Corona*, 5 (1935), 536–62.
Lehmann, William C., *Henry Home, Lord Kames, and the Scottish Enlightenment. A study in national character and in the history of ideas*, The Hague 1971.
Marsak, L. M., 'Fontenelle: the idea of science in the French Enlightenment', *TAPS*, 49 (1959), 1–64.
Schapiro, M., *Diderot on the artist and society*, Diderot Studies, 5, Geneva 1964.
Starobinski, Jean, *L'invention de la liberté 1700–1789*, Geneva 1964.
Wade, I. C., *The intellectual origins of the French Enlightenment*. Princeton 1971.
White, F. D., *Voltaire's Essay on the epic poetry. A study and an edition*, Albany, N.Y., 1915.

2.6 CLASSICISM AND NEOCLASSICISM

Bond, Donald F., ' "Distrust" of imagination in English neoclassicism', *PQ*, 14 (1935), 54–69.
      'The neo-classical psychology of the imagination', *ELH*, 4 (1937), 245–64.
Bredvold, L. I., 'The rise of English classicism: a study in methodology', *CL*, 2 (1950), 253–68.

Cherel, Albert, *Fénelon au XVIIIe siècle en France (1715–1820)*, Paris 1917.

Clark, A. F. B., *Boileau and the French classical critics in England (1660–1830)*, Paris 1925.

Dillon, George L., 'Complexity and change of character in neo-classical criticism', *JHI*, 35 (1974), 51–61.

Draper, J. W., 'Aristotelian mimesis in eighteenth-century England', *PMLA*, 36 (1921), 372–400.

Gallaway, F., *Reason, rule and revolt in English classicism*, New York 1940, 2nd edn 1966.

Haskell, Francis, *The age of the grand tour*, London 1967.

Honour, Hugh, *Neoclassicism*, Harmondsworth 1968.

Johnson, J. W., *The formation of English neo-classical thought*, Princeton 1967.

Marks, E. R., *The poetics of reason. English neoclassical criticism*, New York 1968.

Maurocordato, Alexandre, *La critique classique en Angleterre de la Restauration à la mort de Joseph Addison*, Paris 1964.

Paul, H. G., *John Dennis: his life and criticism*, New York 1911.

Pechter, Edward, *Dryden's classical theory of literature*, Cambridge 1975.

Peyre, Henri, *Qu'est-ce que le classicisme?*, 2nd edn, Paris 1965.

Swedenberg, H. T., 'Rules and English critics of the epic 1650–1800', *SP*, 35 (1938), 566–87.

Tigerstedt, E. N., *Engelsk nyhumanism och nyklassisism under 1700-talet*, Humanistisk kultur, 7, Stockholm 1963.

Wallerstein, R., *Studies in the seventeenth-century poetic*, Madison 1950.

Wood, P. S., 'Native elements in English neoclassicism', *MP*, 24 (1926), 201–8.

   'The opposition to neoclassicism in England between 1660 and 1700', *PMLA*, 43 (1928), 182–97.

2.7   GENIUS

Bundy, Murray W., *The theory of imagination in classical and medieval thought*, University of Illinois studies in language and literature, 12, 2–3, Urbana 1927.

   ' "Invention" and "imagination" in the Renaissance', *Journal of English and Germanic Philology*, 29 (1930), 535–45.

Clough, W. O., 'Reason and genius – an eighteenth-century dilemma', *PQ*, 23 (1944), 33–54.

Currie, Robert, *Genius, an ideology in literature*, London 1974.

Dieckmann, Herbert, 'Diderot's conception of genius', *JHI*, 2 (1941), 151–82.

Eissler, K. R., *Leonardo da Vinci. Psychoanalytic notes on the enigma*, London 1962.

   'Notes on the environment of a genius', *The Psychoanalytic Study of the Child*, 14 (1959), 267–313.

Goldberg, M. A., 'Wit and imagination in eighteenth-century aesthetics', *JAAC*, 16 (1957–8), 503–9.

Grene, Marjorie, 'Gerard's Essay on taste', *MP*, 41 (1943), 45–58.

Kaufman, P., 'Heralds of original genius', *Essays in memory of Barrett Wendell*, Cambridge, Mass., 1926.

Matoré, G., and A. J. Greimas, 'La naissance de "génie" au XVIIIe siècle. Etude lexicologique', *Français moderne*, 25 (1957), 256–72.

Nahm, M. C., 'The theological background of the artist as creator', *JHI*, 8 (1947), 363–72.

   Genius and creativity: an essay in the history of ideas, Baltimore 1965.

Roston, Murray, *Prophet and poet. The Bible and the growth of romanticism*, London 1965.

Rüfner, Vinzenz, 'Homo secundus deus: eine geistesgeschichtliche Studie zum menschlichen Schöpfertum', *Philosophisches Jahrbuch der Görresgesellschaft*, 63 (1955), 248–91.

Thüme, Hans, *Beiträge zur Geschichte des Geniebegriffs in England*, Studien zur Englishen Philologie, 71 (Halle 1927).

Tigerstedt, E. N., 'The poet as creator: origins of a metaphor', *CLS*, 5 (1968), 455–88.

Tucker, S. I., *Enthusiasm: a study in semantic change*, Cambridge 1972.

Watson, G. G., 'Contributions to a dictionary of critical terms: *imagination* and *fancy*', *Essays in Criticism*, 3 (1953), 201–14.

Whyte, L. L., *The unconscious before Freud*, London 1960.

Wiley, M. L., 'Genius: a problem in definition', *Studies in English*, 16 (1936), 77–83.

Willard, Nedd, *Le génie et la folie au dix-huitième siècle*, Paris 1963.

Zilsel, E., *Die Entstehung des Geniebegriffes. Ein Beitrag zur Ideengeschichte der Antike und des Frühkapitalismus*, Tübingen 1926.

2.8 AESTHETICS AND PRIMITIVISM

Amos, F. R., *Early theories of translation*, New York 1920.

Art and ideas in eighteenth-century Italy (lectures given at the Italian Institute 1957–8), Rome 1960.

Atkinson, Geoffrey, *Le sentiment de la nature et le retour à la vie simple (1690–1740)*, Paris 1960.

Babcock, Robert W., *The genesis of Shakespeare idolatry 1766–1799*, London 1931.

Clifford, J. L., *Man versus society in eighteenth-century Britain*, Cambridge 1968.

Cohen, R., 'Association of ideas and poetic unity', *PQ*, 35 (1957), 465–74.

Crane, R. S., 'An early eighteenth-century enthusiast for primitive poetry: John Husbands', *MLN*, 37 (1922), 27–36.

Ehrard, Jean, *L'idée de nature en France au XVIIIe siècle*, Paris 1963.

Foerster, D. M., 'Scottish primitivism and the historical approach', *PQ*, 29 (1950), 307–23.

Folkierski, W., *Entre le classicisme et le romantisme*, Paris 1925.

Formigari, Lia, *L'estetica del gusto nel settecento inglese*, Florence 1962.

Havens, R. D., 'Simplicity, a changing concept', *JHI*, 14 (1953), 3–32.

Hipple, W. J., *Beautiful, sublime, and picturesque in eighteenth-century British aesthetic theory*, Carbondale, Ill., 1957.

Hooker, E. N., 'The discussion of taste, from 1750 to 1770, and the new trends in literary criticism', *PMLA*, 49 (1934), 577–92.

Klein, H., *There is no disputing about taste: Untersuchungen zum englischen Geschmacksbegriff im achtzehnten Jahrhundert*, Münster 1967.

Lenoble, Robert, *Esquisse d'une histoire de l'idée de nature*, Paris 1969.

Lombard, A., *L'Abbé Dubos, un initiateur de la pensée moderne (1670–1742)*, Paris 1913.

Lovejoy, A. O., 'Nature as esthetic norm', *MLN*, 42 (1927), 444–50.

Mann, E. L., 'The problem of originality in English literary criticism 1750–1800', *PQ*, 18 (1939), 97–118.

Manuel, Frank E., *The eighteenth century confronts the gods*, Cambridge, Mass., 1959.

Mazzeo, J. A., ed., *Reason and imagination. Studies in the history of ideas 1600–1800*, New York 1962.

Miller, G. M., 'The historical point of view in English literary criticism from 1570–1770', *Anglistische Forschungen*, 35 (1913), 1–160.

Monk, S. H., *The sublime*, New York 1935.

Nicolson, M. H., *Mountain gloom and mountain glory*, Ithaca, N.Y., 1959.

Pearce, R. H., 'The eighteenth-century Scottish primitivists: some reconsiderations', *ELH*, 12 (1945), 203–20.

Ross, I. S., *Lord Kames and the Scotland of his time*, Oxford 1971.

Scheffer, J. D., 'The idea of decline in literature and the fine arts in eighteenth-century England', *MP*, 34 (1936), 155–78.

Shaffer, E., *'Kubla Khan' and the fall of Jerusalem; the mythological school of biblical criticism and secular literature, 1770–1880*, Cambridge 1975.

Tinker, C. B., *Nature's simple plan*, Princeton 1922.

Tuveson, E. L., *Millenium and utopia: a study in the background of the idea of progress*, Berkeley 1949.

Wasserman, E. R., ed., *Aspects of the eighteenth century*, Baltimore 1965.

Wellek, R., *The rise of English literary history*, Chapel Hill 1941.

　　A history of modern criticism: 1750–1950, vol. 1: *The later eighteenth century*, London 1955.

Whitney, Lois, *Primitivism and the idea of progress in English literature of the eighteenth century*, Baltimore 1934.

'Eighteenth century primitivistic theories of the epic' *MP*, 21 (1924), 337–78.

'Thomas Blackwell, a disciple of Shaftesbury', *PQ*, 5 (1926), 196–211.

Wood, T. E. B., *The word 'sublime' and its context 1650–1760*, The Hague 1972.

Index

Page numbers in italic refer to special discussion of a topic. (Topics indicated in the title of this book are not indexed.)